Totalitarian Space and the
Destruction of Aura

Totalitarian Space and the Destruction of Aura

Saladdin Ahmed

SUNY PRESS

Cover image: Arrow Into Infinity by Milad Safabakhsh

Published by State University of New York Press, Albany

© 2019 State University of New York

For information, contact State University of New York Press, Albany, NY
www.sunypress.edu

Library of Congress Cataloging-in-Publication Data

Names: Ahmed, Saladdin, 1972– author.
Title: Totalitarian space and the destruction of aura / Saladdin Ahmed.
Description: Albany : State University of New York Press, [2019] | Includes
    bibliographical references.
Identifiers: LCCN 2018014128 | ISBN 9781438472911 (hardcover) |
    ISBN 9781438472928 (pbk.) | ISBN 9781438472935 (ebook)
Subjects: LCSH: Space—Philosophy. | Space—Political aspects. | Totalitarianism—
    Social aspects. | Critical theory.
Classification: LCC BH301.S65 A56 2019 | DDC 114—dc23
LC record available at https://lccn.loc.gov/2018014128

10 9 8 7 6 5 4 3 2 1

To the hopeless ones
whose struggle is our only hope.

Contents

Acknowledgments

First, the utmost thanks to Melissa Seelye, who alone knows how much she helped me in everything.

Next, I would like to thank the anonymous readers whose faith in the project and insightful comments on the manuscript encouraged me to make significant changes, especially to the first and last chapters. To Michael Rinella, senior acquisitions editor at SUNY Press, whose professionalism, punctuality, and interest in the project has been unwavering, I extend my sincerest thanks. I also appreciate the work of SUNY's senior production editor, Diane Ganeles; senior promotion manager, Michael Campochiaro; copy editor Laura Tendler; and the other members of the production and marketing teams who saw this book through to completion.

Further thanks, of course, are also due to Douglas Moggach, who was my PhD supervisor at the University of Ottawa. His support was instrumental to my completion of the dissertation, and I am especially grateful for his suggestion to integrate a discussion of Rousseau and Herder. The feedback from the members of my PhD committee, Denis Dumas, Isabelle Thomas-Fogiel, Viren Murthy, and Justin Paulson, as well as my external reader, Samir Gandesha, was also invaluable. Justin was extremely generous with his time and comments, despite the short notice, and Samir's flexibility ensured that the show could go on.

For the indexing, I send many thanks to my friend Vasile-Valentin Latiu, who, as always, undertook the task without a moment's hesitation. I am also thankful to Arezoo Islami, Duncan Rayside, Shahrzad Mojab, Hassan Ghazi, Eric Davis, Andrew Scerri, and Blair Taylor for their interest in the manuscript and encouragement. As well, the help of Sarina Simon Rosenthal, Rose Anderson, and Lauren E. Crain of

Scholars at Risk over the last few years has meant a great deal to me. Here I must also acknowledge friends near and far who have supported me over the years, especially Siyaves Azeri, Ibrahim Bor, Joël Doucet, Alice Constantinou, Eleanor Finley, Amir Hassanpour (whose fight will live on), Greg Younger-Lewis, Anna Markova, Abolfazl Masoumi, Hodan Mohamed, Madalina Santos, Jaffer Sheyholislami, Kamal Soleimani, and Noel Ward.

Parts of the third chapter were published in an article titled "Panopticism and Totalitarian Space" in the *Theory in Action* journal. Thanks to the editor-in-chief, John Asimakopoulos, for kindly granting me permission to republish those here.

Introduction

Recall, for a moment, the wonder with which you once observed the movements of worker ants. Whether visibly united to move a large object or building an anthill one grain of sand at a time, the ant colony at work is an endless source of fascination. To us on the outside, their regimented movements and often frenetic pace seem strange, comical even, but what would we discover if we turned this outsider's gaze on ourselves? Imagine how our urban spaces would be perceived by someone entirely unfamiliar with our dominant socioeconomic norms. At sunrise, the outsider would likely note the systematic division and subdivision of cities by innumerable highways, forming orderly geometric shapes and patterns. She would see the blocks of concrete and glass jutting into the sky, separated, connected, and framed by the grid of city streets. At the appointed hour, these highways and streets would be overtaken by a seemingly endless procession of cars and buses, and she would watch in astonishment as the lines of machines inch their way along. Zooming in closer, the observer would quickly realize that the city is a space of and for machines that orchestrate the mass movement of humans and commodities between points of production and consumption. To her, we would no doubt look like the most domesticated of all creatures, with our movements incomparably more prescribed than the worker ants we gaze down on.

Perceived in its totality, this scene can give us insight into the truth of our spatial lives that we could never otherwise imagine. It would be inaccurate to say that the millions of people who are on the move en masse at certain times of the day are physically coerced in the way that people are forced to work in labor camps. Still, there must be a force behind these highly organized patterns of movement and spatial organization. Behind every hegemonic order, there is a system responsible for its creation and reproduction; nothing in our produced environment is natural. In our case, that hegemonic order is capitalism, and it dictates the organization of human activities as well as the ways in which objects are transformed through those activities and the simultaneous transformation of humans within that process. Indeed, the hegemony of capitalism is such that we have not yet been able to comprehend the scope of our unfreedom, the degree to which our lives are mechanized by the power of capital.

Our obsession with time and history has made us neglect the very pressing question of how the capitalist distribution of space affects our everyday lived experience. The dominant mode of spatiality is fundamentally transparent, which is indicative of our non-freedom. We live in a unified space that is chillingly flat, mechanized, and open to the policing gaze of power. And yet we go along with it. We tacitly accept being watched by unknown individuals whom we view as disembodied elements of the institution of the state and its corporate associates. In fact, we do this despite the commonsensical fact that working in the service of the state does not make anyone more ethical, and it certainly should not make anyone more entitled to penetrate other people's lives. Some of us may comfort ourselves with the belief that we have nothing to hide, and that the surveillance is therefore benign. In doing so, we essentially submit to punishment for a crime that we have not committed. To prove her innocence, the citizen must consent to being naked before the gaze of power, conducting herself in such a way that she would never do anything that could not be made public.

When the body becomes an object of inspection, subjectivity is sieged within increasingly narrow boundaries of a disappearing inner space. This has caused us to lose sight of the fact that each of us is entitled to having things to hide from governments, employers, each other, and even ourselves. Without this, freedom can have no meaning, for any restriction of freedom of thought necessarily negates freedom altogether. Obviously, freedom of action may need to be restricted so as not to infringe on other individuals' freedoms, but only under a system of total domination would people be expected to have nothing to hide. Even in what we would typically identify as traditional totalitarian regimes, there were always underground spaces of resistance, spaces where individuals could eat the fruits of the forbidden tree and enjoy some freedom despite all the laws of absolutism. The totalitarian regimes of the twentieth century relied primarily on human resources, and they therefore never attained anything resembling total domination.[1] In its more advanced stages, however, totalitarianism does not require an omnipresent police force to sustain itself. Instead, it relies on spatial technologies of power and myriad forms of thought policing to wipe out and guard against potential irregularities. For total domination necessarily requires constant policing of each and every individual, and this is virtually impossible without turning people into self-policing inmates confined to a unitary space of complete transparency.

As this book argues, the free world of the market regime has succeeded in obliterating spaces of secrecy and intimacy, achieving a state of hegemony heretofore unprecedented. Let us be clear from the start: no one in her right mind would prefer despotic totalitarianism over liberal democracy. However, something has been destroyed by the capitalist production of space, and it has rendered our contemporary spatial experience fundamentally totalitarian in its transparency and subjugation to technological means of control. This totalitarian space has been so normalized and globalized that critical spatial awareness is imperative for any meaningful emancipatory school of thought or social movement. Notably, this book is not another romantic call for a return to the state of nature, which is neither desirable nor feasible. Regression is not the answer to any problem of modernity, and in fact, romanticizing the imagined lost origins of the past is one of the primary fascist motivations of our time. Rather, the solution is something we cannot hope to discover until we more fully comprehend the scope of the crisis. In other words, for us to be able to imagine and construct different, nonoppressive spaces, we must first be able to articulate what is wrong with the existing spatial order. Though I do not claim to know the path to those other spaces, I believe that for us to know and reject what is wrong, we need not necessarily know what is right.

By the same token, critical spatial theory may not be capable of envisioning the form those other spaces should take, but it should be able to guard our actions against the reproduction of more spaces of domination. This improved spatial awareness may not lead us to spatial emancipation, but without such awareness, we are doomed to eternalize our unfreedom. Perhaps we are not in a position to describe an alternative space, but we must find ways to know/feel what is absent, or, more accurately, to know/feel that *something* is absent. As such, this book aims to problematize our spatial experience, to seek out what has been lost in the unified contemporary space under capitalism, and to name the dominant space of our time. For although we may feel alienated in dominated spaces, the fundamentally spatial nature of this alienation is rarely recognized, in large part because normalcy does not strike us as something to be named. It is rather the abnormal, the pathological, that we insist on diagnosing, naming, and "fixing." Yet, just as the "abnormal" is not necessarily "unnatural," the normal does not necessarily originate in "natural laws" because the norm itself is determined by relations of domination. A critical philosophy of space must necessarily aim to denormalize that which is unquestioned by problematizing the history and functions of our spatial norms, as well as the conditions they help to sustain.

To start, a critical philosophy of space should name the dominant spatial norm, which is so debilitating to thought and so restrictive to our very mode of existence that its threat is not only social and political but also ontological. Living in such a space makes us unable to experience our most crucial existential potentialities. This book simply puts a name to something that we have been living in too deeply and too continuously to be able to accurately perceive. Today, the state of being constantly under watch is no longer a form of control exercised primarily on the incarcerated. The gaze of power follows all citizens wherever they may be. As an individual walks on a street, shops online, or makes a phone call, her actions are recorded in various ways for a range of actual and potential purposes. Particularly in an online context, her consumption history, personality, political orientation, social relations, and much more fall under the never-sleeping gaze of power. Whether manifested in surveillance cameras, drones, or mechanically reproduced symbols of the state, the gaze of power destroys the uniqueness of all spaces to produce a single, lifeless space in which every undesirable body is easily recognizable. Such a space can only be called totalitarian.

Totalitarianism is not exclusively a label to be applied to certain despotic political systems, but rather to any system that aims to achieve the unlimited exercise of power. By the same token, the gaze that recognizes no spatial limit to its vision is inherently totalitarian, as is the resulting produced space. The politicality of social space is not merely a hermeneutical, aesthetic, or epistemological conclusion that theorists of space seek to draw within abstract projects. Rather, social space is inseparable from the question of politics in both the broad and specific senses of the word. Sovereignty, as the state's legitimization of its own use of violence (Lefebvre 1991a, 280), ensures that the subject's perception and experience in space and of space will be continually constrained. Accordingly, what the subject is required to submit to within the borders of a state is more than just a set of laws and regulations; a certain spatial experience is literally imposed on the subject. The state is the master institution that has the decisive say in spatial distribution and thereby determines the movement of bodies between and within the geographies of everyday life.

All states, from the most terroristic to the least undemocratic, affirm their statehood first and foremost by territorializing space, which inherently violates the purportedly communal nature of social spaces. Acting as the commanding brain of the society, the state sees itself as the legitimate engineer of social space. The state's violent spatial politics are manifested clearly at international borders, where the surgical spatial operations are more visible because that is where the subject directly witnesses the shift between two normalized worlds. At a border, the contrast between the two worlds renders the spatial coercion normalized within each state visible, alerting us to the fact that the laws of the state are not the natural laws of the land, as the state's ideological apparatuses would have us believe. Rather, the state is quite literally constructed on the basis of the production and reproduction of space (Lefebvre 1991a, 281), and it continually asserts itself via symbolic materiality. A symbol, by virtue of being a symbol, is never merely a symbol. The function of a flag waving in the wind attributes a political function to the wind and the sky, just as border signs oppressively attribute political functions to the air and the earth.

This fully legitimized, unlimited spatial power of the state is by definition totalitarian, the ultimate result of which is the entrenchment of the belief that the state is the natural distributer of all spaces. What is worse, the more powerful and technologically advanced the state, the more difficult it becomes to find a place to hide or a space to dream. The gaze of the state, and its psychological effects, can penetrate not only all social spaces, but also the very natural solitude we enjoy within the space of our bodies. It can render our bodies an extension of its totally illuminated space of control. People internalize the gaze of power, and the necessity of using physical violence is subsequently minimized. In other words, we ourselves are the daily reproducers and sustainers of the totalitarian space in which we live.

While the hallmark of a traditional totalitarian system may be terror, the more effective the methods of ideological indoctrination

become, the less necessary physical terror becomes. In capitalist democracies, we end up with a form of totalitarianism that is more advanced
in terms of its sustainability and ideological hegemony, as well as its use
of technologies of power. Advanced totalitarianism, or what Sheldon
Wolin terms "inverted totalitarianism" (2010, 213), relies greatly on
ideological hegemony wrought by the culture industry, as opposed to
methods of terrorizing the population. Of course, the state is not the
sole producer of totalitarian space because the state itself is continually
sustained by more fundamental relations of production. Capitalism, as
today's dominant mode of production, is fundamentally involved in the
production of totalitarian space. Under capitalism, the state functions
as the umbrella institution that facilitates the institutional and legal
conditions necessary for production and consumption.

The proliferation of consumerism as a lifestyle has made standardization and repetition desirable aspects of public space. Commodities
have become the flattening agents of space. They reach into all spaces
that consumers use, and they carry with them commodity forms, thereby
creating the conditions for spatial uniformity. Essential to this is, again,
the culture industry, which has molded the mass individual's mode of
perception to fit the consumerist order of things. Familiarity might otherwise be thought of as the addictive appeal of repetition, and the culture
industry achieves exactly that: it simplifies anything and everything it
touches to make it consumer friendly, that is, unchallenging, depthless,
ready to be effortlessly consumed. The culture industry's standardized
patterns of repetition aim to provide a sense of complete familiarity in
all experiences, from shopping and traveling to reading and listening to
music. Spatial experience is no exception.

The question, then, is how we can account for totalitarian space,
given that its production entails much more than simply the employment
of the means of terror. Following the opening chapter on totalitarianism, chapter 2 introduces Lefebvre's theory, being both the historically
and dialectically most important theory of the production of space. His
theory of the production of space opens the door for the kind of critical
thinking essential for capturing the dynamics, contradictions, constant
transformation, and infusion inherent in social space. Lefebvre teaches us
that space is simultaneously perceived, conceived, and lived. He avoids
reducing space to the mental or the physical, but, at the same time, his
theory encompasses both the mental and the physical in a dialectical
relationship that culminates in a third "moment." Symbols and signs play

a pivotal role in this dialectical production of space. In fact, images are crucial determinants of the production of space, especially when those images allude to an existing symbol of absolute power and create endless visual patterns through their proliferation.

Yet before moving on to explore this point further, chapter 3 demonstrates how the technology of power is used spatially. Relying on Foucault's work, I illuminate the principles and functions of the Panopticon as an iconic example of the technology of spatial production. Spatial transparency is crucial to panopticism insofar as it is a technique of observation aimed at total control and discipline. The Panopticon makes the space of the governed subjects transparent, the subjects visible to the gaze of power, and the gaze of power ultravisible to the subjects. In doing so, it cultivates within each subject a state of being continually watched by the disciplinary power, with the chief goal being the implementation of self-policing. Another very important principle that is explored vis-à-vis panopticism is that of maximum utility, which seeks to control the greatest number of people with the absolute minimum number of policing personnel. As chapter 6 shows, these same ideas can be applied to the symbols of the state, namely mechanically reproduced images.

First, however, I further refine the notion of totalitarian space by identifying what is destroyed through its production. Something is fundamentally lost when space is stripped of its uniqueness, and I term that which is lost "aura." Chapters 4 and 5 detail the merits and shortcomings of Benjamin's work on aura. While I would argue that his greatest pursuit was to secularize the notion of aura, emancipating it from its religious/mythological history, he ultimately betrayed his secular version of aura by reassociating it with the cult value. Staying faithful to Benjamin's secular understanding of the concept, I present aura as the negative concept capable of capturing the presence of absence, the appearance of distance, and the trace of what once was. Moving to Benjamin's work on the aura of original works of art, I argue that just as mechanically reproduced works of art are auraless, mechanically reproduced images render the spaces they invade auraless. In this particular context, it is the mechanically reproduced symbols of the state, such as images of a fascist leader, that destroy "spatial aura," thereby turning all spaces into a singular, flat space of totalitarianism.

Having clarified my use of the term "totalitarian," explained the production of space, analyzed panopticism as a spatial technology of power, and defined aura in the first five chapters, chapter 6 brings each of these components together. It reasserts my argument that totalitarian space is produced through the systematic destruction of aura by illustrating the particular case of mechanically reproduced images. More specifically, I show that mechanically reproduced images produce totalitarian space by functioning on four intertwined levels, namely as simulacra creating hyperreality (per Baudrillard), symbolic Panopticons, means of visual hegemony producing an omnipresent cult, and endless repetitive patterns imposing spatial sameness. The systematic distribution of mechanically reproduced symbols renders all spaces auraless. Also in chapter 6, I explain the role commodities play in the systematic destruction of aura. This chapter ultimately aims to provide a concrete case of how the systemic destruction of aura lies at the heart of the production of totalitarian space.

Finally, chapter 7 explores the commodification of public space and the alienation that it engenders. The chapter also revisits the negativity of aura, particularly in relation to the politics of dissent. I argue that commodification simultaneously fragments space, in accordance with the predefined activities of consumerism, and unifies space through the totalizing logic of reproduction. Because familiarity requires repeated duplication, space is both distributed and consumed on the basis of similar patterns. It becomes both a mass commodity and a commodifying force. The resulting spatial patterns of sameness eradicate the conditions for unique, different, individual experiences. This chapter concludes by arguing that the negation of totalitarian space is imperative for regaining the ability to imagine an auratic world. For as much as interrogating the production of space is a question of demasking domination and denormalizing prevailing sociopolitical systems, it is also a matter of imagining spaces of resistance.

1

Notes on Totalitarianism

The word "totalitarianism" evokes a very particular type of imagery. Reflecting the despotism of twentieth-century totalitarian regimes, we associate the term with tyrannical one-party rule, ostentatious celebrations of force, and incendiary propaganda. At the center of it all is a larger-than-life dictator simultaneously feared and revered by the masses. While once considered far-flung for those living in liberal democracies, some of these political attributes are now hitting uncomfortably close to home with the rise of right-wing populism in Europe and the United States. We have seen the protofascist underbellies of political systems long purported to be the bastions of freedom, ushering in a resurgence of militarism, misogyny, xenophobia, and charged rhetoric intent on fabricating an alternate reality. Indeed, the campaign and subsequent election of Donald Trump to the United States' highest office has garnered direct comparisons with totalitarian regimes of the previous century. Following his administration's dissemination of "alternative facts" regarding the size of the crowd at his inauguration in January 2017 (Conway 2017), Amazon even temporarily sold out of Hannah Arendt's *The Origins of Totalitarianism* and saw George Orwell's *1984* top the best-selling book list (Griswold 2017). However, we must be cognizant of the fact that the regimes to which Trump's administration is being compared are just one manifestation of totalitarianism, and they are a crude one at that.

Those who see Trump's ascent to power as an abrupt totalitarian shift in American politics have failed to account for the reality that totalitarianism has inevitably grown more sophisticated since the end of World War II. Disturbing parallels can be drawn between Trump and other autocrats, particularly insofar as his bullying tactics, fragile ego, and disdain for independent media are concerned. Yet conflating such parallels with totalitarianism in the contemporary context speaks to our fixation on the Cold War binary that has immortalized twentieth-century versions of totalitarianism. To be clear, totalitarianism is not, in itself, an ideology or an ideological doctrine, but rather a systemic approach to achieving unlimited domination. As such, it can be adapted by any ideology regardless of whether the ideology's core doctrine is founded on racial hierarchy, universal equality, or individual liberty. Totalitarianism amounts to the use of whatever means proves to be most effective for realizing maximum domination over all domains of public and private life. It would be naive to think that such totalizing forces have lain dormant up until the recent rise of right-wing populism. As an article by the Hannah Arendt Center notes, "The appearance of totalitarianism in the world is not a singular event, signaled by one moment—it is a collection of elements that emerge together under particular historical and material circumstances" (2016). In fashioning Trump and other right-wing populists as isolated threats intent on reviving a political system thought to be dead, we blind ourselves to the more pervasive ways in which totalitarianism has evolved over time.

If we view totalitarianism as a formula for unlimited domination, we can explore the ways in which it has been adapted in increasingly sophisticated ways to systems long considered its antithesis. Although I am not able to fully explicate this here, I would argue that fascism invented and unsuccessfully practiced totalitarianism, state communism further refined it, and liberal capitalism has mastered it. In other words, the new totalitarianism is the totalitarianism of the so-called free market, and in place of Mussolini, Hitler, or Stalin, we have capital. The United States in particular has seen the entrenchment of political power among economic elites who are zealously committed to a "hostile takeover" of American democracy in the name of profit (MacLean 2017, xxxi). According to historian Nancy MacLean, this coalition of billionaires and millionaires "maneuvers very much like a fifth column, operating in a highly calculated fashion, more akin to an occupying force than to an open group engaged in the usual give-and-take of politics" (2017, xxxi). Informed by neoliberal and libertarian ideologies, this fifth column is indicative of the totalitarian underpinnings of capitalism, insofar as it must constantly conquer new spaces yet untapped by the capitalist machine or risk complete collapse.

According to the free-market model, capital must be enabled to overcome all would-be barriers to accrue profit at virtually any cost. We have seen the state in liberal democracies assume the role of facilitating capital's domination, securing a degree of control that no single totalitarian leader could reasonably hope to achieve. This could seem unfathomable if brute force alone were taken to be the primary indicator of totalitarianism, but this chapter demonstrates that advanced totalitarianism relies far more on hegemony than on outright coercion. Against this backdrop, Trump harkens back to an earlier era of totalitarianism, and his wealth afforded him the ability to shun Wall Street with his populist rhetoric. On this level, his campaign was demonstrative of Arendt's observation that the "isolation of atomized individuals provides not only the mass basis for totalitarian rule, but is carried through to the very top of the whole structure" (1979, 407). Trump appealed to the mass individuals whose social bonds have been shattered by the instrumental rationality of capitalism, and he epitomized the mass leader. His outsider posturing, however, was not to last. As Greg Valliere, chief global strategist at Horizon Investments, remarked on Trump's first hundred days in office, "The Goldman Sachs faction in the White House has won" (Long 2017).

The Trump era also signifies the ultimate triumph of the culture industry, which has politicized everything that is nonpolitical and depoliticized everything that is political. This ideological manipulation at the hands of the culture industry has reached such a point that a mass-culture star can now swiftly transition to political stardom. In this brazen merger of mass culture and politics, more tangible signs of totalitarian have surfaced, but nothing substantial has changed. The capitalist system, which both mass culture and official politics mask, has, as a whole, always been totalitarian. Rather than biding our time until things go back to normal, until the real politicians resume the stage, we must ruthlessly interrogate that very sense of normalcy and lay bare the ways in which it is totalitarian. First, however, it is important to unpack the Cold War binary that shapes our understanding of totalitarianism to justify the use of the term to describe the dominant space in today's world.

A Critique of Dominant Understandings of "Totalitarianism"

Admittedly, scholars are deeply divided when it comes to the scholastic usefulness of the term "totalitarianism." While there are many reasons for this divide, a major one is that the term ultimately allowed for communism

and fascism to be grouped side by side. Given totalitarianism's historical association with fascism, it became an especially strong propaganda
weapon for anti-communists to discredit the communist doctrine with a
single stroke (Hobsbawm 1995, 393). The idea is simple: if two entities
are paired together frequently enough to create a pattern, people will
start perceiving them as similar or at the very least comparable entities. Associating communism with a term that is definitive of fascism
inevitably cast doubt on the fundamental legitimacy of the former as
a universalist egalitarian doctrine. Furthermore, grouping communism
with fascism proved especially disquieting for communists, who saw fascism as their opposing ideological pole, and this served to obscure their
prolonged struggle against fascism.

To put it very plainly, as a doctrine, (Marxist) communism rejects
elitism, sectarianism, nationalism, and other forms of stratification of
human society that would create or sustain exploitation. From the Marxist
point of view, the fundamental conflict in societies is not between good
and evil, as theologians believe, or between hierarchical "races," as fascists
believe, but rather between social classes that have conflicting interests.
Because history essentially progresses toward the realization of reason,
per Hegel, and given that exploitative inequality is irrational and thus
historically unsustainable, progressive movements, as most Marxist movements would self-identify, seek to end exploitative inequality. Marxism
views the state as a class instrument that is used to protect the interests
of the ruling class, while the proletariat is considered the largest and most
progressive social class in the capitalist society. In Marxist thought, it is
the proletariat who will eventually take over the state, only to abolish
it altogether after creating the foundations for a classless society.

The fascist doctrine, on the other hand, is founded on the premise
of racial hierarchy among different nations. As the highest manifestation
of the power of the nation, the fascist state is total and supreme. To Mussolini, for instance, "the foundation of Fascism is the conception of the
State, its character, its duty, and its aim. Fascism conceives of the State
as an absolute, in comparison with which all individuals or groups are
relative, only to be conceived of in their relation to the State" (1932).
The fascist worldview maintains that conflict is inevitable when the
power and purity of what is purported to be the innately superior "race"
are challenged by "inferior" races and universalists, such as communists
and liberals. It is because of such fundamental ideological differences
that communists have always seen communism as diametrically opposed

to fascism. Grouping communists with their mortal enemies is therefore considered a grave offence.

From Mussolini's rise to power in 1922, marking the beginning of the fascist reign in Europe, to the Nazi Third Reich (1933–1945) and Franco's coup in 1936, communists were the prominent force of resistance against the hegemony of fascism. Their antifascist history was arguably the most important component of their self-identification, to the degree that opposing communists was often taken to be akin to aligning with fascists (Dallas 2005, 363).[1] Communists played a significant role—if not the most significant—in countering fascism as an ideology and eventually succeeded in rendering fascist a pejorative term. Even now, leftists are often accused of branding all their rivals fascists. While the label was once relatively popular among both ultranationalist mass movements and right-wing artistic and literary elites from Italy to Romania, now it has such negative connotations that even most fascists have forgone it, at least in the public sphere. Yet although fascism's falling out of fashion may have contributed to the popularity of communism as a victorious movement that was definitively antifascist, this was not to last. In the latter half of the 1940s, just as Marxists were looking to build on their symbolic and political victory that resulted from the disgraceful fall of Mussolini and Hitler's regimes, the emerging popularity of the term "totalitarianism" among opponents of communism marked a turning point.

It was used in reference to fascism and Stalinism in the mid-1930s (Christofferson 2004, 4), but only after WWII did totalitarianism come to be viewed as a defining characteristic of the USSR (Hobsbawm 1995, 112; 393). The publication of Arendt's *The Origins of Totalitarianism* in 1951, followed by *Totalitarian Dictatorship and Autocracy* by Carl Friedrich and Zbigniew Brzezinski in 1956, further cemented the popularity of the term in anti-Soviet discourses (Christofferson 2004, 5). Of course, if not for the oppressive politics of Stalin's USSR, totalitarianism may not have become so closely associated with communism in the popular imagination in the West. It often has been retrospectively argued that Stalin's totalitarian rule should have been more widely condemned by Marxists long before the Hitler-Stalin Pact in 1939. Indeed, the Gulags, purges, mass deportations, and political assassinations were prevalent throughout the 1930s. Enzo Traverso explains that many leftist and liberal intellectuals refused to criticize Soviet totalitarianism for primarily pragmatic reasons, insofar as the USSR was indispensable in the war against the Nazis, particularly after the latters' invasion of the Soviet Union in 1941

(2016, 267–68). He writes, "A complex (and perverse) dialectic between fascism and Communism lay at the root of the culpable silence of a large number of intellectuals towards the crimes of Stalinism. First the threat of fascism, then the immense prestige and historical legitimacy gained by the USSR during the Second World War, led a large section of their number to ignore, underestimate, excuse or legitimize Soviet totalitarianism" (2016, 265). Traverso then highlights several more points that are of essential importance in the historical context:

> It is certainly possible to criticize the intellectuals who maintained the myth of the USSR for having lied to themselves and contributed to deceiving the antifascist movement, making themselves propagandists for a totalitarian regime instead of the antifascist movement's critical conscience. But we can also be certain that in Europe (the New Deal in the United States remains a separate case) no mass mobilization against the Nazi menace would have occurred under the leadership of the old liberal elites. The struggle against fascism needed a hope, a message of universal emancipation, which it seemed at this time could be offered only by the country of the October Revolution. If a totalitarian dictatorship like that of Stalin became the embodiment of these values in the eyes of millions of men and women, which is indeed the tragedy of twentieth-century Communism, this is precisely because its origins and its nature were completely different from those of fascism. That is what liberal anti-totalitarianism seems incapable of understanding. (2016, 206; 270)

The resulting reputation of Stalinists was soon generalized to all Marxists in the West, while none of the crimes liberal governments had committed during or after WWII were generalized to all liberals. Marxists found themselves being grouped with their most dreaded enemy based on a notion that historically had been associated with fascists. The term swiftly found a place in the liberal and rightist anticommunist discourse, not so much because of its explanatory or analytic potential, but rather for its obscuring and damning effects.[2] Those whom Marxists had accused of being complicit with fascism during the 1936–1939 Spanish Civil War and with Hitler from 1933 to 1939 now placed Marxists in the same camp as fascists.

Yet in the 1966 preface to Part Three of *The Origins of Totalitarianism*, Arendt noted the significance of Stalin's death and the "authentic, though never unequivocal, process of detotalitarization" that followed (1975, xxv). With some reluctance and skepticism, she concluded that "the Soviet Union can no longer be called totalitarian in the strict sense of the term" (Arendt 1975, xxxvi). To Michael Scott Christofferson, Arendt's reading of the post-Stalin USSR can be seen as an attempt to distance her work from "the Cold War misuse of the concept" (2004, 7). Friedrich and Brzezinski's book lends itself to anticommunist propaganda more easily. Philosophically, their account of totalitarianism is invalid because it stipulates "criteria" that amount to an abstracted description of Stalin's USSR, rendering the notion predeterministic. They posit that all totalitarian regimes have "an official ideology," "a single mass party led typically by one man," "a system of terroristic police control," a party-controlled means of mass communication and armed forces, and a centralized economy (1956, 9–10).

Friedrich and Brzezinski's account can be invalidated quite straightforwardly, namely by determining whether a regime that lacks any one of the criteria could still be called totalitarian. If so, then the criterion in question is false, indicating the invalidity of their account. Taking the first criterion as a case in point, suppose a regime does not officially adopt an ideology "covering all vital aspects of man's existence to which everyone living in that society is supposed to adhere," to use Friedrich and Brzezinski's words (1956, 9). That was the case in General Augusto Pinochet's Chile, yet it would be absurd to exempt it from the class of totalitarian regimes for that reason alone. There was of course an ideology of domination at work in Chile, but only behind the scenes, not officially. Indeed, none other than Milton Friedman, the godfather of neoliberalism and the most influential teacher of the Chicago boys, was Pinochet's adviser (Klein 2007). To the Cold War theorists of totalitarianism, however, the term was never to be applied to liberalism, but only and always to opposing ideologies. In terms of perfecting totalitarianism, ideological hegemony, whereby the dominant ideology becomes internalized and normalized, is far more effective than imposing an official ideology. When ideology is presented, propagated for, and executed as the ideology of the state, this alone suffices to distance people from it, even if they pretend otherwise on the surface. An official ideology that is imposed on people necessarily fosters hypocrisy and public performance, as opposed to anything resembling total domination. As in Romania, the destruction of such a totalitarian state can happen within a matter of days. On the occasion of former President Nicolae Ceausescu's last public speech on December 21, 1989, many in the crowd were still carrying his pictures and banners praising his regime, but the initial warm reception suddenly shifted to booing. Everything started to collapse, and Ceausescu and his wife, Elena, were executed four days later. No one defended them; no masses poured onto the streets to mourn their deaths. Ceausescu's Romania, as an exemplary Stalinist state, met all of Friedrich and Brzezinski's criteria of a totalitarian state, but it was nowhere close to achieving total domination.

This leads into Friedrich and Brzezinski's second criterion, a mass party typically led by a dictator. Would domination not be more totalizing and efficient in the long run if the totalitarian system were not dependent on a single leader? Needless to say, no matter how strong the dictator, eventually s/he either would be killed or die naturally. Especially after Stalin's death, Arendt became aware of the inevitable successor crisis that follows a single totalitarian leader's death, but she saw this as a flaw of totalitarianism as such, rather than attributing it to a pre-advanced stage or type of totalitarianism. Even a slightly more advanced totalitarian regime would be designed in such a way that it would not to be dependent on a single leader or his/her family. As one example, in 1979, the Islamic Republic of Iran established a system that has proven far more successful than its predecessor, the Shah regime, in actualizing extensive and prolonged control over society. Having avoided the traditional formula of a leading political party and dictator when Khomeini died in 1989, ten years after founding the regime, the totalitarian functioning of the system continued without disruption.

Friedrich and Brzezinski's third criterion, "terroristic police control," is also central to Arendt's notion of totalitarianism (1956, 9). The intuitive question this raises is whether the need for terror is indicative of a system that has not achieved total domination. Is it not the case that total domination would rely on indoctrination, rather than resorting to physical force as the primary means of control? Arendt almost reached this conclusion; however, she only went as far as claiming that a totalitarian regime could reach a stage of domination that would no longer require extensive terror and propaganda (1975, 341). In other words, she did not anticipate further development of totalitarianism beyond the existing totalitarian regime of the time, Stalin's USSR.

"[A] technologically conditioned near-complete monopoly of control, in the hands of the party and its subversive cadres, of all means of effective mass communication" is Friedrich and Brzezinski's fourth criterion (1956, 10). Indeed, a monopoly of mass communication does seem to be essential for totalitarianism insofar as it is deemed necessary for ideological indoctrination. However, would it not be even more effective if other agencies were to carry out this indoctrination on behalf of "the party," as we can see in more advanced totalitarian systems? As with an overt state ideology, a totalitarian party's monopoly of the media merely turns the media into a sham that most would only find reliable for relaying state announcements of national holidays, curfews, and the like. On the other hand, when mass communication is left to corporate monopolies, people tune in even during their so-called free time. In other words, while most view party-controlled mass media—much like Trump's Twitter feed—with a healthy dose of skepticism, the corporatization of media is often considered benign, at least comparatively. In a paper he was supposed to present in 1961 at a UNESCO symposium (Kellner 2001, 37), Marcuse noted that "the totalitarian rationality of advanced industrial society makes the problem a purely theoretical one. The transplanting of social into individual needs is so effective that any distinction seems impossible or arbitrary. For example, can one really distinguish between the mass media as technical instruments and as instruments of manipulation, and as instruments of information and entertainment?" (2001, 52–53). Furthermore, the means of corporatized mass communication are now used as exceptionally effective means of surveillance. As Slavoj Žižek predicted more than fifteen years ago, "the digitalization of our lives poses the ultimate threat to our freedom—soon, our daily lives will be registered and controlled to such an extent that the former police state control will look like a childish game: the 'end of privacy' is in sight" (2001, 229). With the proliferation of digital means of communication and surveillance, privacy and private space are invaded with an efficiency that no totalitarian regime could ever reach.

Friedrich and Brzezinski's next criterion for a totalitarian regime is the party's monopoly of the "means of effective armed combat." Let us imagine that the state, as opposed to a particular political party, has the monopoly of arms. Again, would this not result in a more stable, sustainable, efficient totalitarian regime than one tied to the fate of the ruling political party? Such is the case in the Islamic Republic of Iran, further contributing to the regime's endurance. Of course, we have also seen systems wherein the "technologically conditioned near-complete monopoly of control" of all arms, to use Friedrich and Brzezinski's terminology (1956), lies with the state and its corporate partners. Are systems that rely on this shared monopoly of arms inherently less totalitarian than those in which the party or state holds complete control?

The final criterion, a centralized economy, suggests that anything other than a free-market economy is totalitarian by default, speaking to the ideologically loaded nature of Friedrich and Brzezinski's model. To invalidate this criterion, one could simply think of totalitarian regimes that have adopted non-central, free-market economies. In Pinochet's Chile, for example, his neoliberal advisers implemented an extremely unregulated form of free-market economy that no other country, including the United States, has been able to rival (Klein 2007). Neoliberal policies have similarly been in place for more than ten years in Erdogan's Turkey, which continues to advance steadily toward totalitarianism. Even the Chinese regime has learned that adopting neoliberalism is imperative for achieving more complete control. Contrary to neoliberal ideological claims, there is no rational or empirical evidence to prove that an economy monopolized by a small capitalist elite results in less domination and more freedoms.

In sum, a regime that does not meet all of Friedrich and Brzezinski's criteria would not necessarily be nontotalitarian or even less totalitarian, if we agree that totalitarianism ultimately amounts to total domination. If anything, realizing a greater degree of domination would necessarily require going beyond each of Friedrich and Brzezinski's criteria. Even without empirical cases—which can always be dismissed to spare the proposed criteria—we could, with little difficulty, imagine a system that demonstrates none of the six criteria but is nonetheless more efficient as a totalitarian system. This will become clearer over the course of the rest of this chapter, but it should already be evident that the pioneers of the Cold War definition of totalitarianism molded their conception on the least developed of totalitarian systems, without accounting for the conceptual fluidity that is essential in the creation or appropriation of any concept. Recognizing the rigidity of their conceptualization, from the mid-1960s on, Friedrich tried to revise some of their previous assumptions. Brzezinski even announced that the post-Stalin Soviet Union was no longer totalitarian (Christofferson 2004), but this too was a false conclusion, for the USSR was, obviously, totalitarian both during and after Stalin. The concern here is that their conceptualization of totalitarianism could not account for variations of systems that strive for total domination, the advancement of those systems, or historical changes. Crucially, this shortsightedness was not accidental, but rather served the purpose for which the notion was used in the Cold War era. Tailored to Stalinism, it aimed to predetermine that the negation of liberal capitalism would logically and empirically lead to a horrific system of total and arbitrary terror. In a roundabout way, it then became possible for anti-leftists to fully exploit the notion of totalitarianism to delegitimize all Marxian opposition to and critique of the capitalist order, as totalitarianism qua Stalinism was portrayed as the nominal negation of liberal capitalism.

Clearly, many leftists react strongly to the use and abuse of the term "totalitarianism" for this precise reason. For instance, Žižek writes, "[T]he notion of 'totalitarianism', far from being an effective theoretical concept, is a kind of stopgap: instead of enabling us to think, forcing us to acquire a new insight into the historical reality it describes, it relieves us of the duty to think, or even actively prevents us from thinking" (2001, 3). Anyone familiar with Žižek's thought would know that his rejection of the term is motivated not by surreptitious empathy for the communist regimes, but by a desire to speak against its totalizing usage against critics of liberal capitalism. Totalitarianism, as a term, has not only been used to group communists with fascists to demonize the former, but also to obscure the differences between leftist groups and movements and Stalinist regimes. Similar to the function of the religious accusation of blasphemy, the association of Marxist critics with totalitarianism is used as a silencing tactic. As such, it is inherently antidemocratic and, one could even argue, totalitarian. For accusing all critics of liberal capitalism of being illiberal and/or totalitarian is itself an illiberal practice that seeks to elevate liberal capitalism to a position above criticism, thus contributing to its total domination.

Although Arendt's *The Origins of Totalitarianism* brands both communism and fascism totalitarian and perhaps is still the most widely referenced philosophical work on the subject, even she admitted that capitalism has always been totalitarian in its economic manipulation of politics. She states, "The bourgeois class, having made its way through social pressure and, frequently, through an economic blackmail of political institutions, always believed that the public and visible organs of power were directed by their own secret, nonpublic interests and influence" (1975, 336). She goes on to take a Marxian position, adding, "In this sense, the bourgeoisie's political philosophy was always 'totalitarian'; it always assumed an identity of politics, economics and society, in which political institutions served only as the façade for private interests" (1975, 336). Such a statement not only denounces capitalism as inherently totalitarian, but also makes direct use of historical materialism, according to which the state and other political institutions are the ideological superstructure that protects the dominant relations of production. The Marxian view holds that capitalism as a mode of production determines the function of the state, laws, religion, morality, knowledge, and culture, just as feudalism once did the same. That is to say, political, legal, religious, educational, and cultural institutions for the most part help to normalize, protect, and prolong the capitalist social relations as well as the material conditions that sustain those relations. Thus, any theory of totalitarianism that relies on historical materialism would argue that a capitalist system is more totalitarian than its predecessors because of its historical, geographical, and technological advancement.

Theoretically, total domination or the unlimited exercise of power is most often viewed as the definitive characteristic of a totalitarian system (Arendt 1975; Curtis 1979; Conquest 2000, 74). It should go without saying, however, that on a practical level, total domination cannot be achieved. Even those regimes that have unhesitatingly been called totalitarian, namely Nazi Germany and Stalin's Soviet Union, never succeeded in eliminating dissent altogether. Therefore, a crucial indicator of a totalitarian system is the extent of its vision, its aspirations to assume total control, even if, in practice, it cannot completely achieve these aims. Any system, whether strictly political or not, that pursues such unlimited exercise of power, regardless of the methods it uses, is totalitarian.

If we treat totalitarianism as a concept rather than an ideological attribution exclusive to Nazism and Stalinism, it becomes a useful scholastic tool to diagnose totalitarian tendencies as well as advanced totalitarian systems that are not necessarily authoritarian, militant, or terroristic. Just as democracy is ascribed to systems of governance in ancient Greece and contemporary states alike, notwithstanding their myriad differences, there is no reason to reserve the term totalitarianism for labeling a few historical models. In spite of the low voter turnout and overall political apathy of today's "managed" democracies, we persist in calling them democratic.[3] A refusal to entertain similar conceptual flexibility in identifying a system as "totalitarian" is in itself cause for alarm. Aside from Mussolini's fascist Italy, no regime has self-identified with totalitarianism. On the level of official discourse, totalitarian states have historically purported themselves to be the true realization of the people's will. The people, however, while behaving in public "as if" they believed the regime's narrative, were acutely aware of their unfreedom.[4] Only a more advanced totalitarian system could succeed in making the masses believe the lie.

Far from being a fixed ideology that has been discredited, totalitarianism is the will to horizontal and vertical control. As such, it has proven to be adaptable to extremely different ideological and geographical contexts. "[T]otalitarianism," as Wolin writes, "is capable of local variations; plausibly, far from being exhausted by its twentieth-century versions would-be totalitarians now have available technologies of control, intimidation and mass manipulation far surpassing those of that earlier time" (2010, xvii). In this sense, the totalitarianism of the 1930s and 1940s was in its experimental stage, a stage in which the veneration of power along with the expansion of its disciplinary apparatuses was thought to be sufficient to create a nation completely unified behind and submissive to the epoch-making leader. As totalitarianism becomes more advanced, the system increasingly revolves around the maximum mechanization of power, as opposed to the central role of the leader.

Classical vs. Advanced Totalitarianism

The dictatorial leadership, militarization of society, and physical suppression of dissent characteristic of the first generation of totalitarian regimes would prove insufficient for global domination in the age of superpowers. More effective and efficient methods of control were necessary given the vastly expanded spatial field at stake. Therefore, while the tools of classical totalitarianism remained in use to varying degrees in the Soviet Union throughout the Cold War period, a more sophisticated system of control also took shape, a system that Václav Havel termed "post-totalitarian" (1990). The Soviet system that evolved over decades, as Havel wrote in 1975, differed from classical totalitarianism in five main ways: it functioned as a global power; it had "undeniable historicity" as opposed to being a "historical freak"; its ideology provided a more complete rationality and all-inclusive narrative; the exercise of power was systematized, maximizing efficiency and minimizing arbitrariness; and, finally, its citizenry was depoliticized in large part because of the shift toward consumer society (1990, 24–27). In other words, the Soviet Union in its later stages became a more hegemonic form of totalitarianism, both countering and influencing its competing superpower.

Totalitarianism owes much of its advancement to this rivalry between the Soviet Union and the United States, for the Cold War presented the ultimate excuse on both sides to justify the expansion of state power at the expense of political freedoms. Parallel to that was the ideological war to delegitimize the Other and at the same time ensure impenetrable and unbreakable unity at home. Overtly suppressive or terroristic means of control would have been counterproductive in terms of expanding hegemony. Indeed, as Arendt writes, "Violence appears where power is in jeopardy" and "as a last resort to keep the power structure intact" (1970, 56; 146). It was time for totalitarianism to incorporate arenas other than politics, such as the economy, in addition to mechanizing the system of control to ensure the durability of the system independent of the lives and mistakes of leaders. Contrary to the American portrayal of a totalitarian Soviet Union in stark contrast to the supposedly intrinsic freedom and liberty of the American political system, the United States has itself become increasingly totalitarian. It is, in fact, the enduring ideological emphasis on individual liberties in the United States that has served to disguise the development of a form of totalitarianism that is, if anything, more hegemonic than any of its predecessors. Wolin has described the system as "inverted totalitarianism," which, "precisely because of its inverted character, emerges, not as an abrupt regime change or dramatic rupture but as evolutionary, as evolving out of a continuing and increasingly unequal struggle between an unrealized democracy and an antidemocracy that dare not to speak its name" (2010, 213). In addition to sharing an important parallel with Havel's emphasis on the historicity of the post-totalitarian system, Wolin's point helps to elucidate the reasons behind the popular refusal to acknowledge the totalizing tendencies at work in the United States.

While classical totalitarianism targets the citizen as a political agent whose consent is sought as a necessary condition for the legitimacy of the system, in advanced totalitarianism the citizen is targeted as a consumer of both material and cultural commodities. The political mobilization of masses is replaced by economic mobilization in new totalitarianism, as Wolin argues. Thus, in a major liberal democracy such as the United States, much of public opinion is manufactured through the use of corporate money. The most obvious channel for creating the climate of opinion necessary to sustain new totalitarianism is mass media. In contrast to the overtly propagandistic state-controlled media characteristic of classical totalitarianism, a hallmark of advanced totalitarianism is private media that continually portray themselves as independent but ultimately present capitalist liberalism as the nonideological, neutral, objective discourse. Liberalism has been the most successful ideology to date in terms of establishing a nonideological façade, which is precisely why it has been so easily disseminated since the 1980s. Yet this process of creating a world of sameness under the guise of liberal "objectivity," crucial for maintaining and advancing totalitarianism, is more complex than a mere agenda on the part of private media to implement the conditions for the exercise of corporate power. The process takes place within the culture industry, which I explain in more detail later in this chapter. On the most general level, the culture industry adamantly politicizes that which is least political and depoliticizes that which is most political. It is the culture industry that functions as liberalism's ideological machine for disguising the monopoly inherent in the capitalist system. Diffusion is the main strategy: everything is presented as something other than what it is.

The ineffectiveness of state propaganda in classical totalitarianism made the use of force unavoidable to maintain the totalitarian rule. However, advanced totalitarianism has achieved a far greater degree of ideological hegemony, rendering physical violence much less necessary. That said, a striking exception to this pretense of nonviolence is the criminalization of minority groups in liberal democracies, and particularly in the United States, where the prison industrial complex further illustrates the intertwining of state and corporate power. Wolin identifies this as "a strategy of political neutralization" insofar as Black Americans—who are five times more likely to be incarcerated than whites (NAACP 2017)—are "by far the one group that throughout the twentieth century kept alive a spirit of resistance and rebelliousness" (2010, 58). We continue to see this in The Movement for Black Lives, which has demanded "economic justice for all and a reconstruction of the economy to ensure Black communities have collective ownership, not merely access" (2016, 12). Still, as a matter of cost-effectiveness, advanced totalitarianism does prefer to invest in less violent means of control. This logic is nicely encapsulated in a line from The Godfather (1972), when the drug lord Virgil Sollozzo concludes a negotiation with consigliere Tom Hagen by saying, "I don't like violence, Tom. I'm a businessman; blood is a big expense." New systems of unlimited domination have similarly developed less overtly violent means of ensuring compliance that are more politically and economically expedient. Also, in place of crude state propaganda, the culture industry was given the stage to create a nation of consumers of cultural and material commodities.

In contrast, classical totalitarianism relies extensively on cultism. Thus, the omnipresence of the great leader in social space is crucial for producing and maintaining totalitarian space. By placing his ageless images everywhere, the mortal leader hopelessly fights his unavoidable fate. With the passage of time, the great leader's fear of death would increase, and so too would his ensuing absolutism. The more spaces the totalizing power of the leader conquers, the more fetishistic he becomes not only toward his followers, sadistically as their cultic leader, but also narcissistically toward himself. As a pathology, this fetishism only deepens the perilous fragility of the leader's illusion of absolute security and undisturbed prosperity. Indeed, the leader's obsession with himself continually increases his distrust of everyone, which, through never-ending purges, leads to ever more visual demonstrations of loyalty, resulting in a frenzy of fetishism. The ensuing madness is most evident in social space, which becomes the space of endless ornaments of the fetish: the leader. Through endless images, the leader eternally gazes upon the people, whose performance of loyalty functions as an abyss returning his own gaze. Soon every corner of public space would become a Panopticon from which the omnipresent gaze of the leader could enforce everyone's unconditional allegiance.

Classical totalitarianism is perpetually paranoid about possible conspiracies, and this is yet another reason for its reliance on sheer force. This, in turn, creates a social and political environment that renders power the currency for all social rankings. Power hierarchies become the norm, while social space becomes a field for the vulgar exercise of power. The body itself is reduced to a commodity of masculinity to exhibit pure power. Totalitarian leaders become obsessed with showcasing their bodily perfection, and, with the entire state at their disposal, they will stop at nothing to sustain that image. The statues and billboard images of a classical totalitarian leader are nothing but the embodiment of that vulgar masculinity. While the leader would no doubt be presented as the greatest thinker, writer, and artist of all times, it is the hegemony of visibility that is of most concern to the mobs and the leader himself.

Like the imposing façade of classical totalitarianism, by all appearances the leader seems intimidating, but he is in fact extremely insecure precisely because of his obsession with absolute power. The more paranoid the totalitarian leader becomes, the more terror the regime externalizes against its subjects. There is a point when terror becomes both the means and the end, as Arendt noted (1979). When terror too reaches the level of fetishism, the beginning of the regime's end is near. Terror cannot guarantee the complete obedience sought by a totalitarian system simply because there will always be more people who have nothing to lose, some of whom will inevitably form a deadly front against the regime. Furthermore, because classical totalitarianism relies on physical violence to force its potential opponents into submission, violent resistance becomes increasingly justifiable among the oppressed people. Inevitably, when the system begins to show signs of collapse, nearly every member of the oppressed groups becomes an actual enemy of the state. This differs greatly from advanced totalitarianism, wherein terror is not a recognized aspect of the state's apparatuses, making the use of violence as a form of resistance seem unjustifiable to the populace, even among those most oppressed by the ruling groups. Indeed, not even the most radical opponents of the system consider themselves enemies of the state, with the sole exception of anarchists, for whom this enmity is a defining part of their struggle for freedom and equality.

Notwithstanding the differences between classical and advanced totalitarianism, both types of systems produce a space in which individuality qua uniqueness is systematically targeted. In such a space, difference is allowed if and only if it does not represent a threat to the imagined absolute oneness. Thus, certain so-called individual freedoms are permitted under totalitarian systems. In fact, some classical totalitarian regimes have been more socially liberal than their respective societies, and this is a frequent point of confusion for naive observers who measure the merits of political regimes—particularly in the third world—according to simplified abstract standards such as secularism. For instance, some leftists were willing to overlook the atrocities of the Baath regimes in Syria and Iraq because both were relatively secular and socialist, just as the Nazi regime was a secular national socialist regime. Similarly, many liberals have always admired Kemalist Turkish nationalism for its strict policies of secularization and modernization, despite the genocides committed against peoples who were not Muslim Turks. From the outset, the Young Turks pursued a brutal campaign against Armenians, and later Alevite Kurds and other Kurds. Acts of genocide are seemingly minor details when it comes to the reputation of third world regimes. Both Kemalists and Baathists pushed for more personal liberties than their respective societies would have traditionally allowed, but politically, both movements would have readily been labeled fascist had they appeared in Europe.

Even many feminist observers uncritically celebrated the appearance of women in short skirts on the streets of Istanbul, Damascus, and Baghdad, taking this as evidence of those regimes' progressive politics. This served to only further shroud the systematic femicide of those women deemed a threat to national unity merely by virtue of not belonging to the privileged "race."[5]

Yet perhaps we should not be surprised by this tendency to privilege socially progressive freedoms as a gauge of political systems. In advanced totalitarianism, after all, nearly all apolitical and apoliticized freedoms are permitted, while politics itself is depoliticized through the means of the culture industry. Again, this depoliticization of politics is achieved precisely through the politicization of what is least political. For instance, abortion and same-sex marriage, which should be undisputed individual rights, were turned into foundational political questions in the United States, and other countries have increasingly followed suit. Right-wing rhetoric compels voters to believe that they have a moral and political obligation to thwart women's "right to choose" or gay people's right to marry, which then forces those targeted to undertake securing those rights as a political struggle. Indeed, abortion is often made out to be the single most important issue in elections, dating back to the 1970s and 1980s when "the unholy marriage between the Republican Party and the Evangelical Reconstructionist-infected 'pro-life' community was gradually consummated" (Schaeffer 2014). The charged "culture wars" that ensue from the politicization of such issues serve to channel attention away from the totalizing forces that truly shape politics. In advanced totalitarianism, that is, most people have been led to believe that the emperor is not naked, to borrow the famous image from Hans Christian Andersen's story. Under classical totalitarianism, on the other hand, most of the populace only pretends to believe the lie, and therein lies the crucial difference.

Because advanced totalitarianism is more successful in obscuring itself, this chapter endeavors to illustrate the totalitarian features of capitalist liberalism, which enriches the subsequent discussion of totalitarian space. Proving that regimes such as Stalin's USSR are totalitarian is quite straightforward, often self-evident, and thus a less pressing undertaking. In a classical totalitarian country, the traditional benchmarks of totalitarianism are ubiquitous: in city squares, at the entrances to government buildings, on classroom walls, and on state television channels. Wherever one turns, the gaze of the great leader is present, most often looking down upon everyone. In advanced totalitarianism, however, instead of representations of a leader, it is representations of commodities and their promise of happiness that occupy all corners of public space, thereby creating a naturalized world for commodity fetishism. So long as citizens are reduced to consumers, they have a home everywhere they go, and this is the ultimate goal of advanced totalitarianism. The consumer's home becomes those endless spaces of consumption where the flow of commodities ensures the continuity of production elsewhere.

An essential aspect of chain stores and franchised eateries is the fact that they guarantee the continuation of the same spatial experience for the consumer. Home is where one can find one's stores, one's desired commodities, in the most convenient way possible. It is essential for consumers to be able to navigate the sea of commodities and locate the particular commodities they seek. Hence, we see the same layouts replicated again and again, with the spatial distribution dictated by commodities. This is so much so, in fact, that for many consumers, it is often easier to locate things at the store than in their own homes, which have become commodity graveyards.

The big-box stores and chain businesses that have routed out local stores, restaurants, and cafes systematically homogenize the cities they invade. Now, entire urban spaces are transformed into spaces of consumption according to blueprints that are duplicated all around the world. Undoubtedly, the immediate consequence of this mega-reproduction of space is the endless reproduction of similar patterns of spatial experience. Commodities create one vast space predicated on patterns of predictable behaviors. Just as some religious believers await paradise for the realization of justice and the fulfillment of their desires, consumers are promised salvation in the form of commodities. According to the consumerist mentality, there is always another commodity that can deliver the ultimate happiness. Consumerism is a hegemonized lifestyle. Therefore, once citizens are turned into consumers, freedom of expression is no longer a threat insofar as the totalitarian system is concerned. The consumerist is a mass individual, the subject of the culture industry, whose passivity is the vehicle of advanced totalitarianism.

Totalitarian Mechanization and Standardization

The mechanization of society that results from the triumph of capitalist modes of production is itself sufficiently totalitarian to subdue the political realm with little regard for maintaining the façade of political plurality. Systematic alienating processes are part and parcel of the mechanization of social relations, and the monopoly of individual imagination and will to action is the direct result. Ultimately, society is broken down into mass individuals whose social links are bureaucratically massified. The alienated individual's activities, whether during work or so-called free time, further disempower her and perpetuate the conditions of her own reification. Individual freedom is the immediate casualty of the mechanization and technical organization of life, the economy, politics, and mass communication. Accordingly, a society based on individual freedom would necessitate freeing everyday life from exploitive economic relations, social activity from political hegemony, and thought from the apparatuses of mass communication and the culture industry (Marcuse 1968, 4).

Above all, culture is an essential agent of totalization that projects sameness and, thus, creates the standardized patterns of perception needed to maintain the mass personality. At the same time, culture is also a safety valve that releases some sparks of imagination precisely to maintain the pretense of freedom, thereby securing the perpetual domination of the laws of profit. To Horkheimer and Adorno, "culture" is nothing but a commodity. "It is so completely subject to the law of exchange that it is no longer exchanged; it is so blindly equated with use that it can no longer be used" (Horkheimer and Adorno 2002, 131).[6] The culture industry produces mass mentality through the mass production of cultural commodities that, functioning as diffused ideological carriers, ensure indoctrination. Thus, the culture industry domesticates individuals and social groups through the pacification of their potential freedoms. As Horkheimer and Adorno write in *Dialectic of Enlightenment*, first published in 1947:

> Culture today is infecting everything with sameness. Film, radio, and magazines form a system. Each branch of culture is unanimous within itself and all are unanimous together. Even the aesthetic manifestations of political opposites proclaim the same inflexible rhythm. The decorative administrative and exhibition buildings of industry differ little between authoritarian and other countries. (2002, 94)

We cannot have a useful scholarly definition of totalitarianism without considering the global capitalist conditions that gave rise to its various forms within modernism. Not limited to modern technological means of control, these conditions also include the culture industry's means and methods of indoctrination, which function as instrumental rationality that levels all possibilities of individual experience, instead creating and totalizing the absolute commodification of social relations. Such a fragmented social world of pseudoindividuality is based on the mass production of formulas or models of "individuality," and the mere illusion of having choices to make by virtue of being a consumer. Thus, the human-to-human alienation eventually reaches a point when the power of the state as well as its bureaucratic institutions and capitalist corporations will be welcomed into all public and private spheres to organize the social space, protect our rights and private properties from each other, and provide us with a sense of security. This is the point when we will end up in a totality of suppressive and hegemonic power rooted in the entrenchment of social fragmentation and alienation.

In some of the Frankfurt School literature, "mass culture" and "culture industry" are used interchangeably. However, it became especially important to Adorno to avoid using "mass culture" because of its democratic implication (i.e., the suggestion that it is a culture shaped by the masses). Thus, one of the crucial aspects of his account of the culture industry is that it is produced and mass distributed from above with the passive participation of the masses as consumers (Adorno 2006a). Marcuse's distinction between mass culture and high culture is also relevant here. To Marcuse, mass culture is the refusal of "the great refusal" inherent in art (1968, 64). He argues that before the age of mass culture, art and literature were essentially negative insofar as they were a sublimation of alienation, and through that they protested the existing order (Marcuse 1968, 61–62). Furthermore, he adds, "[i]n the realm of culture, the new totalitarianism manifests itself precisely in a harmonizing pluralism, where the most contradictory works and truths peacefully coexist in indifference" (Marcuse 1968, 61). The art that was once part of high culture was the imprint of "the unhappy consciousness" contemplating itself in the world (Marcuse 1968, 61). Art was the sublime product of the troubled souls who had the time and the luxury to think about life, not just to live it in whatever way it imposed itself. Whereas the main artistic heroes of high culture were outcasts and rebels who continually negated the existing order, the protagonists of mass culture are one-dimensional, submissive figures representative of the intellectual poverty and utopian deficiency of which the mass individual suffers. Ultimately, mass culture's stars are not "images of another way of life but rather freaks or types of the same life, serving as an affirmation rather than negation of the established order" (Marcuse 1968, 59).

It could even be argued that the age of the anti-hero has passed, and we now live in the post–anti-hero era. Since around the turn of the century, a type of protagonist has emerged who is a complete failure in the most literal sense without any explicit or implicit tragic element. The post–anti-hero's utter unintelligence is meant to be both unimaginable and familiar to viewers: unimaginable in that everything the character says or does is utterly ridiculous, and familiar because the personality represents a perfect example of resignation from the burden of thinking, which is exactly what makes the product so entertaining at no mental cost. Examples of such products are movies such as *Step Brothers* (McKay 2008) and *The Hangover* (Phillips 2009), and they are more numbing to autonomous critical thought than any totalitarian regime's propaganda could have ever been. Pure entertainment is manufactured in ways that further exile politics into another world, as if all a citizen should and could do besides work is consume commodities that render leisure a constant state of being. In the end, work is conducted as a form of failed leisure and leisure as a sort of mandatory chore, which is exemplified in the state of the worker who listens to popular music, streams videos, or endlessly checks her social media feeds to while away the dreadful hours of work. This behavior offers a window into the worker's leisure time, which is defined by pure and passive consumption. The products of the culture industry represent a thread that ties together the atomized spaceless moments of a mass individual's everyday life.

Heinz Steinert identifies two senses of Horkheimer and Adorno's use of "culture industry": in the first, the emphasis is on the production of culture on the basis of commodity form, and in the second, the focus is on the mass production of cultural goods (2003, 9). I argue that the culture industry is at the heart of the fascist process of flattening social space in a way that makes totalitarianism possible. As Jay Bernstein writes, "While Adorno nowhere identifies the culture industry with the political triumph of fascism, he does imply, both directly and indirectly, that the culture industry's effective integration of society marks an equivalent triumph of repressive unification in liberal democratic states to that which was achieved politically under fascism" (2006, 4). The inquiry in this chapter later takes us to an explanation of the principle of commodity-form, which is an important aspect of new totalitarianism. Then in chapters 5 and 6, I address what to Steinert is the second sense of "culture industry" by explaining Benjamin's emphasis on the mechanical reproduction of works of art, which inevitably leads to the destruction of aura. Only after introducing the political implications and consequences of the destruction of the aura of works of art, and the destruction of spatial aura due to these mechanically reproduced images, can I provide a more complete and specific account of totalitarian space.

The main thesis in Horkheimer and Adorno's theory of the culture industry is that mass culture ideologically and structurally reflects the tendency towards absolute domination inherent in capitalism. They state:

> In reality, a cycle of manipulation and retroactive need is unifying the system ever more tightly. What is not mentioned is that the basis on which technology is gaining power over society is the power of those whose economic position in society is strongest. Technical rationality today is the rationality of domination. It is the compulsive character of a society alienated from itself. Automobiles, bombs, and films hold the totality together until their leveling element demonstrates its power against the very system of injustice it served. (Horkheimer and Adorno 2002, 95)

The overwhelming logic of the culture industry is one and the same as the central drive in capitalism, namely profit. On the other end of the culture industry, according to Adorno and Horkheimer, is the negation of individuality, the destruction of auratic experience (Bernstein 2001, 111), or, in a word, pseudo-individuality (Horkheimer and Adorno 2002, 124–25). One of the points Arendt emphasizes is the essentiality of the masses for totalitarianism; it transforms classes to masses (xxxii, 460). In liberal capitalism, this is exactly what the culture industry does, but in that case, the masses are composed of "dividuals" (Deleuze's term), or individuals who have been simultaneously assimilated (into the system) and isolated (from each other). This mass-ness is defined by mass passive consumption of material and cultural commodities, which serves as an immediate and essential contribution to the totalitarian system. We, as consumers, are supposed to feel politically engaged by making "conscious" choices when deciding from which brands and stores we will purchase. In this vein, purchasing fulfils not only our needs and desires but also our political, moral, humanitarian, and even spiritual responsibilities.

To Milton Friedman and his followers, consumerist freedom of choice is alone sufficient to drive the advancement of all sectors of society, be it education, health, arts, and so forth. In Friedman's neoliberal world, no action need be taken: the Smithian invisible hand of the free market will create the best possible world. One's agency is political only insofar as one is a consumer, but the consumer's power is purely quantitative—that is, it does not require sophisticated political or moral consciousness, because it is merely the power of her money. Those with less purchase power have less political power, and those with the most capital have the loudest say. As such, the neoliberal system is the system of the absolute, unlimited power of capital.

In the years ahead, we will no doubt witness more capitalists, who may also be heroes of the culture industry, push aside politicians from the political stage altogether, and instead take over the highest governmental offices. There is no longer any need for maneuvering behind the scenes. If anything, the vulgarity of certain reality shows and the sheer extravagance of celebrity lifestyles have proven endlessly intriguing to the new masses. With Berlusconi, a new era began, an era in which capital does not buy politics, but runs politics. Up until the end of the last century, the rich had to invest in politicians who were trained diplomats to serve as the façade of the capitalist relations of power. Now, however, thanks to the all-encompassing influence of the culture industry for decades, if anything it is the vulgarity of the bourgeoisie that most appeals to the masses. The new leaders will increasingly come directly from the market with their cash, as opposed to being deemed qualified by virtue of their law degrees from elite universities. Politicians once had to perform a degree of (pseudo)intellectualism, but politics in today's mass society demand openly anti-intellectuals who live the dream life of the mass individuals and speak their language, for better or worse. Just as in the art world, where the mass culture of the 1960s is in many ways today's "high culture," the last century's pseudointellectual populists are now considered too sophisticated to appeal to the populace.[7]

Ultimately, capital determines everything, including the distribution of social space. As Debord states, "Capitalist production has unified space, breaking down the boundaries between one society and the next. This unification is at the same time an extensive and intensive process of banalization" (1983, §165). The dominant space in a capitalist society, or "abstract space" as Lefebvre calls it, is a space unified by the principle of profit, which translates to spaces of production and spaces of consumption. Every other space is produced and measured within that orbit. The cost of dwelling depends on the place's distance from the centers of capital and the areas considered desirable by the upper class. The nature of dominant space under capitalism has nothing to do with the moral values or political views of the capitalists, who have the monopoly of the spatial production. By the same token, those without capital only have their labor to sell, so regardless of who they are, they end up contributing to the system through prolonging their own powerlessness. That is, unless they become aware of their class interests and act accordingly, by transforming from mass to class. To comprehend this issue better, it is worth reviewing the Marxian debates over labor and personhood.

Essentially, the proletariat is propertyless, and, hence, they lack personhood and freedom (because, according to Hegel's *Philosophy of Right*, property is the first condition for personhood). Explaining Marx's argument, Marcuse writes, "If property constitutes the first endowment of a free person, the proletariat is neither free nor a person, for he possesses no property" (1997, 261). Thus, the proletariat represents the falsehood and injustice that exist in capitalist society, a society in which reason is unrecognizable. If truth, to Hegel, is the totality of reason, then the proletariat, to Marx, is a vast abyss in that totality. According to Marx, the realization of reason is situated within the material conflicts represented in the progress of human society, and, as such, the material bases of society determine value systems. Reason must, therefore, be recognized eventually because the contradictions of irrational class society will reach a limit beyond which the conflict between the forces and relations of production cannot continue.

Marx posited that the propertylessness of the proletariat is precisely what makes them revolutionary, namely, because they do not have anything to lose and they are increasingly exploited under unsustainable conditions. Indeed, the second to last statement of the Manifesto famously reads, "The proletarians have nothing to lose but their chains. They have a world to win" (Marx and Engels 1972, 500).[8] For the first time in the history of capitalism, since the mid–twentieth-century insurance companies and banks in the United States have managed to alter the proletariat's consciousness of being propertyless, thereby de-revolutionizing the proletariat. Workers have been made to believe that they have a great deal to lose if the capitalist order is destabilized. They have been coerced into a process of metamorphosis, gradually transforming from propertyless to property owners (losing wings and gaining roots) in exchange for their future labor. Maintaining the dream of owning property arguably functions more effectively than truly having property in terms of transforming the subject into a conformist fearful of any disturbances to the existing order and, hence, the dominant social conditions of which the subject herself is a victim. This declassing process is accomplished by enabling people to *have without owning*, with a perceived status *would own*.

After all, what is a mortgage but the idea that the individual has a house without owning it, and that she is in the process of becoming a property owner? As such, the mortgagor is given the opportunity to live as if she owns the property in question, all while reflecting on her future identity as a property owner. Politically speaking, it is more likely that she will act even more conventionally than a person who inherited property. The mortgage essentially functions as a contract according to which the individual is promised to eventually own her house if she guarantees paying the cost of the house within the next X years, which in turn amounts to selling the individual's labor for X years. In effect, she must keep working hard to conform, to purchase her personhood, but obviously on the path to winning the promised personhood she must surrender her free will, which in turn negates the very essence of her personhood. She is someone whose personhood is a promise to be fulfilled in the future while she is in the process of becoming a property owner.

Of course, there is always the argument that the person enters such contracts freely. The problem with this liberal and libertarian idea of freedom is that it is abstracted to the degree that it could easily collapse into its opposite in any real social and political context. In this particular setting, yes, the worker would enter the contract freely, but only insofar as she must have shelter. The freedom of the worker who sells her future labor to mortgage a house is similar to the freedom of a woman who "chooses" to work in prostitution to pay back her traffickers who helped her reach a safe place. The person who is deprived of the necessities of life (food, shelter, clothing, etc.) is only free in the most existential sense (e.g., free to try to rob a bank and face the consequences or to attempt suicide). Only cynically can we call the freedom to choose between selling your future freedom or choosing to rob a bank freedom and equate it with the freedom of a well-off person.

On a more general level, by agreeing to sell her future labor, a worker could partake in some of what the rich enjoy such as driving a luxury car, eating at high-end restaurants, traveling for pleasure, etc.

An American or Canadian worker, for example, may be able to afford to go to South America, Asia, or Africa for a week or two to enjoy treating others the way she is treated throughout the rest of the year. The worker is given a temporary passport to travel through classes to a higher class. Once she realizes what it is like to be the one to look down on others by virtue of being a member of the bourgeoisie, she will commit faithfully to her role as a surplus value maker drawing her strength from concentrating single-purposely on the promised future. In fact, the worker's ability to have other things she cannot own is dependent on how far into the future and how well she can submit to the capitalist order. The ability to live the illusion of being rich is dependent on the worker's submission to live as an exploited worker, precisely because her obedience as a worker who works for less than the value of her labor is her only way to be awarded credit.

For many workers in the "developing countries," the capitalist promise is that they too could one day earn enough trust to find buyers for their future labor. The privilege of being able to sell one's future labor is dependent on finding the right capitalist conditions wherein the worker is given the opportunity to prove her trustworthiness (a person's credibility as determined by the capitalist relations of production).[9] Eventually, this privileged worker would create surplus value two times over: by working for less than the value of the products of her labor and by paying interest on the money for which she sells her future labor. To be situated in those capitalist conditions whereby a capitalist is willing to employ the worker and to invest in her future labor, the worker must have proven to be a committed double surplus creator. Capital can only be made by exploiting nature and/or exploiting (underpaying) labor. All the profit made in capitalism is made by direct exploitation of natural resources and/or by surplus value, which is the value of unpaid labor. A laborer today considers herself privileged to be given the chance to enter a social contract according to which she commits to being exploited twice: by working for less than what her labor is worth (paid less than the actual value of her labor) and being forced to pay interest on the money she receives in return for her future underpaid labor.

Capitalist competition revolves entirely around how to win money for which one does not work, that is, to steal the value of someone else's labor. To climb the ladder from the bottom, the worker not only has to work for most of her life to make money for the capitalist who does not work, but she also has to hope that the capitalist relations of production will not collapse. Therefore, any proposed change to win the worker's approval must first guarantee her conditions of ownership, which means any alternative relations of production are rejected from the outset. Far from being revolutionary subjects, workers in most of today's capitalist world faithfully sustain the existing social conditions.

Thus, while under classical totalitarianism most people are aware of their oppression and therefore are detached from the system, under capitalist totalitarianism the oppressed are inseparable from the system. Classical totalitarianism inevitably antagonizes most of the oppressed, so that they are incentivized to organize resistance as soon as they know they have a chance to regain their freedom. Everyone knows that a classical totalitarian regime will sooner or later collapse, so the ability to dream of another social and political space is kept alive. There is always another way to see the world under violent totalitarian regimes. Capitalist totalitarianism, on the other hand, is more secure because the oppressed are atomized and each is situated in her own odyssey of would-own, would-be-free. It restricts dreaming to a single condition, namely, profit: gaining without working. One's freedom is determined by one's capital, that is, by other people's unfreedom. The dreamt space is not another space, but just another place, for the dreamer, within the same totalitarian space.

For Hegel, the human *being* is a product of human labor. But in the case of capitalist society, wherein the very act of labor only alienates the laborer further, the proletariat represents a fundamental contradiction to this Hegelian principle. In this setting, the product of the laborer's labor renders her world unsocial, fragmented, cruel, and alienating. The more the laborer produces, the less free she becomes. "The *increase in value* of the world of things is directly proportional to the *decrease in value* of the human world. Labor not only produces commodities. It also produces itself and the worker as a *commodity*" (Marx 1967, 289; italics from original). Not only does the object not represent the realm of self-realization for the subject, but it also estranges and enslaves her. The social system in capitalism is such that labor necessarily and directly empowers the capitalist by accumulating more capital for the capitalist. This, in turn, results in the direct enslavement of the laborer. In other words, alienation is the result of both the process and the outcome of production (Marx 1967, 261). To Marx, the laborer is forced to treat her own labor as a commodity and sell it to the capitalist, who is free to decide whether or not to buy it. The capitalist buys the cheapest labor to make maximum profit, so, like any other commodity, the value of labor is determined by the power of capital. In the competition among workers, the value of labor continually falls, allowing for the highest degree of exploitation by the owner of capital. To Marx, this process amounts to the prostitution of the laborer. In fact, he states, "Prostitution is only a *specific* expression of the *general prostitution of the laborer*" (Marx 1988, 101; italics from original). Because of their lack of property, the proletariat as a class is forced into selling their labor: "Prostitution of the non-owning class in all its forms" (Marx 1988, 31). Drawing on Marx, Benjamin states that the commodity "stands in opposition to the organic. It prostitutes the living body to the inorganic world. In relation to the living it represents the rights of the corpse. Fetishisation, which succumbs to the sex appeal of the inorganic, is its vital nerve; and the cult of the commodity recruits this to its service" (quoted in Gilloch 1996, 120; Benjamin 1973, 166). Gilloch further analyzes Benjamin's notes on prostitution and the commodity and writes, "Just as the body of the worker becomes 'mechanized' in modern society, so that of the prostitute is commodified" (1996, 162). Buck-Morss writes that "advertisement images attempt to 'humanize' products in order to deny their commodity character" (1991, 184), but what should be added is that at the same time advertisements also objectify humans in order to establish their commodity character. Under capitalism, the female body is objectified insofar as commodification transforms it into an object of sexual fetishism, and simultaneously the object is humanized insofar as commodification gives it social identity. Gilloch notes, "Modern capitalism involves both the sexualization of the commodity and the commodification of the sexual" (1996, 120). The commodity as sexual and the sexual as commodity are deeply embedded in the capitalist relations of exchange. Thus, as Gilloch puts it, the prostitute is one of the primary expressions of the dehumanizing effect of mechanization and of Benjamin's "heroic, proletarian figure in the metropolis" (Gilloch 1996, 161). Prostitution is the labor that directly aims to increase the chances of the fetishization of the prostitute's body, thereby transforming it into an ideal form of commodity. It is the prostitute body's where the capitalist means and relations of production, labor, and commodity meet the laborer and the fetish. Explicating Benjamin, Buck-Morss writes, "Prostitution is indeed an objective emblem of capitalism, a hieroglyph of the true nature of social reality in the sense that the Egyptian hieroglyphs were viewed by the Renaissance—and in Marx's sense as well" (1991, 184). The prostitute's body, thus, is a unique space where the capitalist mode of production is concentrated. To Marx, what is more important than defining prostitution in terms of labor is defining labor in terms of prostitution. Prostitution amounts to selling the body of the prostitute to fulfil/meet the desires/ needs of consumers/customers in exchange for money needed for liveli- hood. A laborer essentially does the same thing; selling one's own labor is nothing but selling one's own body.[10] The only difference is that the relationship is immediately clear in the case of prostitution.

To Lukács, the central problem of all the structural aspects of capitalist society is the problem of commodities, and hence commodity- relations is the model according to which the objective-subjective forms in bourgeois societies and relations can be read (1971, 83). Through a totalizing process of mechanization and rationalization under capitalism, time has lost its experiential qualities and instead has become abstract and calculable based on the speed of productivity. Indeed, the measure of production is one and the same measure that determines the value of each unit of time. Moreover, the function of the laborer is determined by the function of the machine, and because the function of machine, by virtue of being a machine, is nothing but the endless repetition of the same motion, the function of the worker must also respond to the same pattern of movement and hence endless repetition. Perhaps the factory scenes in Charlie Chaplin's *Modern Times* (1936) are the best depiction of this relationship between the machine and the worker. In some of those scenes we can see how every worker's speed has to correspond exactly to the speed of the machine, and by increasing the speed of the machine, the operator can also increase the speed of all the workers from another room. Significantly, the film's elements of "science fiction," such as the total surveillance inside the factory, are not fictional by today's standards. When Chaplin is in the washroom trying to light a cigarette, it is the angry face of the manager that appears on a big screen in the washroom watching him and ordering him, instead of Chaplin appear- ing on a screen in the manager's office. The twist makes the symbolic omnipresence of the capitalist, or the gaze of power, even more strongly embodied in the scene. As the following scenes go, only by going crazy does Chaplin become free from being the "automatic motor of a detail operation," to use Marx's expression (Marx 1990, 481). The mechanization of production paired with the determinist role of capital in all aspects of human life will inevitably lead to flattening social space to a degree that every unconformity is mechanically spat out from the social system.

Lukács emphasizes the totalizing effect of mechanization and ratio-nalization of all social relations in the capitalist modernity. He writes:

> But this implies that the principle of rational mechanisation and calculability must embrace every aspect of life. Consumer articles no longer appear as the products of an organic process within a community (as for example in a village community). They now appear, on the one hand, as abstract members of a species identical by definition with its other members and, on the other hand, as isolated objects the possession or non-possession of which depends on rational calculations. (1971, 91)

The immediate social reflection of this is the breakdown of the organic bond among individuals as members of a community. Thus, we end up with the absolute social fragmentation of individuals, as the Frankfurt School philosophers also show. Again, the danger of reification is that it has a totalizing effect over all social relations. Lukács thinks the logic of the commodity movement, that is, from its mass production to its calculability, fragmentation and isolation, and exchangeability according to the naturalized laws of the market, predetermines all social relations. The atomization of individuals in capitalist society is the direct outcome of the totalizing nature of the laws of capitalist production embodied in commodity forms (Marx 1990, 481–82). "For the first time in history," Lukács adds, "the whole of society is subjected, or tends to be subjected, to a unified economic process, and that the fate of every member of soci-ety is determined by unified laws" (1971, 92). The totalitarian aspect of capitalist modernity is intrinsic in the determining aspect of these unified laws.[11] In short, commodity relations are both isolating and totalizing; they isolate particulars and totalize objectification.

This total objectification and hence alienation are continually increasing as the processes of rationalization and mechanization are increasingly expanded through the intellectual labor of armies of specialists who have already been reified within, by, and for the sake of the system of capitalism, who in turn maximize profit by investing in methods that maximize the totalizing capabilities of mechanization and instrumental rationalism. In the final picture, what we have is the limitless deter-mining power of capital over all aspects of society, including education, moral values, political topography, and the state. Commodity relations and their reifying effects on society produce and reproduce a particular consciousness everywhere, a unified structure of consciousness that is unable to step outside the limits of the world of servitude to capitalism because its way of experiencing the world is limited. It is a consciousness that is unconscious of its confines as a predetermined, totalized, and quantitative form of consciousness. Thus, it is simply a consciousness against consciousness. As Lukács writes, "The distinction between a worker faced with a particular machine, the entrepreneur faced with a given type of mechanical development, the technologist faced with the state of science and the profitability of its application to technology, is purely quantitative; it does not directly entail *any qualitative difference in the structure of consciousness*" (1971, 98; italics in original).

Further, according to Lukács's account, this consciousness is shaped by and located within the bourgeois systematization or rationalization, a rationality that postulates its own universality through a series of other assumptions in modern thought. The two main intertwined, or rather circular, assumptions are 1) the world is rational; and 2) human subjects possess a system of perception that corresponds to, and is capable of grasping, that rationality. The system determines its principles in such a way that the consequences are already guaranteed. Born into the normalized world of capitalism, the normalcy of the domination of capital and neutrality of the principle of exchange are encoded into our social institutions, such as family and school, which in turn encode them into our mode of perception.

Lukács contends that rationalism is not limited to modernity, but what is different about modern rationalization is that it claims the discovery of the principles of social and natural laws. Hence, the totalitarian aspect of this rationalization is intrinsic in its essence (1971, 113). He goes on to write, "The situation is quite different when rationalism claims to be the universal method by which to obtain knowledge of the whole of existence. In that event the necessary correlation with the principle of irrationality becomes crucial: it erodes and dissolves the whole system. This is the case with modern (bourgeois) rationalism" (Lukács 1971, 114). It is in this sense that the capitalist modes of production totalize a one-dimensional consciousness in a way that is ultimately comparable to the uniformity of belief systems produced by imperial religious doctrines whose conception of all humans is mass-based; and, as a result of that, the space for unique individual experience of life is continually abolished. The predictability and calculability provided by rationalization is crucial in social engineering, not only under authoritarian capitalism, but also in democratic capitalism (to use Pollock's terms [Jay 1984, 37]). The totalitarian world is only the outcome of this continual rationalization of all aspects of social life under the uniformity of the commodity form. In such a world, not only are aesthetics, values, dreams, desires, and needs mass produced, but rationality and irrationality are also redefined and indoctrinated through ideological apparatuses such as educational institutions. A popular film such as *Titanic* (Cameron 1997), for instance, continues to serve as a source of reforming the romantic experience for millions throughout the globe, regardless of their habitat. There are, on the one hand, those individuals who are alienated by their very everydayness, helplessly sustaining the conditions of their suppression, and desperately trying to meet the demands of a postponed happiness. On the other hand, a capitalist industry manufactures a spectacle, a wordily paradise, where labor is nonexistent, boredom is unknown, desires are magically fulfilled, and, most importantly, spatial experience is freed from the oppressive flow of time.

Now, what if all aspects of life are continually targeted with endless such media in addition to, and intertwined with, the mass production of material objects appealing to mass-produced desires? A product of the culture industry represents a collective enterprise designed, produced, and distributed through powerful capitalist enterprises; yet the target is a repressed individual often deprived of even the ability to comprehend the conditions of her unfreedom. When an individual, who is usually already suppressed in various ways because of existing oppressive social institutions such as family, is targeted by such massive industries of spectacle, the chances of her authentic imagination and will to unique individual life surviving are next to nothing. The sway of, for instance, a popular Hollywood movie is the result of the aggregate of tremendous and resourceful means (e.g., vast capital, facilities that can include an entire mini-city constructed especially for this purpose, specialists, and marketing apparatuses, actors who perfect acting) to create a piece that essentially targets the individual, inevitably intervening with her thoughts, dreams, wishes, and needs without changing anything in the material conditions of her life. The hyperreal dimension created by endless such visual media pieces in an individual's daily life will most likely affect her entire reality through meddling in her image of herself. While the means to hyper-reality are always improving, the target remains an individual, more and more fragmented, isolated, and alienated.[12] In short, the culture industry functions as a centralized and aggregated means of indoctrination, necessarily producing standardization and sameness resulting in social hegemony, and hence reproducing and sustaining social uniformity. In other words, mass mentality (characterized by standardization and patterns of repetition) is the direct ideological outcome of the culture industry that perpetually feeds its consumers commodities produced for mass consumption through targeting individuals in their social alienation and isolation.

What Horkheimer and Adorno call instrumental rationality in their *Dialectic of Enlightenment* is strongly connected to Lukács's idea of the production of a unified structure of consciousness through what he called rationalization in capitalist society, or bourgeois rationality. However, the two notions are not identical even though both indicate totalitarian aspects of capitalist modernity. To clarify, instrumental rationalism is the specialized and pragmatic threads of bourgeois rationality that are put to work aiming at specific social and economic goals.

Marcuse, in his *One Dimensional Man*, focused on the same totalitarian outcomes of this form of fatal rationality from the angle of the applications and implications of technological means of production in capitalism. In the introduction to his book, he states, "In this society, the productive apparatus tends to become totalitarian to the extent to which it determines not only the socially needed occupations, skills, and attitudes, but also individual needs and aspirations" (1968, xv). In advanced industrial societies, "[t]echnology serves to institute new, more effective, and more pleasant forms of social control and social cohesion" (Marcuse 1968, xv). Thus, in advanced industrial states the totalitarian means and methods are even more hegemonic because they are less political and less aggressive on the surface. In both authoritarian capitalist regimes and democratic capitalist systems, both means of cohesion and hegemony are systematically used to establish and maintain totalitarianism. For example, in a totalitarian state where various coercive forms of social control are effective in state institutions, a gigantic machine of more infused means of social control, such as mechanically reproduced images of the totalitarian leader, is also used. Mechanically reproduced images are used to target social space, and the result is totalitarian space. In the case of democratic capitalist states, both the non-pleasant and what Marcuse calls "more pleasant" (1968, xv) forms of control are also systematically used in the ideological state apparatuses. However, because of the advanced methods of the second form, that is, more pleasant forms of control or perhaps what we might call the "means of ideological hegemony," the apparatuses of the first forms of control become less apparent. It is for this reason that it is easier to call regimes such as Fascism, Nazism, Stalinism, and Baathism totalitarian, but to most of us it might sound like a metaphoric exaggeration to call a democratic capitalist state "totalitarian." New totalitarianism has moved from propaganda and control to indoctrination and hegemony, which is precisely why it is harder to conceive it as totalitarian and which why we need unorthodox analysis to reconceptualize totalitarian/ism in relation to its historical development.

Marcuse also points to the totalitarian effect of capitalism in countries that are on the periphery of the global system of capitalism, which is a claim not strange to anyone familiar with the theories of World Systems Analysis (Wallenstein 2005). Marcuse writes, "The totalitarian tendency of these controls seems to assert itself in still another sense—by spreading to the less developed and even to the preindustrial areas of the world, and by creating similarities in the development of capitalism and communism" (1968, xv–xvi). The hegemonic effect of this totalitarian rationality structurally reshapes human affairs from politics to even more fundamental issues of perception. In Marcuse's own words, "Technological rationality reveals its political character as it becomes the great vehicle of better domination, creating a truly totalitarian universe in which society and nature, mind and body are kept in a state of permanent mobilization for the defense of this universe" (Marcuse 1968, 18).

In this sense, Žižek argues that capitalism is truly universal rather than Eurocentric (2008, 79–80). As a "neutral matrix of social relations" (Žižek 2008, 158), capitalism has the ability both to be global and to sustain its globalization. Capitalism, therefore, is not only "worldless," but it also is deworlding. Moreover, capitalism does not offer an alternative meaning because it does not have a philosophy or a worldview, as Žižek argues (2008, 80). Thus, capitalism does not replace a local topography of meaning with another; rather, it perpetually flattens all spaces to turn them to a single space of one-dimensional experience.

Closing

As the domination of technological rationality transforms a once varied landscape to geometrical blocs, it also produces a one-dimensional consciousness incapable of negative thinking and creative imagination. With advanced forms of communication, states have become more powerful than ever by virtue of their totalizing power of standardization, systemization, and unification. This advanced technological communication not only led to the unification of forms and measurements of knowledge, a direct example being the education *system* within the state, but it also resulted in the standardization of history itself via a certain ideological, usually nationalist, narrative of the past. Similarly, it is the state apparatuses that decide what can and will become the event of the day by nationalizing it, by putting its celebration into practice in every household in the country. When all the people are fed the same information at the same time, and when they are subjected to the same ideological state apparatuses even in their so-called free time, the result is most likely to be not only a nationalist identity, but also a one-dimensional consciousness. The production of this one-dimensional consciousness, of mass mentality, is dialectically involved in the production of totalitarianism.

If totalitarianism is defined as imposed uniformity throughout the social arenas and power that recognizes no limits, then the combination of the culture industry with instrumental knowledge amounts to the actualization of totalitarianism. Through standardization, repetition, and predictability, the culture industry has been "infecting everything with sameness" (Horkheimer and Adorno 2002, 94). As for "knowledge, which is power, [it] knows no limits, either in its enslavement of creation or in its deference to worldly masters" (Horkheimer and Adorno 2002, 2). Here Horkheimer and Adorno mean instrumental knowledge because they add, "Technology is the essence of this knowledge. It aims to produce neither concepts nor images, nor the joy of understanding, but method, exploitation of the labor of others, capital" (2002, 2). This is the dark side of the dialectic of Enlightenment, and it is in this sense that "Enlightenment is totalitarian" (Horkheimer and Adorno 2002, 4). Then the question is how this relapse into unreason, essentially into another form of religion, can be so passively accepted to make totalitarianism possible. The culture industry has effectively deactivated the creative potentialities of resistance. Again, in Horkheimer and Adorno's words, "Under the leveling rule of abstraction, which makes everything in nature repeatable, and of industry, for which abstraction prepared the way, the liberated finally themselves become the 'herd' (*Trupp*), which Hegel identified as the outcome of enlightenment" (2002, 9). Therefore, not only works of art,[13] but also forms of localized revolt have been turned into commodities for profit. For instance, one day, a group of people supposedly rebelling against the dominant norms creatively produce what appears to be abnormal music, and the next, their abnormality, if it attracts enough fans, will be mass produced and sold to create more capital. In fact, even symbols of most serious forms of resistance can easily become part of the larger system of the culture industry. Adorno writes, "Mass culture allows precisely this reserve army of outsiders to participate: mass culture is an organized mania for connecting everything with everything else, a totality of public secrets. Everyone who is informed has his share in the secret, just as under National Socialism the privilege of esoteric blood-brotherhood was actually offered to everyone" (1991, 83).

The hegemony of this instrumental knowledge and the domination of the culture industry, in fact, determine even the forms of "revolt" in such a way that the outcast ends up functioning as another choreographed confirmation of the supposed freedom and plurality within the existing order and as more raw material for the culture industry to feed on. Perhaps the most dangerous part of the culture industry, though, is that it has determined the limits of utopia by limiting our ability to imagine, both qualitatively and quantitatively. Hence, not only do forms of revolt fail to accomplish any emancipation in such a system, but they also seem to be precisely the new blood that revives the culture industry, both in terms of more accumulation of capital and deepening the existing ideological hegemony. The degree of the hegemony and dominance is so paralyzing that it seems we cannot even imagine a way out. Perhaps that is why, as Fredric Jameson noticed, it is easier for people to imagine a natural catastrophe that would bring an end to life on Earth than to imagine an end to capitalism (2003, 76).[14]

Now I go back to another crucial aspect of the culture industry, which is the mass production of individuality itself, resulting in a fake sense not only of unique identity, but also of plurality. It may seem ironic that the culture industry provides enough variety for everyone to have a "sense" of uniqueness in choice, and thus individual identity to the extent that it seems as though the industry mass produces authenticity. The following example perhaps helps to illuminate this absurd contradiction: describing the upholstery in his car, Max Goldman, played by Walter Matthau, in *Grumpier Old Men* (Deutch 1995), tells John Gustafson, played by Jack Lemmon, "I went to Nate's Auto Body Shop. Had all the seats refinished . . . It's authentic imitation leather." Likewise, the individual produced within the culture industry can also be considered an "authentic imitation" individual. In Horkheimer and Adorno's words,

"Each human being has been endowed with a self of his or her own, different from all others, so that it could all the more surely be made the same" (2002, 9). It is this sameness and, at the same time, sense of self, that provides a crucial condition for totalitarianism: the condition of uniformity. "The unity of the manipulated collective consists in the negation of each individual and in the scorn poured on the type of society which could make people into individuals" (Horkheimer and Adorno 2002, 9).

Political totalitarianism is only an outcome of the totalitarian world of the culture industry. Once more in Horkheimer and Adorno's words, "The relentless unity of the culture industry bears witness to the emergent unity of politics" (2002, 96). Moreover, we can now depict the dialectical relationship between the culture industry and instrumental rationality: the more individuality is liquidated, the more mass mentality replaces critical thinking. On the other hand, the more this one-dimensional consciousness is normalized, the easier the task to control becomes for the state apparatuses. Parallel to this liquidation of individuality at the hands of the culture industry, instrumental rationality expands and deepens the power of the state through putting in place more effective instruments and methods of surveillance and social engineering. Hence, the state has continually been gaining more ground in its capacity of exercising power over the society, even though the degree of the state's reliance on the techniques of terror or direct physical means of control as opposed to ideological hegemony and advanced technologies of surveillance vary greatly between classical totalitarian states and postindustrial capitalist states. At any rate, this continuing weakening of social relations alongside the limitless empowerment of the state apparatuses already indicates the perfect path to totalitarianism in its different forms.

To have any functioning societal order without the police apparatuses of the state has become almost unimaginable. However, what we often fail to realize is that the state's naturalized patronizing rule over social arenas is precisely what jeopardizes the autonomy of social relations. Although portrayed as the maintainer of social order, the state, in truth, is a sociopolitical tumor that thrives on the deterioration of society's micro and macro joints. Natural systems contain immense brutality, violence, and use of force, but they are essentially systems of collaboration, as opposed to domination. Every species develops organic multiplicities within deeper, broader, and more nuanced life systems free of the exercise of power for the sake of sheer control. The social and spatial engineering that ruling groups achieve through their use of the state's apparatuses, on the other hand, operates on the basis of a one-dimensional rationality of control. Furthermore, the state has managed to uproot everything that is not fundamentally dependent on hierarchy to the degree that even "nature" has come to be perceived as a hierarchical system.

The state strives to reify everything, extract force, abstract time, and monopolize space for the sole purpose of control, developing technologies of power to those ends. At the heart of every enterprise of control is an oppressive production of space, and the state itself is inherently both a spatial production and a system of control. This has always been so, but spatial production under capitalism is without precedent in its uniformity. Capitalism has perfected the state's technologies of power, rendering the totalitarian drive for total control more robust and sustainable than it has ever been. Thus, we cannot understand how totalitarianism is maintained without grasping the capitalist modes of spatial production. It follows that understanding the production of space is essential not only to our spatial literacy, but also to resistance against totalitarianism.

2

The Production of Space

What we continue to call public space, without the accompanying irony that such labeling should elicit, is public only in the sense that chronic consumers need not (usually) pay to "use" it. However, in a world principled on profit, freebies are calculated to encourage further consumption, which in the case of public space is achieved by conditioning consumers to seek out consumption-oriented activities disguised as leisure or entertainment in their so-called free time. Space has been depublicized in an ongoing process under the hegemony of capitalism, resulting in the normalization of the capitalist distribution of space.

The value of any space is measured by its production-consumption capacity in relation to other actual or potential commodities. That is to say, space itself is always quantified, to the degree that its quality becomes one and the same as its quantifying/quantified value in terms of the abstraction of money. In essence, all spaces become one insofar as they have exchange values. Though ostensibly broken down into more or less self-contained cells (e.g., spaces of production, consumption, leisure, transportation, and communication) according to the mechanisms of the market, totalitarian space has at the same time ultimately been united by commercial as well as state totalizing powers, or what Debord calls the "integration of state and economy" (1990, 12). The proliferation of the technological means of surveillance, sorting, and ordering combined with the domination of the capitalist modes of production and the hegemony of capitalist ideology produce totalitarian space. Our experience of space is systematically replicated whether in airports, shopping centers, or chain coffee shops. Consumers' desire for complete familiarity has ushered in the replication of space parallel to the mass production of commodities. Ultimately, space is produced as a commodity to further sustain the world of commodities.

The familiarity of spaces of consumption maximizes consumption and in so doing commodifies the labor force of consumers, who must sell their labor to gain and sustain so-called purchasing power. Essential to this system is that the same subjects who labor in the "spaces of production," producing surplus value for those who own the means of production, must also spend their wages in the "spaces of consumption," completing the cycle of profit making for capitalists, and thus sustaining the capitalist system. The spaces demarcated for leisure, communication, and rest therefore are simply recharging zones for the labor power and the spaces in which consumers' buying habits are shaped. As Marx observed in his *Economic and Philosophical Manuscripts* (1844), it is not just the labor, but also the laborer that become commodity. The more the laborer works, the more alienated she becomes because of the objectification involved in the process of capitalist production. He analogizes the relationship between the laborer and the product of her labor to that between a worshiper and God. Just as attributing more powers to God makes the believer weaker, the more labor the laborer puts into the product, the more alienating the product becomes (Marx 1967, 287–90).

The alienation of the user of space corresponds to her desire for greater familiarity. Patterns of sameness, in turn, continue to proliferate, ironing out differences that would be seen as irregularities and thereby expanding the totalitarian space. It is precisely this predictability of spatial patterns of sameness that renders the auratic experience of space impossible. As Adorno writes,

> The sacrifice of individuality, which accommodates itself to the regularity of the successful, the doing of what everyone does, follows from the basic fact that in broad areas the same thing is offered to everybody by the standardized production of consumption goods. But the commercial necessity of connecting this identity leads to the manipulation of taste and official culture's presence of individualism which necessarily increases in production to the liquidation of the individual. (2006c, 40)

This account can easily be applied to space as well, particularly when it is produced as a consumable good. The result is indeed "the liquidation of the individual." In a world orchestrated by the culture industry, the destruction of spatial aura goes hand in hand with the massification of the individual. Beyond the point of alienation and closer to the point of nullification, the mass individual's feelings, experiences, and actions must all follow predesigned patterns. Just as mass-produced greeting cards are organized by occasion according to the contrived messages already printed within, spaces are mass produced for mass behaviors.

The mass individual participates in the production of totalitarian space through both the culture industry and commodity fetishism. Just as there are predetermined times for the mass individual's celebrations, there are designated spaces for the mass individual to have specific experiences. There are spaces for spirituality, entertainment, tourism, romance, and so on. All such spaces are commodified, and it is precisely this commodification that allows for fetishism, which is necessary for the fulfillment of the individual's purchased experience. The mass individual is incapable of having an individual experience even if the space in which she functions is a potential auratic space simply because commodity forms have become her a priori conditions of experience. In fact, even in their social relationships, mass individuals mechanically apply the rules of commodity forms. We can see this clearly in cyberspace, with its popular "markets" where those who seek love can list their own specifications as well as those they wish to find in a potential lover, and algorithms arrange the matching either for a price or in exchange for the personal information exchanged.

Cyberspace has become the hyperreal space wherein millions of feelings are announced universally. Rather than literature or art, social media is where we now turn to reach out to the world in times of social and personal crises. Having access to dozens, hundreds, or thousands of other people who are hyperreal friends in the spectacle that has replaced physical spaces of social interaction has changed our psychic development. Loneliness is escaped through a medium that is perhaps the ultimate testament to loneliness. The more immersed one becomes in the digital medium known as social media (which should more accurately be called antisocial media), the more dependent one becomes on the hyperreal world. Millions of people exercise two lives: their undesirable, boring, suppressive, and intolerable daily lives in the physical world, and the lives they wish to live, as broadcast on Facebook or Instagram. Social media eventually becomes the only refuge, but it is a refuge that cannot shelter any real feeling or actual body. Instead, feelings are exhibited to the world in a prescribed number of characters and abbreviated forms, and in this placeless space the body is completely disembodied through images, whether digital or imagined. Now, in addition to the paradise promised by the Absolute, there is another paradise: a hyperreal, digital one that is sandwiched between ads laced with still more promises. This space is fashioned as a retreat from the physical world, which has in turn fallen into even further neglect. As cyberspace has become the hyperreality par excellence, social space has been even more ruthlessly administered, sliced, fragmented, sold, bought, and used within a totalitarian system that is the ultimate source of legitimacy.

Totalitarian space inherently implies the totalitarian tendency of an oppressive, anti-auratic, and hegemonic power that recognizes no limit. It is important to clarify, however, that neither power nor space can exist abstractly, as we seem to conceive them in the linguistic discourse through which we (hope to) study them. Therefore, it would also be misleading to try to define totalitarian power exclusively through totalitarian space. What we can do, however, is explore the relationship between aura and totalitarian space, which seems to be a negative relationship that will help us grasp the totality of power and the destruction, void, and alienation power creates in relation to individual everyday experience of and in space. Thus, my goal is to find the absent, the spatial aspect that is being destroyed under and because of totalitarianism.

It should be expected that totalitarian power is inherently destructive, and the spatial trace that destructive force will leave behind must be something negative in its essence (because it is a reference to an absence). Therefore, it makes sense to have a name for that thing, that absence, and "aura" (itself a negative notion devoid of any positive truth claim) seems to be the best potential concept to designate that negativity. Of course, the choice of the word, aura, is not arbitrary; the concept of "aura" is open enough for theoretical findings, and that is the point. However, only in a longer discussion devoted to aura can I show the necessary philosophical conceptualizations of aura, which is the topic of fourth and fifth chapters. Thus, until aura is, at least minimally, conceptualized, I do not use it in any defining way in terms of totalitarian space, nor do I use totalitarian space in the first occasion of conceptualizing aura.

Both the production (of space) and a spatial technology of power are already implied in the theme of "totalitarian space." Therefore, it is necessary first to problematize the production of space, which brings us to Lefebvre. However, as it becomes clear toward the end of this chapter, Lefebvre's theory lacks a clear account of the spatial technology of power, which gives us an additional reason to consult Foucault.

Hence, Foucault's work on the technology of power with regard to the production of space is discussed in chapter 3.

Space as Production

Human experiences are all spatial. Even imagined and mythological variations of human existence, including underworld or afterlife, are necessarily grounded in the spatial mode of being in the world. Therefore, problematizing space is as challenging as conceptualizing history. While there is a robust tradition in the humanities and social sciences of creating an awareness of the complexity of history, space has remained on the nondialectical level, as Lefebvre discovered. From Lefebvre and Bachelard we learn that space is complex and dialectical like history. However, even with Lefebvre and Bachelard a new term has not emerged to designate the more complex notion of space. When we think of "history," we think of how living beings, things, ideas, and events correlate to each other on the grand scale of their evolvement and their temporal relations with each other. Thus, normally we do not equate between time and history. Whereas time is understood to be linear and measurable, history is understood to be nonlinear, complex, multidimensional, and immeasurable. The fact that we still lack a concept to designate the study of complex spatial relations of living beings, things, ideas, and events on the grand scale of their evolvement and their locational relations to each other shows our lack of spatial awareness.

Just as we make sense of history by qualifying different historical eras, it is essential to designate characteristic spatialities that give a particular space its distinct mode of being. For that, we must see space as both a product and a production. Space is not something in itself; rather, it is a social production, and as such, it requires theory to explore and grasp the production and the product in their totality and their perpetual dialectical contradictions on all the levels of the physical, mental, and social. The problem with the formulas we find in traditional philosophy about space is that they focus only on a partial aspect or dimension of space, such as geometrical or architectural space. This essentially leads to an absolute notion of space and ultimately the fetishism of that reductive, and thus necessarily erroneous, notion.

Lefebvre criticizes the typical philosophical approaches to space, which were mostly geometrical, metaphysical or epistemological. By way of understanding one of the roots of the problem, Lefebvre explains that mathematics, considered a self-sufficient science by mathematicians, produced what can be called mental space. Mental space is the abstract notion of space as a multidimensional empty area (Lefebvre 1991a, 1–3). Accounts of mental space depend on sets of semblances and produce their own logics, but contemporary epistemology has generally adopted the concept of mental space as it has been revised by mathematics. "No limits at all have been set on the generalization of the concept of *mental space*: no clear account of it is ever given. . . . We are forever hearing about the space of this and/or the space of that: about literary space, ideological spaces, the space of the dream, psychoanalytic topologies, and so on and so forth" (Lefebvre 1991a, 3; italics in original [2000, 9–10]). The gap between the epistemological and the practical, the intellectual and the social, is often overlooked without sufficient questioning. For example, Lefebvre argues that Foucault's concept of a "space of dissensions" is never clearly defined, nor is it differentiated from other spaces (1991a, 4 [2000, 10]). Lefebvre also criticizes Chomsky, Derrida, and Kristeva for dismissing "an abyss between the mental sphere on one side and the physical and social spheres on the other" (1991a, 6 [2000, 13]).

The common assumption is that the epistemological sphere structurally corresponds to the spatial sphere, including social space. This account, which assumes direct discursive representation of reality, dismisses the world of the subject and its unique experience by naming the subject from a god-like position. In philosophical cogito and scientific discourse, which are shaped by a super-structural logos, the subject is stripped of personhood and is instead depicted and presented as "the impersonal pronoun 'one'" (Lefebvre 1991a, 4 [2000, 10]). However, the subject was needed to advance various philosophical and linguistic theories, so the ghost of the Cartesian subject and the cogito has continued to exist under "'neo-' forms: neo-Hegelian, neo-Kantian, neo-Cartesian" (Lefebvre 1991a, 4 [2000, 10–11]). At the same time, the gaps that are dismissed between the mental space, as pure theoretical speculations, and the social space, as practice, have only become larger. If there is one overarching aim of Lefebvre's book, it is to address this precise problem. In Lefebvre's words, "The project I am outlining . . . does not aim to produce a (or *the*) discourse on space, but rather to expose the actual production of space by bringing the various kinds of space and the modalities of their genesis together within a single theory" (1991a, 16; italics from original [2000, 24]).

The leap from the mental space to the social space is often taken unconsciously. Theoretical practice then becomes more and more rooted in mental space with the assumption that the latter is one and the same with social space, even though any thinker would acknowledge the inherent distance between the two. Lefebvre writes, "The philosophico-epistemological notion of space is fetishized and the mental realm comes to envelop the social and physical ones" (1991a, 5 [2000, 12]). The problems being dismissed and the ones created because of this jump from the mental to the social concern Lefebvre. Without a unitary theory that can encompass all aspects of space, or at least a theory that would allow that kind of potential for unlimited inclusion of all the dimensions of space, we will unavoidably lapse back into a reductionist account of space that will start to go astray after a certain point.

Lefebvre would not deny that there will always be forms of mental space that claim representation of physical and social space. Rather, Lefebvre's project seeks to emphasize the fact that there is a social, political, and historical process of constructing the theoretical practice according to which the identification between the mental and the social is presumed. The more complicated part of the problem is that mental space itself is endlessly divided and subdivided as an immediate reflection of capitalist modes of production, which are mainly based on the divisions of labor. Lefebvre shows that social space is a social production and that under the domination of capitalism, production is highly defused in favor of social domination itself. This entails the critical part of the project. The more positive part of the project aims at overcoming the existing fragmentation and diffusion of space by relinking the levels of space in a way that can enable us to reproblematize the realms of politics and knowledge dialectically. That is to say, to Lefebvre, dialectics is the only way to proceed if we wish to overcome all these problems of fragmentation and reductionism.

Lefebvre's approach is highly dialectical and genealogical, so he traces coding and decoding in their moments of emergence and disappearance on the immanent plane of interactions between multilayered spaces of experience and thought (Lefebvre 1991a, 18). The project is simultaneously and dialectically immersed in the parallel processes of showing the multiplicity of levels of space and the interconnectivity of those levels. Lefebvre avoids definitions of and clear distinctions between concepts and expressions for reasons that I explain later. Therefore, it is a very challenging project to comprehend, but that is so because, in

Lefebvre's defense, space itself is not easy to comprehend. Furthermore, as mentioned before, while no scholar would equate history to a physical notion of time, space is still commonly understood in some Euclidean-Cartesian-Newtonian (geometrical, physical as extension or a container without content, and absolute) sense, or as a priori condition of perception (Kant). With the emergence of relativist theories in physics in the nineteenth century, new approaches to space emerged, but they could not account for social space. Finally, in the twentieth century, endless accounts of social space appeared, but they were fragmented accounts reflecting the fragmentation of specialties and disciplines (Lefebvre 2003b, 206–7). In contrast, Lefebvre tries to preserve the complexity of the subject of space and attacks previous attempts of reductionism, abstract conceptualization, and simplification. Hence, the most promising locus for explicating Lefebvre's project is its dialectical method, which is meant to deal with the multiplicity of spatiality, complexity of spatial production, and the contradictions among spatial moments.

So far, Lefebvre argues, philosophy, architecture, literature, and science have failed to provide us with a universal notion of space. With this in mind, Lefebvre proposes the concept of production as the paradigm for founding a unitary theory of space. To Lefebvre, the concept of "production" is a "concrete universal" and a direct indication of social practice (Lefebvre 1991a, 15 [2000, 23]; Stanek 2008, 63). Lefebvre, therefore, tries to reappropriate the concept of production to pave the way for a theory of the production of space. At first glance, referring to the *production of space* may sound odd, or even metaphorical, in the best case. Thus, the main point to keep in mind at this stage is the double-sidedness of Lefebvre's preliminary attempt to account for space simultaneously: as logico-mathematical and practico-sensory (Lefebvre 1991a, 15).

Lefebvre's objective is not simply to decode space, because that alone would again reduce space to a static text to be read. Rather, his theory is also meant to trace the codes genealogically in terms of their emergence, life-cycle, and disappearance as an integrated part of spatial practice and production. The continual attempts to attribute forms of geometrical and architectural structure to space must be seen as spatial practices that conceal the production of space as much as they reveal logico-mathematical tendencies within a history that can be described best as "qualitative chaos" (Lefebvre 1991a, 17 [2000, 25]).

The unitary theory that can address all these spatial multiplicities without repeating the problems of the past approaches must be a dialectical one, which can then be called spatial dialectics. Hence, Lefebvre tries to integrate spatial studies with historical materialism. Both David Harvey and Edward Soja think that Marx, like many other Hegelian thinkers, shaped his theories around the theme of history at the expense of geography (Harvey 1982; Soja 1989, 31–33). In fact, even before *The Production of Space*, Lefebvre continually tried to reappropriate Marxism to apply it to spatial questions. For example, in his article "Space: Social Product and Use Value," Lefebvre states, "Although space is not analysed in *Capital*, certain concepts, such as exchange value and use value, today apply to space" (2009, 192; italics in original [1976]). Harvey and Castells, however, thought Lefebvre made spatial relations so central to his social theory that he substituted the central position of class struggle in the Marxist theory with spatial conflicts. These orthodox Marxist critiques went so far as to accuse Lefebvre of being a "spatial separatist" because, supposedly, his project amounts to space fetishism (Soja 1989, 76–77). Soja, however, argues that Harvey and Castells missed Lefebvre's dialectical view and that they set limiting boundaries of spatial interpretations without presenting convincing reasons for such limitations (1989, 77–78).

Furthermore, Soja thinks the Marxists of the 1970s, including Harvey, despite the latter's helpful emphasis on Lefebvre's works, did not do justice to the Lefebvrean Marxist analysis of space in terms of its dialectical richness. To Lefebvre, Soja argues, spatial relations must be read within the conflicts and contradictions of historical materialism. In other words, an accurate reading of Lefebvre would not subject him to rigid categorical logic and causality, because that is not how he saw spatial relations (Soja 1989, 77–78). The wrong interpretation begins when we expect Lefebvre to take one of two positions: either depicting space as a determinant of social relations or social relations as the ultimate birth giver of space (Soja 1989, 77–78; Elden 2001, 814). Instead, Lefebvre presents the dialectical alternative. Because social and spatial relations are dialectically indissoluble and are both rooted in the modes of production, the relations of production are at the same time both spatial and social (Soja 1989, 78). The following quote from Lefebvre shows the dialectical compound of which Soja speaks:

> There is one question which has remained open in the past
> because it has never been asked: what exactly is the mode
> of existence of social relationships? Are they substantial?
> natural? or formally abstract? The study of space offers an

answer according to which the social relations of production have a social existence to the extent that they have a spatial existence; they project themselves into a space, becoming inscribed there, and in the process producing that space itself. Failing this, these relations would remain in the realm of "pure" abstraction—that is to say, in the realm of representations and hence of ideology: the realm of verbalism, verbiage and empty words. (Lefebvre 1991a, 129; [2000, 152–53])

Lefebvre goes on to explain that space as a product of the modes of production and as a capitalist means will produce its own contradictions, embodying the dialectics that surface over time. These spatial contradictions do not eliminate the contradictions that emerge as a result of the passage of time, but dialectically elevate them to a higher, more contradictory, and, thus, more complex level (Lefebvre 1991a, 129). Therefore, the characterization of Lefebvre's work as spatial determinist is dismissive and unfair. Especially in *The Production of Space*, Lefebvre continually insists that he speaks of space as production and of production as it is dialectically argued for in historical materialism. Besides, Marx and Engels applied a material (in terms of sociohistorical conditions) framework to Hegel's temporal logic of dialectics as part of their historical materialism. Thus, there is no reason to see Lefebvre's spatial application of the dialectics as a countertheory to historical materialism, especially when this application is not implying any generic separation of space from the rest of the components of historical materialism. On the contrary, Lefebvre's most obvious thesis on space entails that social space is a product of conflicting social forces and relations. Moreover, as it becomes clear in what follows, Lefebvre showed that space itself is not merely spatial, in the narrow physical or geometrical sense of the word, so the danger of reductive determinism in Lefebvre's project on space is ruled out right from the beginning. Before engaging more in the discussion of possible and actual misunderstandings and shortcomings of Lefebvre's theory of space, it is time to present his spatial dialectics.

Lefebvre's Spatial Dialectic

Lefebvre continued working to improve his dialectic beginning with his early works as a young student and even after publishing *Dialectical*

Materialism in 1936 (1974). However, his most significant application of his dialectic is found in *The Production of Space* (Schmid 2008, 31). It was in this work that Lefebvre made his most original contribution in terms of his dialectic with his addition of the third dimension. In this way, he hoped to improve on both the Hegelian idealist dialectic and Marx's material appropriation of the Hegelian dialectic. Essentially, Lefebvre proposed representational space, or the lived space, as the third element of the dialectic. This dialectical anatomy then opened the way for Lefebvre to solve the problem of the closed system of the perceived and the conceived. He states, "The philosopher, 'caught in the web of words', is left behind as soon as meditation begins to deal with time and space instead of being imprisoned by them" (Lefebvre 1991a, 406 [2000, 466]). His third way makes it possible to reopen the dialectical system that was caught up between "the concept of truth and the truth of the concept" (Lefebvre 1991a, 406 [2000, 466]). At its most basic level, the three-dimensional dialectic is a movement between antipodes, each of which simultaneously negates the other two and none of which can stand on its own separately without falling into abstraction (Schmid 2008, 33).

Thus, Lefebvre's critique combines Hegel's dialectic, Marx's critique of Hegel, and Nietzsche's notion of art. As Lefebvre puts it: "This critique is rooted on the one hand in social practice (Marx), and on the other hand in art, poetry, music and drama (Nietzsche)—and rooted, too, in both cases, in the (material) body" (1991a, 406 [2000, 467]). In an article titled "Hegel, Marx, Nietzsche," Lefebvre conclusively focuses on the trinity that encompasses Marx's *social*, Hegel's *state*, and (to overcome their contradictions) Nietzsche's concept of art in relation to *civilization*. Lefebvre's goal is to grasp these three projects in their relational contextualities as three mediations, or as three interconnected moments of becoming, to capture the contradictions and tendencies of modernity (Lefebvre 2003a, 44).

Lefebvre explains that only with Hegel were the binary oppositions rectified as the third element appeared (Lefebvre 2003c). This triadic structure always existed in Logos, but the moment of its emergence was the Hegelian moment (Lefebvre 2003c, 50). Lefebvre states, "Is there ever a two-term relationship except in representation? There are always Three. There is always the Other" (2003c, 50 [1980, 143]). He goes on to write, "The third term, here, is the *other*, with all that implies (*alterity*, the relation with the present/absent other—*alteration*—*alienation*)" (Lefebvre 2003c, 51; italics in original [1980, 225]). This takes us back to Nietzsche's art as the third moment in Lefebvre's philosophical trinity. Christian Schmid notes, "At a general level, the fundamental dialectical figure in Lefebvre's work can be understood as the contradiction between social thought and social action, supplemented by the third factor of the creative, poetic act" (2008, 33). Art for Nietzsche represented precisely the kind of vision that is higher than truth, a negation of reality to enable the subject to affirm life (Deleuze 1983, 102–3). Nietzsche states, "We possess *art* lest we *perish of the truth*" (1968, 435 §822; italics in original). Hence, according to Nietzsche, art is what makes life livable despite the parallelizing effect of truth. In this sense, Lefebvre contrasts life as art with modern everydayness, which is one of the main themes of his *Critique of Everyday Life*.

Lefebvre divides space into three interrelated dimensions: 1) Spatial practice or perceived space, 2) Representations of space or conceived space, and 3) Representational spaces or lived space (1991a, 33, 38–39; [2000, 42–43]). This ternary is at the heart of Lefebvre's dialectic, and therefore the three moments cannot be defined independently without referring to the sublate—the inner contradiction and intercontradictions among them. Before diving into an explanation of these three moments of spatial production, however, it is extremely important, as Schmid insists (2008, 29), to note that there are no clear and distinct definitions of any of the three moments. For this reason, Lefebvre tries to describe the dialectical moments in terms of their movements and approximations within the totality of the dialectical process. Thus, each explanation will preserve that continual motion in the form of ambiguity. Keeping in mind this problematic method, I present a summary of Lefebvre's approximations with regard to the three dialectical moments.

Lefebvre seems to suggest that the physical and mental spaces are transcended dialectically to produce the social space. Soja emphasizes that Lefebvre's three-dimensional dialectics led the way out of the realism-idealism dualism by conceptualizing the third space. He writes, "[Lefebvre] sought to transcend, via his inclusive dialectical or, better, *trialectical* materialism, the stubborn bi-polarity and dualism that had developed between Marx's historical materialism and Hegel's philosophical idealism" (Soja 1996, 36; italics in original). Spatial practice, or perceived space, is associated with the physicality of space (Lefebvre 1991a, 40: Soja 1996, 10). It encompasses the perspective of a measurable and mappable space. Yet, in spite of the relative cohesiveness of spatial practice, it is not comprehensive intellectually, and so any attempt to disclose it must involve the decodification of space (Lefebvre 1991a, 38). Lefebvre writes, " 'Modern' spatial practice might thus be defined—to take an extreme but significant case—by the daily life of a tenant in a government-subsidized high-rise housing project" (Lefebvre 1991a, 38 [2000, 48]). He leaves the example unexplained, so we can only speculate as to the significance of the example, and thus the definition of spatial practice itself. The aspects Lefebvre seems to intend to emphasize directly with the example are everydayness, urbanism, class identity, and the state's social politics. Taking that one step further, the interaction between these aspects within the context of the everyday life of the individual continually codes and recodes space. Here Lefebvre is actually speaking of spatial practice specific to capitalism, represented by two opposing poles: the urban, designed, collective, administrative, and instrumentally rational, on the one hand, and the unique, individual, and subjectively experiential, on the other hand. On this multilayer of contradictory interactions, space is constructed continually through the daily spatial practices of individuals.

Representations of space make up the space that is "conceived in ideas about space" (Soja 1996, 10); it is the mental representation of our spatiality (Lefebvre 1991a, 40). In other words, "representations of space" are *representations* of perceived and lived space, and they are produced by experts: "scientists, planners, urbanists, technocratic subdividers, and social engineers" (Lefebvre 1991a, 38 [2000, 48]). This space is the creation of specialists who reconcile what is experienced in everyday life with what is conceived. Representations of space are also the dominant space of every society because they reflect the dominant mode of production, and they are discursively and intellectually constructed because they embody the ideological hegemony in any society (Lefebvre 1991a, 39, 45). The space of artists who have a positivistic attitude toward art and life is an exemplifying case of representations of space.

Finally, representational space is "space as directly *lived* through its associated images and symbols, and hence the space of 'inhabitants' and 'users' " (Lefebvre 1991a, 39; italics in original). At the same time, it is also the space of creative artists and philosophers (Lefebvre 1991a, 39 [2000, 49]), the space of the organic intellectuals who are not part of the hegemonic machine of the state. Representational space is the dominated space, the space that is experienced passively, but for that very reason it is also the space where creative forces of dissent seek to occupy and hence re-create. At this point, there are two definitive aspects of representational space that are important to emphasize: 1) "It overlays physical space, making symbolic use of its objects"; and 2) It "tend[s] towards more or less coherent systems of non-verbal symbols and signs" (Lefebvre 1991a, 39 [2000, 49]). These two aspects respectively reflect transcended aspects of perceived and conceived space, because in the first case (perceived space) we have spatial practice that is infused in space through the daily lives of individuals within the mass-produced and managed space, and in the second case (conceived, or representations of, space) we have ideologically and lingo-discursively articulated and systemized space through the ideological state apparatuses. Hence, representational space is the realm of passivity and potential resistance, silence and intelligibility, repetition and re-creation; in short, it is the space of contradictions and transformations where humans make their history.

Each of the three moments (spatial practice, representations of space, and representational space) partakes in the production of space in various ways depending on their qualities, the dominant mode of production in the society, and the historical period. Each historical change in the modes of production brings about a new change in social space because each mode of production establishes its own space (Lefebvre 1991a, 46). For example, when the mode of production shifts from feudal to merchant capitalist, Lefebvre argues, a new space is also produced that immediately implies different spatial practices and representations of space. This was embodied in the Renaissance town where the new spatial code became determinant of an entirely new social reality (Lefebvre 1991a, 47). With this historical shift, the city became spatially recoded in terms of both ideology and knowledge. The government and public buildings became the loci around which the rest of the city was reorganized, and, in short, the new code became the new mode of the production of space.

A city square is the embodiment of the passive experience of space at its purest insofar as it is the direct product of the state's social engineering, represented by the division of space into private and public spheres. The state positions itself as the organizer of our public experience via the absolute organization of these public spaces, which are subdivided into spaces of shopping, entertainment, leisure, and so on through the repetition and mimicry of signs to direct and restrict people's activities in each space. Thus, the state insures the presence of its symbolic power and social order in city squares and streets. Of course, we are all expected to obey the policing power of the state, which insures that this order of things is continually sustained. Indeed, even where the police are physically not present, surveillance cameras render us visible to their omnipresent gaze. The state automatically assumes a public division of space into political-institutional and social-apolitical. The former functions as the organizer and sustainer of the latter and takes its legitimacy from a form of the assumed or actual consensus of the social-apolitical. In terms of this division between the political and the social, systems of representational democracy are not fundamentally different from authoritarian regimes because the fundamental assumption is that the elected politicians are designated to manage the political aspects of our lives as a society. Once consent is given to a certain group of politicians, who usually represent the highest level in the hierarchy of political parties, citizens have very little or no say in the nature of the police apparatuses. Order, security, public safety, and the rule of law are the kind of fetishized specialties that become 1) the fields of enormous abstraction and reproduction of more and more abstract specialization and their corresponding experts, which make public affairs less and less "public" and more and more alienating; and 2) the sources of legitimization for anything from installing a totalitarian system of surveillance to the militarization of the society. Under such democratic authoritarian circumstances, the organization of city squares, and public spaces in general, belong to us only insofar as we agree to passively go about our daily lives, the limits and nature of which are qualitatively predetermined by the state apparatuses. We normally get immersed in this repetition and mimicry until a moment of rapture when a creative political act disturbs this perfect rationalization of space.

What happened in the 2011–2012 movements of dissent, from Tunisia and Egypt to Greece, England, Spain, the United States, and Canada, exemplify this the actualization of the potential forces of creativity, the innovating praxis. At a historical moment of resistance, these social forces abolished the predetermined and passive spatial experience of city squares in many cities, such as Cairo, New York City, and Montreal. They have rejoined the political and the social by turning the space upside down with regard to the contradictions of the political and the social. In Tahrir Square in Cairo, Zuccotti Park in New York City, and the downtown streets of Montreal, the predesigned spaces for the passive experience of endless repetition and mimicry were transformed into spaces of political action in opposition to the normalized spatial politics of the state. In each of these cases, the social order that had been sustained by the policing power of the state was disturbed intentionally to accomplish the goal of toppling down an authoritarian regime or resisting and changing the economic politics of the state. In each case, it was possible that the negation of the representational spaces would become a swiping locus of spatial transformation. The fault lines of a dialectical leap in the perceived, conceived, and lived spaces became clear, of course with relative variations. To Lefebvre, dialectical determination is "the negative that contains the positive, negates the past in the name of the possible, and so manifests it as totality" (1982, 55 [1974, 49]).

On a winter day in 2010, a group of Tunisian police beat up a young man for resisting them after they had confiscated his unlicensed cart, with which he sold fruits and vegetables to support his family. Then, on December 17, 2010, in front of the municipal office of the central town of Sidi Bouzid, the young man set himself on fire as a political action of protest, not knowing that with such a hopeless act he would bring decisive contradictions and widespread unrest to the surface throughout the region. Simultaneously and throughout that same day, people in the town stormed the streets intent on breaking the imposed order and rationality, enraged against the regime for all that the lonely burned protester symbolized in their lives. Within ten days of that first moment, acts of public protest had reached the poor regions of the capital city as well. Images of the first protest and the following demonstrations (both spontaneous and organized) in Sidi Bouzid, and the resulting police violence, spread around the whole country and the rest of the world. Ordinary citizens provided public and instantaneous media by using their cellphone cameras and YouTube and Twitter, and the movement grew. Thus, the state's totalitarian control of the media in the country lost all influence within two weeks of the revolution's launch. Even more significant, on January 15, 2011, Bin Ali, the notorious head of one of the most notorious totalitarian states, fled the country.[1]

In every case of city square transformation during the prodemocracy movements of 2011–2012 there was also a dialectical interaction between digital space and the urban space, with each side growing exponentially to new explosive dimensions through the other. Each image of protest or police violence that left a city square returned only to make the new and innovative politicization of the city square more actual. At the same time, each major spatial reorganization of a city square created and reorganized new digital spaces of and for political action. If these city squares had not been decentered through digital means of communication, they could not have overcome the larger totalitarian systems that had contained them for so long. The digital dimension gave the city squares international breadth, which ultimately freed them from the grip of the local totalitarian claws. In other words, without the digital space, these pockets of civil resistance could not have possibly been emancipated from their totalitarian geopolitical chains.[2] Traditional totalitarian regimes in the Middle East and North Africa seem to be especially vulnerable to this digital dimension because they have for so long relied on the total visibility of space within, while remaining isolated from the outside world. Within the borders of the state and at the same time bridging the so-called national space to the international space beyond the borders of the state, digital space opened routes for constructing spaces of resistance.

Of course, we cannot designate the actual beginning of the spatial transformation of these and other city squares. It is more accurate to say that, like any other historical moment, these movements do not have beginnings; instead they have ideological interpretations of beginnings. By the same token, it is important to note that many of the spatial techniques of these political actions can also be found in the 2009 Green Movement in Iran and the 2010–2012 Anarcho-communist protests in Greece. In fact, we can trace many aspects of these spatial revolts even back to the 1960s movements, including the student movement of 1968 in Paris. The common underlining principle is that through occupying the most symbolic space of domination, political and social domination itself can be challenged and transformed. Furthermore, the realization of a public urban space as a space of political acts of protest by a certain group, such as students, can re-create the spatial dynamics throughout many other urban centers as well. For instance, what took place in Montreal with regard to the Student Strike Movement in 2012 reemerged in Chicago with similar symbolism (the red square) and modified political goals. Likewise, what happened in Egypt in the form of creating a free city within the city square, including mobile service centers such as hospitals, in the same year played out in a modified form in New York City during the Occupy Wall Street Movement. Of course, what is unclear is what kind of acts of protest make the initial spark and why. It seems that the moment the spatial order is somehow disturbed, the chaotic contradictions can surface and then spur an explosive plane of events that would lead to a new dialectical transformation of the order of things. Both history and spatiality float on a sea of contradictions, and only after the actual transformations take place can we theorize what exactly led to what. What we can be sure of is that the creation of history and the production of space are equally rooted in contradictions that cannot be accurately understood through any theory that does not entail dialectical logic—the logic that accounts for contradictions.

Both democratic and authoritarian governments react immediately to the political demonstration of the body. Lefebvre writes, "The bourgeoisie and the capitalist system thus experience great difficulty in mastering what is at once their product and tool of their mastery, namely space. They find themselves unable to reduce practice (the practico-sensory realm, the body, social spatial practice) to their abstract space, and hence new, spatial, contradictions arise and make themselves felt" (1991, 63). Taming the body is the state apparatuses' main task, and the moment the body regains its politicality, the state responds with violence. In the case of large demonstrations, governments do not hesitate to use the pretext of public safety to justify violent policing, but the truth is that the antagonism against the politicality of the body is ingrained in the system. Feminist groups such as Pussy Riot and Femen have shown how paranoid the state is when it comes to the untamed or rebellious body. Patriarchy demands unconditional respect for its symbols of power because of its fragility, and the genius of these two movements in particular is that their members target the most symbolic, and often sacred, spaces of patriarchy. To accomplish this, they mobilize the female body, a potentially devastating spatial weapon when it steps out of its predetermined role.

The historical suppression of the body of the condemned has charged it with potential negativity. It is this potential negativity that has the power to shake the foundations of the sacred at virtually any moment. The body of the condemned, in other words, can expose the fragility, the empty core, of the sacred simply by breaking the sacred taboos, most of which are attached to the body itself. By declaring its freedom from the spell of the sacred, the body can disrupt the patriarchal system with all its sacred symbols, myths, powerful institutions, and value systems. Indeed, radical feminists in some of the world's most patriarchal societies have done exactly that. In doing so, they use the body to negate representational space, sending shock waves all the way down to the spatial foundation of the system.

The body is the last corner of space that has not yet been completely subsumed into the totalitarian space, and, therefore, it is also the last hope for overturning it. When gradual reform is not possible, the revolutionary technique of negating representational space becomes the most effective method of change. Although such action will most likely not lead to changes in the modes of spatial production (because that would require emancipating the means of spatial production and changing society's spatial practices), it might very well create cracks in totalitarian space that future movements could then pry open. The very presence of the body of the condemned in certain spaces is more than disrespectful; it is an existential threat. Intuitively, one should realize the power of the negativity embedded in the body of the condemned. All the body needs to do is boldly and unapologetically announce its presence where it is not supposed to be and in ways that it is not supposed to be seen.

The state's violent reaction to the political demonstration of the body represents the existing order's automatic aggression toward any attempt to meddle with the existing spatial economy. At such moments, we see how the state treats public space as its own private space: as soon as its ownership is challenged politically by members of civil society, the state reacts with the disproportionate force of its armed agents against people who are often carrying nothing but banners. Even in the most democratic countries, demonstrations that try to accomplish even a partial debourgeoisification of space are met with the deployment of the armed forces. The body is free to be in public space only insofar as it does not represent a threat to the ownership of the means and relations of spatial production. What constitutes such a threat is interpreted in different ways depending on the means of control, discipline, and hegemony at work in a given society. Of course, the bourgeois public space allows for greater individual freedoms compared to, say, feudal or aristocratic public spaces, but it is an illusion to think that it would allow for any segment of the public to debourgeoisify space.

Nonetheless, there seems to be a common assumption that free public space can be constructed and made available for people to use if, when, and how they like. As the assumption goes, the space is available whether people use it or not, and the mere fact of its availability is taken to meet the spatial conditions for a democratic society. In a typical North American city square, for instance, on a sunny afternoon, one can find a cacophony of activity: people relaxing and socializing, musicians and performance artists trying to attract audiences, vendors selling food, wide-screen televisions running commercial advertisements, and groups demonstrating to raise awareness about issues they think deserve public attention. There is some art, some leisure, some socialization, and some politics taking place within a safe and diverse atmosphere. That kind of scene might be precisely the picture that comes to mind when one thinks of a free and democratic public space. The only issue is that, everything else being equal, such a space does not make any of its users freer than those who live in another city with no city square or public park. While space to some degree does determine the nature of social activities, it is more so social practice that determines social space. In other words, it is the practices of the users of space that, both instantaneously and over time, shape that space. Only if we decide to obey a certain set of rules or conventions can we say that the social space determines social activities. Of course, there are always regulations and conventions, but the question is how democratically those regulations and conventions are decided on.

It is counterintuitive to take the existence of a place designated by administrators for a select category of activities as a sign of our freedom. As Malcolm Miles strongly argues, "[D]emocracy happens where people are not in predetermined spaces" (2014, 108). In the same article, Miles states that "the task is not to reclaim public spaces but to reclaim the state itself as a public sphere of societal determination, and as where the public interest, once it is identified, can be protected" (2014, 113). Miles's position is aligned with the Lefebvrian perspective that what determines social space, including public space, in any society is the dominant modes and relations of production. In a capitalist society, city squares and public parks remain part of the dominant space until the users of those spaces actively and consciously alter the modes of spatial production. That is to say, if the users of space are situated within the capitalist modes of production, their daily spatial practice will invariably contribute to the production and reproduction of the capitalist abstract space. Even for an individual who does not need to work, that is, whose time is entirely "free," the capitalist abstract space is just as totalitarian because it is the social relations of production, rather than her individual way of using space, that is at stake.

Furthermore, what makes a system totalitarian is not the lack of public space, but the system's unlimited spatial power, whereby the types and ranges of spatial practices are centrally determined by the ruling elites. Free public space is a vague notion at best, and it is not overly useful for a critical spatial theory. When the establishment dictates what freedom is as well as where and how it should be exercised, freedom does not necessarily negate totalitarianism. For example, in Saddam Hussein's Iraq, every university had a designated wall called "the free wall" where students could publish anything they wanted. Of course, everyone knew that it was also the wall that was most watched by the regime's agents.

If there was one place that political activists had to avoid, it was "the free wall" simply because it was the least free of spaces.

The point here is not to equate totalitarian regimes with liberal democracies, but to emphasize the fact that whenever any spatial practice threatens the existing spatial economy, those in power will react with sufficient violence to prevent any change in the ownership of the means of spatial production. Capitalist abstract space is more advanced in its totalitarian nuances than space under a classical totalitarian regime. The latter would take issue with anything, from antiestablishment music and resistance theater to unauthorized demonstrations. However, in downtown Toronto, for example, antiestablishment performance and music would not be an issue, but anything approaching the debourgeoisification of space would fall well outside the limit of people's freedom. This was evident in the brutal police response to the protest against the 2010 G20 summit in Toronto, during which more than one thousand demonstrators, including a number of journalists, were arrested. That kind of anticapitalist demonstration directly exposes the spatial tyranny that otherwise serves as the façade of freedom. Whether in the 2010 Toronto riots or the 2017 Hamburg riots, a broken store window or ATM wins much more attention than any protester's broken leg or arm. When we repeatedly see pictures of the same damaged storefront in news reports, the implicit message is clear: the demonstrators crossed the line demarcating the legitimate use of space, and therefore the state security apparatuses' use of violence was justified. The body falls under attack the moment it is conceived as a threat to the clearly defined spatial hierarchy of power.

Here it is worth revisiting the experience of the Occupy movement. While its very name suggested an intention to occupy the heart of Wall Street, the movement never came close to accomplishing this. With no sense of irony or humorous intention, the mayor of New York at the time, Michael Bloomberg, said, "[P]eople have a right to protest, and if they want to protest, we'll be happy to make sure they have locations to do it" (quoted in Colangelo 2011). The spatial totality of the exercise of power is seemingly so secured and neutralized that it did not occur to Blomberg that the organizers of the movement already had a very particular location in mind. The universal rule of power is unchanging: everyone is free if they obey the rules. Of course, the rules are usually precisely what negates freedom. In the case of the Occupy movement, Bloomberg's statement unintentionally exposed the normalized absolutism that frames the management of space.

Granted, the Occupy movement could have tried harder to force itself into the sacred spaces of capital, but to do so, they would have needed to respond to violence in kind, and they surely would have failed regardless. Because of their adherence to the principles and pragmatics of nonviolence, the movement stayed clear of any actions that could have justified the police's use of more force. This naturally required them to focus on a less contentious space for their protest. As a result, the implicit goal of the movement almost immediately became merely metaphoric for sympathizers, utopic for the general public, and ridiculous to the elites.[3] Of course, the democratic space the movement created in Zuccotti Park was of historical importance, especially in terms of its innovative peacefulness. The mere creation of such a space for democratic debate among various social and political movements was a significant accomplishment, but, unsurprisingly, as soon as the spatial practice ceased, the production of the new space also collapsed.

For the sake of analysis, we can say there were two distinct phases of the movement: the first directed toward the symbolic space of the iconic Charging Bull at One Chase Manhattan Plaza, and the second toward Zuccotti Park. In the Charging Bull phase, with the goal of occupying Wall Street, the movement tried to trigger dialectical change in the production of space from above, namely by changing representational space, which might have eventually resulted in a fundamental change in social spatial practices if the public at large followed suit. In the Zuccotti Park phase, the dialectics shifted to inventing new spatial practices that would eventually lead to a change in representational space. The continued endurance of new spatial practices is crucial for negating the dominant space and achieving change in lived space. Of course, in each phase the top-down and bottom-up dialectics could, in theory, occur. However, the first phase was meant to move from negating representational space to negating spatial practice. In the second phase, the primary dialectical motion was reversed: from negating spatial practice to negating representational space. Nonetheless, Occupy remained to some extent an attempt to trigger a change in representational space insofar as it was still a protest taking place in capital's stomping ground of lower Manhattan.

Despite the rich array of opinions about the movement, it is still worth asking whether it was possible for the movement to accomplish more than what it did. Diana Boros and Haley Smith offer a strong critical analysis of why the movement faded away so quickly. "The goal of the movement," they state, "was never simply to present a system of reforms and fit neatly within current political processes, but rather it was to construct an alternative public space, one with greater and more influential access for all citizens, regardless of socioeconomic positioning" (Boros & Smith 2014, 216). They argue that the positivization, commodification, and "pop-culturalization" of the movement by means of the culture industry reduced its radical dialectical critique into a simple image (Boros & Smith 2014, 228). Although social media played a major role in bringing attention to Occupy both in the United States and abroad, it also swiftly derevolutionized the movement as a result of transforming its initial discourse into something digestible by the positive (as opposed to negative or dialectal) mentality of the public. Boros and Smith's critical, and sound, account of the domination of the culture industry and the one-dimensional mentality it fosters seems to suggest that the movement did not stand much chance of initiating a substantial shift in the dynamics of public space, even though it did succeed in providing an example of an egalitarian alternative to the existing hierarchical order.

Historically, the failure to sustain a democratic participatory space has been a problem for all progressive revolutionary movements. There always seems to be a moment when space is left to the old or newly forming relations of domination. Even revolutions that successfully change the ownership of the means of production only achieve a temporary cessation of the domination of space. In the midst of the chaos that initially surrounds popular revolutions of the kind we have witnessed since the October Revolution, another system of domination immediately starts to crystalize. It is only during the relatively short time just before any political force gains enough power to reactivate the state that public space is emancipated. That is when we experience spaces such as city squares as political innovation at its purest. Arguably, the 1936–1939 anarcho-syndicalist revolution in Spain is the only significant exception to the relapse of progressive revolutions. Both ideologically and in practice, it tried to persist within and perpetuate that free revolutionary space, resisting any possibility of reestablishing the power of the state and, hence, the redomination of space. The Rojava movement in northern Syria has followed a comparably promising trajectory with its aims to provide a peaceful, diverse, egalitarian mode of spatial production based on everyday direct democracy. However, particularly in the context of an economic embargo and a lack of international support, it is uncertain how much longer the movement will be able to survive the hostilities of the Turkish state, jihadists, and Syrian nationalists.[4]

The first major premise that is implied in the concept of "totalitarian space" is that space is a production. Totalitarian space is, first and foremost, a space that is both produced and dominated. Despite the indispensability of Lefebvre's theory of the production of space to any critical spatial theory, as it stands, it is not sufficient to identify what makes a particular space totalitarian. Specifically, in the production of totalitarian space, the spatial uniqueness of each individual place is destroyed as a necessary condition for flattening space, which in turn leads to the emergence of totalitarian space. Lefebvre's three-dimensional theory of the production of space cannot account for the destruction of spatial uniqueness. However, there are more concepts in Lefebvre's *The Production of Space* that can be used to illuminate the destruction of a place's unique spatial features in the march toward totalitarian space.

Dominated Space

In chapter 6, I argue that mechanically reproduced patterns of signs, images, and symbols are used effectively to dominate space and produce totalitarian space. Lefebvre uses the term "visual space" to refer to the spatial product of these signs, images, and symbols. In this sense, totalitarian space is a space that is shaped by visual systems of repetitive semiological patterns or, in other words, the engineered repetition of signs within a unifying canon of totality linked dialectically to cycles of mimicry. The mechanically reproduced semiological patterns eventually demolish natural space and create an artificial one; they turn space against itself for the sake of deepening and sustaining the existing relations of domination. Lefebvre states, "A sign has a repetitive aspect in that it adds a corresponding representation. Between the signified and the sign there is a mesmerizing difference, a deceptive gap" (1991a, 135 [2000, 158]). Then he states:

> Space is also felt to have this deadly character: as the locus of communication by means of signs, as the locus of separations and the milieu of prohibitions, spatiality is characterized by a death instinct inherent to life—which only proliferates when it enters into conflict with itself and seeks its own destruction. (Lefebvre 1991a, 134 [2000, 159])

Here Lefebvre hints at the spatial aspects of destruction, the destruction of spatial elements, and the dialectics of destruction and creation. This is the closest Lefebvre comes to bringing together the dialectics of spatial production with the destruction of a specific spatial aspect that is inherent in natural, or appropriated, space and necessary for authentic experiences of space: aura.

The bourgeoisie aims at the complete domination and abstraction of space, and the extent of the subsequent destruction should be measured by the degree of violence committed against nature. After all, nature is our only fundamental and universal point of reference simply because, in its least disturbed form, space is defined by nature. Deviation from nature is a marker of civilization, but we have now reached a point where the appropriation is no longer tenable insofar as it amounts to the universal destruction of nature as such. Despite the intrinsic brutality of life in general, embodied most clearly in living beings feeding on each other, non-human animals' spatialities do not violate the ecological frame of being. All animals leave traces, but those traces are part of the natural space. Humans, too, for most of their history have appropriated natural space according to their needs for food and shelter without stripping natural space of its essential naturalness. The Finnish architect Juhani Pallasmaa states, "Construction in traditional cultures is guided by the body in the same way that a bird shapes its nest by the movements of its body" (2005, 26). Like a den, a traditional mud house does not waste space, nor does it violently create abstract space using geometrical lines and sharp angles. It projects the body's mode of dwelling in space, adapted to the natural conditions.

A traditional home is an artistic spatial projection of the ontological mode of being. The home used to be the body's corner to hide *in* nature. Any traditional village, whether in Sub-Saharan Africa or the Himalayas, emphasizes the naturalness of the natural space, in the same way that a white cloud emphasizes the blueness of the sky. In such a village, the paths flow around boulders and trees, keeping the traces of the accumulated, everyday movements across multiple generations. Such paths do not violently cut through everything like bullets on their way to murder. In human history, the shift from leaving traces in nature to eliminating every trace of natural space is very recent and begins with the emergence of industrial capitalism. Ancient and medieval cities destroyed natural space to varying degrees, but, for the most part, they preserved a substantial degree of their spaces' naturalness. Admittedly, this was largely the result of the limitations of the dominant modes of production of the time, as opposed to ecological awareness. A town's houses would, as a matter of course, be built of limestone, mud, bamboo, or whatever else was naturally available in a given place. The spatial outcome was, therefore, not a drastic departure from the natural environment around the town. While no two mud houses, traditional villages, or naturally shaped paths look the same, the same cannot be said about concrete houses, modern cities, and highways. This is the main difference between auratic and non-auratic spaces.

Industrial capitalism commodified everything it could reach by any means possible. The usage of signs under capitalism is not for marking the natural space but for abstracting, flattening, and commodifying it. The violence committed against space by semiotic patterns is not side or unconscious effects; rather, it is "*intrinsic to* [the] *abstraction*" it commits against nature (Lefebvre 1991a, 289; italics from original [2000, 344]). Historically, this comprises the "hegemony of vision" (Lefebvre 1991a, 140 [2000, 165]), the generalization of violence represented by the state and carried out by the bourgeoisie, and the domination of the abstract and visual space, which are interconnected (Lefebvre 1991a, 280; 289; 290). These theses of Lefebvre's sound more profound when they are integrated with some of the relevant themes of Benjamin's "The Work of Art in the Age of Its Technological Reproducibility."

Benjamin presents a history of the transitions of visual art in terms of the reproduction of works of art. He explains that the ancient Greeks knew founding and stamping to reproduce identical pieces such as coins and terracotta. The mechanical reproduction of art has a more recent history. Mechanically reproduced art first emerged with the invention of woodcut and graphic art, even before the invention of print (Benjamin 2006g, 252). In the Middle Ages, engraving and etching were also invented as means of mechanically reproducing art. In the nineteenth century, lithography appeared, and this can be considered a leap to a much more advanced method of mechanical reproducibility. Finally, photography was the ultimate revolution in this realm (Benjamin 2006g, 252–53), which was then followed by the current age of the digital reproduction of art and the whole invention of cyberspace, which Benjamin did not live to see.

What I want to pause on shortly, and at length in chapters 4 and 5, is the concept of "aura" in Benjamin's article. When it comes to mechanically reproduced works of art, Benjamin realizes the absence of the authentic presence of the original context, space and time. He sub-sumes this missing feature with the concept of "aura" (Benjamin 2006g, 253). Hence, aura is supposed to designate the relationship between the original work of art and its original space and time. In Adorno's words, aura is "the presence of that which is not present" (2006a, 102). Elsewhere Benjamin defines aura as "a strange weave of space and time: the unique appearance or semblance of distance" (2005b, 518). Two things should be kept in mind at this point: first, mechanically reproduced works of art are auraless (Benjamin's main thesis). Second, I argue, these auraless objects must have some auratic (or rather anti-auratic) effect on space where they are located.

Now we can define Lefebvre's "visual space" in terms of Benjamin's concept of auraless-ness. The visual space is a space in which spatial violence is totalized by means of the installation of numerous auraless images, signs, and symbols. These mechanically reproduced and distrib-uted auraless semiotic patterns destroy the aura of space.[5] That is to say, the visual space is produced through a totalitarian spatial application of auraless signs, symbols, images, and objects, which destroy the spatial uniqueness of the places where they are installed. This process involves the standardization of social space, administrative division of private and public space, spatial centralization as part of social engineering, and spatial flattening through the repetition of visual patterns that create the visual thread that imposes one spatial dimension on all places. All this has a major political consequence; namely, it prepares the space for totalitarian governance embodied in the project of the state.

Finally, Lefebvre also differentiates between "dominated space" and "appropriated space." He borrows the concept of "appropriation" from Marx and reappropriates it. While Marx used the concept in opposition to private property, Lefebvre claims he never made his understanding of appropriation clear. Lefebvre defines appropriated space as simply the space that has been appropriated according to the essential needs of its dwellers (Lefebvre 1991a, 164–65). Lefebvre's examples include igloos, straw huts, peasant dwellings, traditional Japanese houses, and traditional Norman and Provençal houses. "Peasant houses and villages," in Lefebvre's words, "speak: they recount, though in a mumbled and somewhat con-fused way, the lives of those who built and inhabited them" (1991a, 165 [2000, 192]). This is what Gaston Bachelard would call "the poetics of space," where the dweller roots in her "corner of the world," her "first universe" (Bachelard 1994, 4).

What Lefebvre calls "appropriated space" is a space adjusted to fit the essential needs of its dwellers and users, functioning in accordance with the natural environment, not despite it. Naturally, people appropriate their spaces according to the climate as well as their ways of life, leisure, communal relations, and so on. Obviously, the use value is the most essential, but an aesthetic value also emerges as a result of the dweller's direct sculpting of the space. This appropriation of space in accordance with the natural needs of its dwellers, be that space a wigwam, mud hut, or any traditional peasant house, exudes an aura of its own that enriches the existing aura of its surrounding habitat. Every appropriated space carries a unique signature corresponding to its natural environment and expressing an existential statement made by its creators.

However, when capital becomes a determinant factor in housing, transportation, labor, production, and consumption, the human relation to space shifts from one of appropriation to domination. The dull and alienating space Lefebvre terms "dominated space" is engineered through instrumental rationality and produced to meet the needs of capitalism. Capitalist modes of production essentially divide social space into spaces of production and spaces of consumption, both of which exemplify dominated space. The state functions as both the umbrella institution of other institutions and the executive institution that actualizes the ideal conditions for sustaining the capitalist modes of production.

In the course of capitalist history, domination has prevailed over appropriation. Dominated space is violent, dull, and alienating, whereas appropriated space is harmonious, inspiring, and inviting. Furthermore, dominated space is not separate from the exploitive enterprise of social domination. It is the space that has been commodified, and thus it is necessarily alienating. Appropriated space, on the other hand, contains the innovative dialectical moment that negates the repetition and mimicry. Now the connection between these sets of concepts will become even more interesting.

To Lefebvre, an example of dominated space is a motorway that "brutalizes the countryside and the land, slicing through space like a great knife" (Lefebvre 1991a, 165 [2000, 191]). Other examples of dominated space, which has become dominant because of the proliferation of technological means of reproduction, are "military architecture, fortifications and ramparts, dams and irrigation systems" (Lefebvre 1991a, 164 [2000, 191]). What about city squares? Because the state is the master of the spatial codes of dominated space, and because dominated space is always the production of that master (Lefebvre 1991a, 162; 165), it is only through revolutionary, innovative acts of spatial revolt that spaces such as city squares can be decoded, recoded, and thus reappropriated to become auratic space once more, emancipated from the totalitarianism. Again, in Lefebvre's words: "Any revolutionary 'project' today, whether utopian or realistic, must, if it is to avoid hopeless banality, make the reappropriation of the body, in association with the reappropriation of space, into a non-negotiable part of its agenda" (1991a, 166–67 [2000, 193]). However, he also cautions that reappropriation can only temporarily stop domination (1991a, 168). Therefore, the truly emancipating revolution is the one that can put an end to the systemization and rationalization of space, thus opening up space for direct interaction with its users planet-wide. The model of this human-specie space would be nothing less than art itself: continual creativity and the transformation of everyday life in a way that would not be in destructive conflict with ecology (Lefebvre 1991a, 422).

Finally, to combine concepts of both Lefebvre and Benjamin, auraless-ness also seems to be inherent in the concept of "dominated space" (with its violence, dullness, and alienating features). On the other hand, the concept of spatial aura perfectly captures the uniqueness that is intrinsic in "appropriated space." What Lefebvre is speaking of in his examples of appropriated space, such as Provençal peasant houses, oriental straw houses, and igloos, is in fact "aura." The same applies to Lefebvre's criticism of mental and abstract space as well as logico-mathematical representations of space; in other words, one could claim, Lefebvre's problem with them is that they cannot express or represent the aura of space. In fact, Lefebvre states, "An appropriated space *resembles* a work of art" (1991a, 165; italics in original [2000, 192]). Now, if Benjamin's concept of aura is associated with works of art (because works of art can be looked at as loci of aura), we can safely claim that appropriated space is auratic space, as opposed to dominated space, which can be defined as auraless space (like mechanically reproduced works of art for Benjamin). In later chapters I return to "aura," and with it I eventually reach the open end of this journey, but for now I move on to the essential role of spatial technologies of power in the production of totalitarian space.

3

Spatial Technologies of Power

The proliferation of unmanned aerial vehicles, otherwise known as drones, in recent years for purposes ranging from extrajudicial executions to policing and surveillance has drawn attention to the increasingly boundless nature of power. Drones free the all-seeing eye of power from the limited mobility of the body as well as the constraints of the built environment, geographical topographies, and state sovereignty. In doing so, drones have taken the totalizing enterprise of power to the very limits of spatiality on this planet. Yet the maximization of vision is a very old goal of power, with documentation dating back to Ancient Greece (Levin, 1993). Even in its most abstract form, power entails visibility, and because vision is inherently aggressive, the hegemony of vision is synonymous with the very functioning of power. It was not until the Enlightenment, however, that a plan for actualizing unlimited visibility began to crystallize.

All at once, everything—from the "laws of nature" to isolated tribes whose only fault was not being privy to the Parisian way of life—had to be made visible. The only place where so-called laws of nature could be proposed and approved was Western Europe, but these norms were nonetheless imposed on the rest of humanity, especially the populations of Africa and the indigenous peoples of the Americas. Not surprisingly, these purportedly universal laws were such that the Other was irrevocably situated on the lowermost rungs of nature's hierarchy. According to the new morality that accompanied these laws, the social was only a mirror of the natural: those at the lower levels of the natural hierarchy could be exploited by those who were naturally and, therefore, socially superior. Of course, in reality Europe managed to overlay a constructed hierarchy of nature on an existing social hierarchy. Slavery, for instance, was subsequently justified by the pseudoscientific paradigm of race, but the practice itself predated the scientific "discovery" of the superiority of certain races. However, it is those with the best view who inevitably know the most, and who could see better than those in Western Europe, where the facts were manufactured?

In antiquity, vision was understood to mean a hallucination, a dream, a metaphoric glimpse of a divine reality, or perhaps a coded prediction of the future. For the prophets of modernity and their Frankensteinian creatures, however, vision entailed molding the world according to the laws of nature. Nationalism was the first major vision to be realized. In the beginning of the new age, there was Napoleon and his French empire. He was followed by innumerable and often catastrophically malformed imitators: Hitler is just one example from the twentieth century of such a man of vision, as are Ataturk, Mussolini, Stalin, and many other national heroes.[1] Those who did not fit into the modernist vision were, in the best cases, social pathologies who needed to be cured and assimilated or, in the worst cases, natural errors who had to be physically eliminated.

The new messianic meaning of vision correlates with the modern means of totalizing visibility. This is no longer merely epistemological ocularcentrism but a hegemony realized through the totalization of vision. The hegemony of vision runs through all aspects of modern social and political life, including arenas that are supposed to be premised on the metaphysical superiority of the invisible.[2] The goal of making everything visible both inside and outside, macro and micro, conscious and unconscious, material and spiritual is at the heart of the violent conquering of the world. Ancient tombs are to be penetrated to the level of DNA and exhibited to the public, whose lives are defined by their role as spectators. Embryos are to be viewed long before they even acquire eyes. Soon potential parents who have their own visions for their perfect babies may be able to place orders for gene editing.

The fascination with zoos is just one manifestation of this invasive drive for visibility. Well before and even after Nazism, human zoos were erected in Europe: non-European individuals would be shipped from America and Africa for public exhibition. There is something intrinsically fascistic in the modern desire to see, something that goes far beyond the fascism of the first half of the twentieth century. While the first generation of historical fascists were fascinated by self-presentation, imagery, performance, and appearance, the general tendency among dominant modern and postmodern groups is toward total visibility. In fact, the visual subjugation of the Other is at the heart of the process of othering itself, and once the Other is made a subject of the oppressor's sight, she will be deprived of her space. Othering by visional violence is therefore a form of spatial domination.

We see this in media coverage of isolated societies, which proliferates aerial images of these societies, serving to visually colonize their spaces. It is as if those of us who are trapped in the global plane of transparency enviously chastise them for their freedom. Or perhaps we so badly want to look back onto the time of our own freedom, which we lost the moment we felt we were being watched, when we became the subject of the inspecting gaze of God. We are the isolated ones, not the Amazonians. Transparency has isolated us. Being exhibited to the gaze of the Other takes away the ability to see oneself from the point of view of oneself. Transparency, in this sense, objectifies one not only to the other but to oneself as well. Being beautiful in the society of exhibition amounts to pleasing the consuming gaze of the other, transforming one's own being into a pure exhibition value in the abstract space of commodities. The gaze deports the self from the body and turns the body into a refugee in a spectacle that is placeless. Even worse, the gaze of a camera lens disrupts the process of becoming and freezes one's being in a moment that lacks history or future. Stripped from becoming, a being is no longer seen as a being, or even an object. A photographically defined person is, instead, mere data. Technologies of transparency thus deontologize us through our deworlding. Their function is to strip us from the right to being, transform us from a knowing and feeling being into a placeless piece of processable, classifiable, calculable, storable, sellable, and deletable information.

Today the digital means of surveillance do what God used to do: they can see without being seen. With the death of God, the ruling elite needed a replacement that would function in the same way but more effectively. People had to be made to feel that they were always watched, and with that the panoptic technology, the vision of one of the Enlightenment's loyal sons, was born. The panoptic technology obliterated physical and psychological barriers, granting unprecedented powers to vision and limitless vision to power. It was the panoptic technology that could for the first time transform our spatial condition into such a state of helplessness that our sole source of comfort would be to tell ourselves that we have nothing to hide. What we forget is that constantly living in such a condition is to always already be a prisoner because we are punished before even committing the potential crime. This mirrors the first theological arrangement, whereby we are charged with an original sin we never committed and subjected to constant monitoring to deter us from further sins we are purportedly destined to commit.

By forcing nature into the plane of total visibility, we lost our own naturalness as well. There are two reasons for this: 1) every exposure of a human secret is an exposure of the part of all humans' secrets (the golden rule of psychoanalysis); and 2) seeing further into the Other amounts to facing one's own abyss. We have effectively given the machine every map it could ever need to navigate our exploited inner spaces, from our genes to the psyche. Aware of the fact that the visual occupation of external space correlates to losing internal space, a yogi meditator closes her eyes to stop the shrinking of her inner space. Seeing outwardly is spatial conquest, and, as such, one would presume that it would expand the inner horizons of the self. On a subjective level, however, seeing amounts to what can be best termed spatial bleeding, as the self loses spatial ground to the external world.

The obsession to obtain a better view has also divested most of today's architecture of its homeness. It is this drive for a better view that, as an exemplifying case of fetishism, ultimately pursues a totalizing vision. Architecturally, this could only mean the glassification of walls. However, walls made of transparent glass essentially destroy wallness, and, in doing so, they also annihilate windows, which can only exist when they are framed by walls that visually separate the inside from the outside. What is forgotten in this age of glassification is that the view from inside only has value when it returns the viewer's gaze through a window. When an entire wall is made transparent, the dweller is deprived of her solitude along with the experience of distance that is at the core of homeness.

A home with transparent walls causes spatial bleeding from within and, from outside, it lends itself to spatial prostitution. As Byung-Chul Han states, "[W]hen the world becomes a display room, dwelling proves impossible" (2015, 12). By housing ourselves in transparent spaces to see the outside world, we become zoo occupants, permanently at the mercy of others' gazes. The spectacle's spell is lethal: it draws the spectator into its objectified mode of being, eliminating the grains of texture. This is detrimental to "[a]ll the senses, including vision," for, as Juhani Pallasmaa states, they all "are extensions of the tactile sense; the senses are specializations of skin tissue, and all sensory experiences are modes of touching and thus related to tactility" (2005, 10). Modern vision, on the other hand, is the vision of the inspector, whose primary goal is to control, colonize, and exploit.

Transparency

Nowhere is a totalitarian system's limitless exercise of power more pronounced than in its domination and regulation of social space for the purposes of self-preservation. Yet while classical totalitarian regimes rely mainly on propagating the fear that they could acquire whatever information they seek, the corporate state has achieved the closest thing to omniscience that we have ever known. The intelligence in the form of Big Data that has already been amassed has overwhelmed traditional means of data processing, with much of it awaiting future, unknown uses. What we can be sure of is that with unmanned aerial vehicles (UAVs), better known as drones, surveying even the most remote regions of the world and intelligence agencies determined to circumvent unbreakable encryption, contemporary spatial technologies of power leave us with "no place to hide" (O'Harrow 2005, 2; Greenwald 2014, 21).

The degree to which contemporary social space has been made transparent to the gaze of power, controlled by the state's apparatuses and corporate partners, is unprecedented. Today the state of being constantly under watch is no longer a form of control exercised primarily on the incarcerated; the gaze of power follows all citizens wherever they may be in urban space. As an individual walks on a street, shops online, or makes a phone call, her actions are recorded in various ways for a range of actual and potential purposes. Particularly in an online context, her consumption history, personality, political orientation, social relations, and much more all fall under the never-sleeping gaze of power. This totalizing visibility has produced a unity of space, the completeness and transparency of which can best be described as totalitarian. A state that recognizes no limit to its power is the quintessential feature of totalitarian regimes (Conquest 2000, 74). By the same token, the gaze that recognizes no spatial limit to its vision is inherently totalitarian, as is the resulting produced space.

The obsession with transparency is inseparable from power's tendency to control. The idea that an all-powerful god is an all-seeing god is deeply rooted in monotheism and other mythologies that predate it (e.g., Horus in ancient Egyptian deities, and the Hindu god Shiva). To the emerging modern state, investment in the idea of God proved to be too inefficient for the purpose of controlling increasingly heterogeneous societies, so it was time for scientific knowledge to be put to work to actualize total domination. Intrinsic in the project of Enlightenment is the goal of illuminating everything everywhere. As Foucault once stated in an interview, "A fear haunted the latter half of the eighteenth century: the fear of darkened spaces, of the pall of gloom which prevents the full visibility of things, men and truths. It sought to break up the patches of darkness that blocked the light, eliminate the shadowy areas of society, demolish the unlit chambers" (Foucault 1980, 153). In this sense, the instrumental rationality that aims to invent technologies capable of providing limitless visibility and, thus, totalitarian space, dates back to the Enlightenment. Acquiring the knowledge and technique for high-resolution individuation of bodies and thorough inspection of society was set in motion by the Enlightenment project (1980, 151–52).

"Enlightenment Is Totalitarian"[3]

The Enlightenment project was, of course, a revolution in knowledge, but it was, for the same reason, a revolution in the means of control too. It sought both the emancipation of society from irrationality and the transparency of social space, both the destruction of the authority of the church and the construction of the command of the state. It ended the Dark Ages, but it also brought a nightmarish age of total illumination, limitless transparency, and fetishized visibility. The French Revolution quickly placed the means of knowledge, illumination, and power in the hands of the new ruling elite, the bourgeoisie. Thus, the realized transparency was mainly of the social space for the gaze of the bourgeois state and to a significantly lesser degree of official politics to the eyes of the public. Through instrumentalizing knowledge, power reached a much higher level of complexity rendering social space cornerless, paving the way for the creation of totalitarian space, a space in which the body could have no place to hide, no place to commit freedom. By the second quarter of the twentieth century, after the establishment painfully had shed its final aristocratic skin in favor of advanced capitalism and the direct rule of the bourgeoisie, not only was everything being used against the interests of the oppressed majority, but the oppressed majority itself was monopolized to act against itself. To use Arendt's words again, a transformation of classes into masses took place, and that was the first distinct phase of totalitarianism. Power began finding ways to move from control to hegemony.

Specialists implanted in all state institutions became the new gods, deciding on what was best for social groups in all arenas, from their relations to each other to their use of space. Social engineering, taking absolute legitimacy from the superiority of science according to this new hegemonic ideology, is premised on the authority of the state over society. Born from the capitalist modes of production and their power relations, this new absolutism set out to standardize all societal affairs with little or no consideration for the remaining organic relations that had evolved over time within various ecosystems. To instrumental rationalism and the "invisible hand" of the market, the efficiency of administration and the principle of profit are the sole parameters. Thus, not only is uniqueness not seen as an essential element of every ecosystem, but each exception to the patterns of sameness is wiped out, isolated, or "treated" as a pathological case. Normalcy is defined by the limits of the bourgeois rationality, which requires unlimited transparency of social space in order to standardize everything in accordance with its vision.

Douglas Moggach argues that Herder considered tyrannies "inherent in modern society as connections and relationships break," a result that Bruno Bauer also considered a not abnormal product of mass society (Moggach 2005, 57; 58). Of course, there are other philosophers who have voiced comparable criticism of or concerns about modernity, but Herder is both among the earliest critics and arguably the most passionate in his rejection of positivistic rationality as a means for creating political organization of societies and, thus, relations of control. Herder was also an early critic of standardization and mechanical distribution of labor, which in his time were just emerging (Moggach 2005, 56; Berlin 2000, 200–1). He laments "that *everything* fell into *small connections, divisions,* and *orderings-together,* and so *many, many* limbs arose!" (2002a, 301; italics in original). "Now, is it better," he asks, "is it *healthier* and *more beneficial* for humanity, to produce mere lifeless cogs of a great, wooden, thoughtless machine, or *to awaken* and *rouse forces?*" (2002a, 301; italics in original).

Isaiah Berlin argues that no other thinker has influenced European thought more than Herder in terms of developing the contrast between local/regional plurality and diversity and despotic universality and uniformity (2000, 201). To Herder, human diversity is rooted in nature itself;

thus, every individual naturally has a harmonious and unique position within the universal order (Herder 2002a, 335–36). In other words, the only healthy form of universality is natural universality, which is a system that links all individuals organically in accordance with their uniqueness. Herder's notion of universality can be analogized to what we now call ecosystem in both its sophistication and fragility. Unlike many of his contemporaries, Herder does not feign understanding of this complex system, and he strongly objects to any mechanical, rationalist, or partial approach to it. From this point of view, Herder argues that modernity's rationality is destructive to individual uniqueness and, thus, to the entire natural system (Herder 2002a, 318; 320). Herder is also against all forms of governmental suppression—for example, "political calculation" (Herder 2002a, 320)—of the rich diversity and natural complexity of societies, which is why, in opposing Kant's statement "man is *an animal who needs a master*" (Kant 2003, 46; italics in original), Herder states, "a man who needs a master is an animal" (Herder 2004, 127). To him, it is impossible to accurately label the sociohistorical richness of complex local circumstances that surround and shape people's characteristics (Herder 2002a, 292), and he therefore rejects every form of political despotism because it would destroy this organic richness fostered by nature. Moreover, Herder consistently expresses his disgust for any form of domination of one group of people over another under whatever motivation, including conquest, enlightenment, religion, and so on (Herder 2004, 126; 128; Herder 2002b). For similar reasons, he is against colonialism (Herder 2002b), which would result in "the flattening out of human beings," according to Berlin's reading of Herder (Berlin 2000, 202).

Even though Herder is commonly considered the godfather of nationalism, he is strongly against not only the stereotypical, and even positivistic, categorization of people, but also any steamrolling notion of universality. As for his conception of nationalism, it is extremely important to take note that for him it is rooted in his celebration of the uniqueness, particularity, and equality of people, as well as their natural right of self-determination, as opposed to the positivistic and Eurocentric notions of universality (Herder 2002a, 292–96; 328; Herder 2002b). Hence, he is unequivocally against the idea of one language, one nation, and one destiny. On the contrary, to Herder, national character is, or should be, precisely the force that resists the abolition of plurality (Herder 2002a, 329). All these aspects of Herder's philosophy make him arguably the most passionate critic of instrumental rationality, "the machine of state" (Herder 2004, 128), and human-to-human domination in his era. Foucault's project of critiquing the Enlightenment, thus, can be seen as the postmodern echo of Herder's vigorous attacks on modernity in its infancy, including its political systems of control (Herder 2004, 128).

Herder gives an essential weight to communal relations as the necessary and healthy environment for individual freedom; in fact, he sees the community itself as the protective medium that shields individuals against the oppressive power of the state. Subsequently, the collapse of organic communal relations amounts to the exposure of individuals to the aggressive power of the state. In Moggach's words, "Deprived of communal support and the buffering of corporate bodies, isolated individuals are thrust back on their own resources and narrow self-interest, and encounter the naked power of state" (2005, 57). Because Herder is against such direct individual exposure to the power of the state, one can argue that Herder's philosophy is also intensely against transparency, especially of the kind Bentham proposes and Foucault criticizes. In short, Herder's criticism of modernity shares two main points of contention with Foucault's criticism of panopticism: the exposure of the individual to the power of the state, and the fragmentation of social bodies into isolated bodies at the mercy of centralized power.

At the other end of the spectrum we have Rousseau, the Enlightenment's philosopher of transparency. What comes less easily, though, is determining whether we can hold Rousseau responsible for what might be thought of as yet another twist in the French Revolution regarding the nightmare to which transparency quickly turned. To Rousseau, transparency was associated with the authenticity of the general will as much as it was also a fundamental principle throughout his writings, including *Confessions*, as Jean Starobinski contends (1988, 8–14). Starobinski famously argues that Rousseau's central dream was "total transparency and immediate communication" (1988, 41), not only in terms of social and political life, but with regard to all levels of personal life as well (Marks 2005, 170). Moreover, it is on the basis of transparency as unrestricted communication that Rousseau rejects representative systems, maintaining that any form of representation would function as a medium preventing total transparency, fragmenting the community, and, eventually, privileging particular wills over the general will. He instead advocates a sociopolitical system based on the active and continual participation of the citizens (Rousseau 2008, 126–29). Explaining Rousseau's rejection of representation, Starobinski writes, "If nothing is represented, then space is a free vacuum, the optic medium of transparency: mind is directly accessible to mind without intermediary. And if nothing is represented, then everyone can represent himself and see the representations of others" (1988, 96). Thus, every member of the community's freedom (the premise of freedom being individual autonomy, nondependency [Ferrara 1993, 63]) would be guaranteed by total social transparency throughout the community. From there, only through the realization of the general will as the embodiment of total social transparency can alienation, social fragmentation, and tyranny of opinion be avoided (Rousseau 2008, 73–75; Starobinski 1988, 32). Transparency, to Rousseau, also amounts to immediate (unmeditated) communal communication on all levels of society, through which society can overcome moral decay and reconcile culture and nature within a new social totality saved from disintegration (Starobinski 1988, 32; 96).

To Rousseau, the sovereign is the overseer only insofar as everyone is a member of the sovereign. In fact, Rousseau thought this would prevent not only the tyrannical practice of political institutions imposing the interests of the advantaged over the rest, but also the emergence of such institutions in the first place. Yet Foucault insists that the Benthamian enterprise of total transparency stems from the Rousseauian project.[4] According to Foucault (1980, 152), if the statement "'each comrade becomes an overseer'" is Bentham's dream, the equivalent Rousseauian formula would be "each overseer should become a comrade." "Thus," Foucault writes, "Bentham's obsession, the technical idea of the exercise of an 'all-seeing' power, is grafted on to the great Rousseauist theme which is in some sense the lyrical note of the Revolution. The two things combine into a working whole, Rousseau's lyricism and Bentham's obsession" (1980, 152). Ultimately, through illuminating all dark spaces and eliminating all the shadowy social areas, the new order is born.

Foucault's critique is alluding more to the moral component of absolute social transparency—everyone's visibility to everyone—than to Rousseau's fundamental idea of citizens' continual involvement in the legislature and in general political life through unrestricted communication.[5] To further protect the personal sphere from the ill-application of the ideal of general will, Rousseau actually makes a distinction between public and private (2008, 68; 70). Still, much of the problem comes down to the limits of Rousseau's transparency in terms of making a clear distinction between private and public. The implied compulsory transparency imposed by the practical power of the general will, effectively the sovereign, remains a problematic aspect of Rousseau's social and political thought, especially if we read Rousseau with the fear we now have of totalitarianism. It is true that Rousseau had concerns that were rooted in his historic time, and his work should be read in that context, but one can also understand why, to Foucault, having witnessed Fascism's political spirituality in Europe and elsewhere, total transparency is a nightmare.

To Foucault, the transparency and visibility of society and social space are simultaneously an enterprise of power and of knowledge. At the same time that specialists in prisons, hospitals, schools, and factories produce the sociological knowledge necessary for power to implement and sustain its relations of domination, the relations of domination put more aggregate apparatuses of effective exercise of power in the hands of privileged specialists. It was on this aspect of the Enlightenment that the Frankfurt School thinkers mainly focused. For example, perhaps when Horkheimer and Adorno wrote, "Enlightenment is totalitarian" (2002, 4), the principle of visibility for the sake of domination was one of the things they had in mind. The visibility, as Foucault writes of it, is "organ-ised entirely around a dominating, overseeing gaze" (1980, 152 [1977, 16]). In fact, Foucault's position can easily be included in the Frankfurt School's critical theory. For instance, Foucault argues, "It was on the basis of the flamboyant rationality of social Darwinism that racism was formulated, becoming one of the most enduring and powerful ingredients of Nazism. This was, of course, an irrationality, but an irrationality that was at the same time, after all, a certain form of rationality" (Foucault 1984, 249). Those two statements would fit perfectly with Horkheimer and Adorno's writings. Moreover, the quotes "Knowledge, which is power, knows no limits, either in its enslavement of creation or in its deference to worldly masters" (Horkheimer and Adorno 2002, 2) and "For enlightenment, anything which does not conform to the standard of calculability and utility must be viewed with suspicion" (Horkheimer and Adorno 2002, 3) are perfectly in line with Foucault's writings on power and knowledge. At any rate, with each of the Frankfurt thinkers I have discussed in chapter 1 and along with Foucault, we arrive at the conclusion that inherent in the Enlightenment was a totalitarian aspect. The difference with Foucault is that he specifically and genealogically demonstrates the technologies of power and their spatial application for the production of what can be called totalitarian space. To put it more precisely, by combining the Frankfurt School's philosophical critique of the Enlightenment (a major claim of which is that "Enlightenment is totalitarian," with the focus on the critique of instrumental rationality/ knowledge—which is power) with Foucault's genealogical findings on the modes of spatial contribution that stemmed from the Enlighten- ment and are embodied in panopticism, we can conclude that the space produced through the dynamics of knowledge-power can ultimately be called totalitarian.

The essential modern relations of spatial production are relations of power. Moreover, the umbrella institution of the institutions (e.g., schools, hospitals, religious institutions, and prisons) that produce the knowledge and means necessary for the function of power is the state.[6] Hence, the state is the master producer of space. Thus, the conclusion at which I am about to arrive can actually be expressed in the following words by Lefebvre: "This space was of course the birthplace and cradle of the modern state. It was here, in the space of accumulation, that the state's *totalitarian vocation* took shape, its tendency to deem political life and existence superior to other so-called 'social' and 'cultural' forms of practice, while at the same time concentrating all such political existence in itself and on this basis proclaiming the principle of *sovereignty*—the principle, that is to say, of its own sovereignty" (1991a, 279; first italics added [2000, 322]). In short, the modern state, like premodern states, strives for absolute power, but, unlike premodern states, it has at its disposal the techniques to render its "totalitarian vocation" real. Now, because the state is also the master of the dominant space (by virtue of its production of that space), the dominant/transparent space is ulti- mately totalitarian.[7] As I explain later, Ellul draws the same connection between techniques and totalitarianism, but before I discuss his argu- ment, I elaborate on a major technological formula of the production of totalitarian space.

Panopticism

I

As advanced as today's technologies are, the logic behind them often strikingly resembles that of pre–digital age technology. For example, we can clearly see the enduring reliance of spatial technologies of power on the principle of maximizing visibility in the case of drones. Described as "persistent stare capability" or "the unblinking eye" (*Newsweek* Staff

2008), drones have used the latest technology to realize a centuries-old aspiration of power: to see all. The hundred-eyed guard, Argos Panoptes, in ancient Greek mythology is an embodiment of an early desire to perfect vision by abstracting the ideal function of the human eye and multiplying it. In spite of the cartoonlike quality of Panoptes (which literally means "all-seeing") compared to today's CCTV cameras and other eyes of power, the exact same rationale is at work, as further demonstrated by the adoption of Panoptes as a name for drone technology companies.

In the context of the evolution of spatial technologies of power, the Panopticon, which likewise owes its name to ancient Greek, is a demonstrative model aimed at maximizing the disciplinary effects of the gaze of power through a technological formula reliant on the standardization and mechanization essential to the capitalist modes of production. Panopticism exploits instrumental rationalism to realize the dream of unlimited control as well as the capitalist goal of maximizing profit. Thus, the difference between panoptic technologies and the spatial technologies of the corporate state is primarily one of degree. Whereas in the disciplinary societies studied by Foucault power strived to render contained spaces transparent to the gaze of power, the limits of vision today are the limits of geography itself. For that reason, the principles underlying spatial technologies of power are in many ways more comprehensible when explored within a closed system such as the Panopticon.

The surveillance sector today, especially compared with that of the nineteenth century, is both immeasurable and inaccessible as a cohesive whole in large part because the state and corporations operate so clandestinely. It is precisely the Panopticon's smaller scale and more overt methods that make it perfectly demonstrative of the instrumentality through which power seeks to produce spaces of control. As Foucault made clear, the Panopticon is a mechanism, a technology of power in its ideal and abstract form, for generating relations of domination (1995, 205). Thus, the significance of the Panopticon does not lie in its architectural realization or institutional installation, but rather in its principles of spatial distribution, which reflect the drive toward transparency, standardization, and mechanization that has its roots in the French Revolution.

II

Brothers Samuel Bentham, as the initial designer of the Panopticon, and Jeremy Bentham, as its chief promoter, sought the fulfilment of the ultimate goal of power. This, as they saw it, was to achieve complete control of all spaces, ranging from schools, factories, and hospitals to prisons, which they intended to deliver through the maximum use of visibility and with minimal labor. The Panopticon embodies the major irony of the Enlightenment: a revolution in rationality that turns instrumental from the beginning. It also represents a perfect example of knowledge produced and used by the dominant class for the sake of further domination. The French Revolution enthusiastically embraced the idea of the Panopticon—with Jeremy Bentham even being granted honorary French citizenship in 1791.[8]

Derived from the Greek words *pan* and *optikos*, "Panopticon" literally means all-seeing. As envisioned by the Bentham brothers, the Panopticon as an architectural model would take the form of a circular building composed of an inspection tower at the center surrounded by vacant space and separate cells that would be built adjacent to each other to form rings around the center. The design was to allow light to travel through each cell, making the resident of each cell visible to the inspector, who could be watching at any given moment without being visible to the cell residents. However, it is the desired outcome of this design that is of the utmost interest here, namely to fulfil the dream of an all-seeing technology of power. In that sense, CCTV and drones have the same aim, with the difference being that they are the outcome of drastic technological advancement. This advancement will continue until panopticism reaches its ultimate goal: absolute and most efficient control of social space.

To show how panopticism both ideologically and technologically aims to produce totalitarian space, below I discuss the Panopticon's principles. First, the Panopticon renders power at once "visible and unverifiable" (Foucault 1995, 201 [1975, 235]). The spatial arrangement gives the supervisor in the inspection tower the power of "*seeing without being seen*" (Bentham 1843, (vol. 4) 44; italics in original), while at the same time preventing the inmate from seeing anything but the absolute dominance of the power center (Foucault 1995, 201–2). In other words, the space is structured in such a way that the eye of power penetrates it as a single flat surface on which every subject and object, as well as their activities, can be identified by unidentifiable and invisible over-seers at any moment. The absolute visibility of inmates paired with the invisibility of the person monitoring the power apparatus situates the inmate as "the object of information, never a subject in communication" (Foucault 1995, 200 [1975, 234]). This dynamic produces in the inmate a continual state of alert, which then guarantees "the automatic functioning of power" (Foucault 1995, 201 [1975, 234]). Therefore, this feature of the Panopticon is less about ensuring continual and actual observation and more about creating the permanent feeling in the inmate that she may be watched at any moment. With the subject's permanent state of consciousness so altered by this anonymous gaze of power that she perceives the space as a single flat and completely exposed field in which everything is visible to those in power, a space that betrays its dwellers through its transparency, through surrendering them to the omnipresent eye of the spying power, continual and active surveillance becomes unnecessary. What this means is that the Panopticon economically guarantees the perfect function of power, namely by establishing a form of power relations that can function independent of even the physical/active exercise of power. Thus, the space under the invisible gaze of power becomes the field of the absolute exercise of power insofar as the intended effects of the technology are concerned. This technology of power therefore ushers in a spatial environment that is unmistakably totalitarian in the refusal of the system to recognize any limit to the exercise of its power.[9]

Power is disembodied and technologically autonomous. By virtue of the design and the function of the inspection house, it is absolutely insignificant what kind of person (e.g., a moral philosopher or a psychopath) is left to monitor the inmates. Instead, the spatial arrangement of the Panopticon ensures the distribution of the bodies in such a way that the relations of power trap everyone according to predetermined mechanisms of power itself (Foucault 1995, 202). In other words, the spatial production itself is sufficient for the perpetual and effective function of power. Subjecting the entire space to the gaze of power amounts to imposing a single form of spatial practice, thereby eliminating any possibility of individual spatial experiences. The ultimate goal of technology is perfectly autonomous functionality. The panoptic technology of power aims at the perfection of totalitarianism imbedded the spatial distribution.

In its subjugation of individuals, power isolates each individual from the rest. According to Bentham's design, the cells making up the periphery ring should be isolated from one another by sidewalls. This feature ensures both the singularization of the observation, or what can be called the designating power of the inspecting eye, and the segregation of each inmate (Foucault 1995, 203). In such a space, the subject finds herself trapped in the light that continually reduces her to an object of the visible exercise of an invisible power. The consciousness produced by these material conditions of space is the consciousness of total subjugation. Thus, this kind of spatial technology of power, through imposing multiple forms of isolation and partitions, and through its pinpointing capacity, paves the way for both the material and the psychological conditions of totalitarianism. "Totalitarianism is, first of all," Anthony Giddens states, "an extreme focusing of surveillance" (1985, 303).

In his project of the Panopticon, Bentham, as the founder of utilitarianism, had in mind what Foucault calls the increase of "the utility of power" (1995, 208 [1975, 243]) and "the possible utility of individuals" (1995, 210 [1975, 245]). In addition to designing a disciplinary structure aimed at controlling the greatest possible number of people with the fewest possible supervisors, Bentham developed a detailed plan for penal servitude to ground his profit-driven economic model. First, he suggested contracting out the management of the Panopticon to whoever offered the best terms. This contractor would then, according to Bentham's proposal, impose conditions under which each inmate, isolated from the rest and fed a diet of bad bread and water, would submit to the role of a "prisoner-workman" in return for below-market wages (Bentham 1843, (vol. 4), 50; 54). The panoptic pecuniary economy, structured as it is around maximizing surplus value while paying lip service to liberal ideals, thus constitutes an ideal example of capitalist relations of production at work.

Panopticism, because it amplifies the effects of power and, in so doing, renders power more economical, permits the transformation, mobilization, fortification, and regeneration of power in increasingly larger spatial fields. Through its gaze, power turns social space into a space of potential total obedience by generalizing the sociological knowledge gained in the space of discipline. The Panopticon, as Bentham dreamt of it, is the formula that has allowed/inspired the transformation of enclosed spaces of discipline "into a network of mechanisms that would be everywhere and always alert, running through society without interruption in space or in time" (Foucault 1995, 209 [1975, 243]). Panopticism, therefore, is the spatial technology and production that effectively allow the total application of power in any chosen field of surveillance. As Foucault notes, spaces of discipline existed throughout the classical age, for example, in some armies or plague-stricken towns, but the technology of power represented by the Panopticon has provided the formula for generalizing what used to be exceptional and temporal measures in distinct places. The technological transformation of power is a historic one with fundamental political and social consequences. This transformation has also taken place alongside the rise of new challenges to governmental rationality, especially with regard to more sophisticated population management, economics, and security.

Of course, the rationalization for legitimizing the device does not so blatantly call for the total domination of state institutions for the sake of domination. On the contrary, Bentham contends that morality, health, education, productivity, the rule of law to ensure public prosperity, and so on are at stake. Thus, he appeals to the well-being of society by advocating efficient governance through the principle of visibility as a crucial aspect of the new technique. Bentham's central concern is the problem of governance within the duality of power-population. In a 1979 lecture, Foucault again explains that only in the beginning was Bentham's Panopticon seen as a formula for specific governmental institutions, whereas toward the end of his life, Bentham presented the project as a utilitarian formula for entire governments (2008, 67). Thus, Bentham's self-appointed task was to provide a formula that positions a population in the most efficient relations of domination, a formula that would allow the domination of the largest number of people by the fewest number of supervisors, and this, for him, is ultimately a question of utility and efficiency (Foucault, 1980, 151).

Today's panoptic technology has rendered the traditional Panopticon as an architectural distribution of space obsolete. Digital surveillance has enabled the installation of the gaze of power everywhere without the need for inspection towers. This, in turn, has revolutionized the panoptic principles of 1) unverifiability of inspection (there is no way to know when one is being watched, by whom, and for what purpose); 2) psychological effects of being watched (most people now know that they could be under some sort of surveillance wherever they may be at any given time for their entire lives, which amounts to universalization of the consciousness of an inmate with immeasurable policing effects); 3) autonomous function of power (the data-collection process is very much mechanized, and there is no way for ordinary people to know who would watch them, where, when, and why); 4) individuation of people under surveillance (there are innumerable individual imprints—which are left behind as traces on daily bases by ordinary citizens—functioning as fingerprints as far as the new technology is concerned);[10] 5) utility of power (with recording and storing capacities of digital surveillance systems, the number of supervisors now can be reduced to near zero while the number of people put under surveillance is not limited); 6) spatial totalization of visibility for the purposes of governmentality (places that are out the scope of CCTV and the surveillance means that are embedded in the World Wide Web can be reached by various types of drones, including microdrones of the size of a fly). Panopticism is about to transform the world to a large Panopticon, producing a single space of total transparency.

What used to be social space is now continually under extreme individuating inspection, which alone is sufficient to say that social space has been totally panopticized, thereby fulfilling the ultimate Benthamian dream of the universal application of the formula. The domination of capitalism and the technological development of the state made it possible to transform the entire social and political landscape into segmented, abstracted, and monitored spaces, confining inmates who do not even consider themselves inmates. What makes the contemporary exercise of power perfectly automatic is not only the inmate's consciousness of being watched, but also, more importantly, the ideological hegemony of capitalism, the perpetuation of which is arguably the culture industry's most significant task within the existing order. Of course, technologies of thought policing have also been developed through the installation of invisible eyes of power in cyberspace (e.g., monitoring emails and conversations), but that has only complemented (not replaced) the Panoptic technology.

Edward Snowden's leaks of National Security Agency (NSA) secret documents showed that the surveillance systems of Western governments and especially "the five eyes" target their entire populations.[11] Although necessarily more diffused than the traditional panoptic gaze, the centrality of the gaze of power is still maintained given how smoothly the collected data are transmitted to the various policing centers of the state. Glen Greenwald's book on mass surveillance explains how Snowden's leaks exposed the extensive collaboration between the US government and giant Internet and telecommunication corporations to collect information about consumer-citizens. The fact that billions of private emails, chat logs, photos, and phone conversations are indiscriminately collected, viewed, stored, and exchanged between corporations and policing apparatuses (O'Harrow 2005, 2; Greenwald 2014, 21) indicates that surveillance has infiltrated even the most private spheres. This does not mean the principle of the visibility of the eye of power to the inmates to create the consciousness of being watched has been abandoned. Many eyes of power do continue to function visibly and unverifiably in what is considered public space, often in concert with more advanced cyber technologies.

The network of panoptic technology in today's capitalist democracies has enabled the extraordinary registration of knowledge regarding each individual's identity, personal history, health, financial status, communications, and social relations. Through this vast registration of knowledge, the state's (in)dividuating capacity is becoming absolute. Each social security number, credit card, bank account, medical record, email account, mobile phone, or laptop can function as a transparent cage not only for the individual's body, but often her mind as well. Moreover, this penetrating gaze is not simply bestowed on a supervisor in an inspecting tower; unknown numbers of spying agencies, analysts, and data collectors are granted access to information that could be used for any number of economic and political purposes. In short, digital and cyber panopticism have allowed the state and its capitalist partners to eliminate both public and private space, creating what can only be called totalitarian space.

III

Deleuze contends that we are no longer living in disciplinary societies (which continued from the eighteenth to the twentieth century, according to Foucault [1980]), but rather in societies of control (1992, 3). The disciplinary society was composed of enclosed spaces, and individuals were continually trapped in one or another of those spaces (family, school, factory, army, prison, hospital) that molded them (Deleuze 1992, 3–5). The duality of the disciplinary society, Deleuze maintains, was individual and mass, or signature and number (number designating the individual). On the other hand, in societies of control, "individuals have become '*dividuals*,' and masses have become samples, data, markets, or '*banks*'" (Deleuze 1992, 5; italics in original). The "dividuals" in societies of control are coded and administered through placeless files, and factories are replaced by corporations, schooling by training, and machines by computers. The deforming spaces of control "modulate," and, as a result, the "dividual" lives in a perpetual state of deformation imposed on her by complex systems that incorporate the distorting powers of older institutions, such as schools and armies (Deleuze 1992, 5). In disciplinary societies, each enclosed system was transparent to the center of power, whereas in societies of control, Deleuze argues, all spaces, from familial, educational, and professional, to those of the military and police, are not only centralized, but also deformed in an interchangeable manner. In Deleuze's words, "The family, the school, the army, the factory are no longer the distinct analogical spaces that converge towards an owner—state or private power—but coded figures—deformable and transformable——of a single corporation that now has only stockholders" (1992, 6).

The Panopticon is, first and foremost, a technique exactly in the sense the French philosopher Jacques Ellul defines technique: "In our technological society, *technique* is the *totality of methods rationally arrived at and having absolute efficiency* (for a given stage of development) in *every* field of human activity" (1964, xxv; italics in original). Accordingly, Ellul would call Foucault's surveillance or disciplinary society, or Deleuze's society of control, "technological society." Moreover, Ellul argues that "the accumulation of techniques in the hands of the state" amounts to totalitarianism (1964, 284). Techniques in the technological society blanket all human activities and abolish individuality in a network that transforms or obliterates the qualitative. Essentially, technique, as a "mass instrument," categorizes, labels, and deindividualizes by transforming all that is qualitative into numbers (Ellul 1964, 286–87).[12] Then, because the state gains increasing command over the network of techniques, the state gradually transforms into a totalitarian one. "Even when the state is resolutely liberal and democratic, it cannot do otherwise than become totalitarian" (Ellul 1964, 284) because "technique is totalitarian; and when the state becomes technical, it too becomes totalitarian; it has no alternative" (Ellul 1964, 287).

Ellul then goes on to argue that a state that reaches complete totalitarianism would not be physically violent. The use of torture is a sign of arbitrariness, for which there is no possibility in a truly totalitarian state. When technique reaches its full capacity of control, the resulting totalitarian state tolerates no waste of power utilities;[13] everything is instrumentally invested without any form of arbitrariness, "for the arbitrary represents the very opposite of technique, in which everything 'has a reason' (not a final but a mechanical reason)" (Ellul 1964, 287). In this perfect system of the totality of technical methods, whenever irrationality in terms of the utility of power does take place, it is undoubtedly a human error resulting from a person's or group's ignorant intervention in the technology (Ellul 1964, 287).

Additionally, the technically matured totalitarian state has no need for a totalitarian theory (nor does it strive for one), for it is *technical* in its very essence; its functionality is inherently systematized and instrumentally structured. Older forms of totalitarianism (say the dictatorial form), on the other hand, consciously exploit the network of techniques (Ellul 1964, 287–88). The dictator and her/his appointed circles of power control the techniques, which only prevents the network of techniques from reaching its totalitarian perfection. Furthermore, even if the dictator is not brought down by means of physical violence, which is already entrenched in the sociopolitical relations because of the imperfection of the totalitarian system, s/he will inevitably age and die, and with her/his death the entire regime would be put at risk. In technological totalitarianism, on the contrary, parties and leaders come and go, but the system continues to improve its methods of domination uninterrupted. If there is one common element between the discipline or surveillance society, the society of control, and the technological society, that element is the space produced under the contemporary technology of power, which can be called totalitarian par excellence.

The Gaze

I have discussed the model of the Panopticon in terms of "*seeing without being seen*," to use Bentham's words (1843, [vol. 4] 44; italics in original), and its oppressive psychological consequences. However, given the significant role the gaze plays in later chapters, this psycho-technique of control warrants further discussion. After all, "seeing without being seen" is arguably the most prominent characteristic attributed to God. For God to have functional omnipresent power, to be both all-knowing and all-powerful, it was necessary to attribute to him the absolute ability to see everyone at all times without being at the mercy of his subjects' inquiring eyes. Obviously, God was not endowed with the ability to see for the purpose of discerning shades of colors or admiring works of art; God's gaze is an inspecting one, and its object is us as potential wrongdoers. The emphasis in religious discourse on God's ability to see and the absence of mentions of his other senses (with the exception of hearing, which, like seeing, functions as a surveillance technique) is demonstrative. Believers are essentially warned that God wields policing powers amounting to a universal Panopticon.

Likewise, a state aspiring to acquire limitless power over its citizens would need to invent means that could produce the same psychological effects as an all-seeing God. This was especially visible in monarchies, which sought to portray the monarch as the embodiment of the divine will, so that disobeying the monarch would be akin to rejecting God's will. However, this arrangement still relied on the popular belief in God and the monarch's subsequent divine sanction in order for the necessary power relations to be established. The effectiveness of panoptic technology, on the other hand, does not rely on this metaphysical belief in God or the monarch's divine right to rule. Rather, the Panopticon draws its omnipresent power directly from its physical reality, from making its center of power overwhelmingly visible to the ruled population, who are in turn perpetually visible to its never-sleeping and oppressive eyes. Therefore, one could argue that with the spatial production represented by the Panopticon, unlike architecture inspired by the idea of God (such as houses of worship), the power of God is architecturally harnessed and put to work for the mighty state. In such a space, the state no longer needs to seek or even allude to God's approval to be legitimate in the eyes of its subjects; rather, the state itself has become God in such a way that its existence, unlike the dead theological God, is not a question of a metaphysical belief.

Rather, the state's omnipresence and corresponding omnipotence are continually asserted through the visual proliferation of its marks. The sole function of these marks is often to remind the subject that the space in question is, in some capacity, overseen by the state. One could be walking in a forest and come across a sign displaying a warning, directions, or instructions, but the main function of the sign is to reassert the presence of the state. Similarly, in city squares the state endeavors to make its presence unmistakable; this can take various forms, whether through a statue of the totalitarian leader, a military monument, or a tribute to a founding political figure, depending on the degree to which totalitarianism has advanced. This same logic applies to government headquarters, where the imposing nature of the architecture towers above the physical existence of the subject and appears to take priority over the building's other functions. The sovereign's architecture is intended to awe the spectator precisely because the state seeks to harness the powers of God in the visual realm.

The power of the gaze and the gaze of power transform space into disciplinary space, a space in which everything is controlled by a system that functions automatically. In the Panopticon, "the principle of the dungeon is reversed; daylight and the overseer's gaze capture the inmate more effectively than darkness, which afforded after all a sort of protection" (Foucault 1980, 147 [1977, 10]). Hence, wherever the means of spatial visibility and surveillance are applied, they tend to transform space into a single visible, controllable, and accordingly totalitarian sphere. Indeed, what Foucault unearthed in his vast genealogical project is even more relevant now to the study of social space, given that the principle of transparency and the technological means of observation have advanced exponentially with digital and computerized technology. These more powerful means of surveillance (such as surveillance cameras used in almost all spheres of social space) only further attest to the spread of the panoptic technology of power and its tendency toward unlimited control. This particular dream of the Enlightenment, essentially the dream of illuminating all darkened spaces, has been nearly accomplished. The power of the gaze, being everywhere at all times, functions as a psycho-technique making the individual internalize surveillance and thus become her own police. It is then the "politics of the gaze" (Foucault 1980, 162 [1977, 28]) installed in the "apparatus of total and circulating mistrust" (Foucault 1980, 158 [1977, 23]) that paves the way to spatial hegemony and, hence, the production of totalitarian space.

Heterotopia or the Poetics of Spatial Aura

As we learned from Lefebvre, we can do justice to space only through a dialectical, unitary, and interdisciplinary theory that avoids reductionist and abstract accounts of space. Despite the hegemonic and oppressive relations of power, we cannot claim that our lived spaces are entirely homogeneous. In this chapter, I have argued that the technology of power, through consolidating its controlling gaze (within the capitalist relations of production), strives to produce totalitarian space. However, that is not to say this totalitarian production of space has indeed reached its final goal. While it is true that the power relations resulting from spatial technologies of power, with their psychotechnical means of manipula-tion, provide the conditions for the perfect and automatic functioning of power, there will always be dialectical contradictions that safeguard spatial experience from total one-dimensionality, no matter how perfect the totalitarian domination becomes in terms of its horizontal expansion. In Lefebvre's terminology, because there are countless spatial practices, representations of space, and, thus, forms of representational, or lived, space, in which imagination seeks creative change, it is needless to say that there are endless potential processes of the production of space.

Thus, to better articulate what differentiates totalitarian space, I now turn toward the opposite end of the spectrum.

Ultimately, there will always be spaces of hope and daydream. In fact, hope (I address daydreams later with Bachelard) is inherently more present in hopeless times and spaces.[14] Hope, in other words, is always already an outcome of its own negation, for the negation of hope *is* hope itself. This dialectical relationship between hope and hopelessness is perhaps best expressed in Benjamin's statement "Only for the sake of the hopeless ones have we been given hope" (quoted in Arendt 1969, 17). No matter how narrow, unbearable, and disciplinary the space of our everyday experience becomes, there will always be that Other space, that mythical yet real space, that dark, private, and protective cave. Nevertheless, that space of hope and daydream, that space of utopia, is in fact a placeless space (Foucault 1986, 24; 1994, xviii). Foucault's heterotopia, on the other hand, is a form of the Other space that is not placeless.

Foucault delivered a lecture in 1967 based on an essay that was later, in 1984, published under the title "*Des Espaces Autres*" in *Architecture-Mouvement-Continuité*. The main concept advanced by the article is "heterotopia," which is Foucault's notion of the Other-space, "a space that is other, another real space" (Foucault 1986, 27 [1984, 1580]), a space that is neither merely mental nor physical, a space where a genuine form of otherness manifests itself, a space ultimately capable of returning the gaze of the self (Foucault 1986, 24 [1984, 1575]). Heteropology, according to Foucault, can be described "as a sort of simultaneously mythic and real contestation of the space in which we live" (1986, 24 [1984, 1575]). This is strikingly similar to Lefebvre's spatial dialectics, according to which "lived space" appears as the third term, that is, when the contradictions between conceived and perceived spaces transcend the real and the mental, as I explained in the previous chapter.

Thus, heterotopia has a physical dimension to it even though it is not defined exclusively by that dimension. Heterotopia allows us to escape the unbearable repetition of the alienating spatial experience of everyday life and bring an element of utopia into the physical space. Foucault suggests the experience of the mirror manifests dynamics similar to those of utopia and heterotopia. About this experience of the mirror and heterotopia he writes:

> In the mirror, I see myself there where I am not, in an unreal, virtual space that opens up behind the surface; I am over

there, there where I am not, a sort of shadow that gives my own visibility to myself, that enables me to see myself there where I am absent: such is the utopia of the mirror. But it is also a heterotopia in so far as the mirror does exist in reality, where it exerts a sort of counteraction on the position that I occupy. From the standpoint of the mirror I discover my absence from the place where I am since I see myself over there. *Starting from this gaze that is, as it were, directed toward me*, from the ground of this virtual space that is on the other side of the glass, I come back toward myself; I begin again to direct my eyes toward myself and to reconstitute myself there where I am. The mirror functions as a heterotopia in this respect: it makes this place that I occupy at the moment when I look at myself in the glass at once absolutely real, connected with all the space that surrounds it, and absolutely unreal, since in order to be perceived it has to pass through this virtual point which is over there. (Foucault 1986, 24; italics added [1984, 1575])[15]

We can begin our interpretation of this passage with Lacan's statement "I think where I am not, therefore I am where I do not think" (2001, 183). However, if in heterotopia my gaze is returned, then I am where I think; body and thought reunite in the here and now. That is to say, the gaze travels to where I am not, only to return to where I am, re-presenting my absent dimension, the ideal dimension that always flees my immediate/material/bodily existence. This reunification of the opposing dimensions sparks the dialectical becoming, and, thus, the result is sublime. In this third moment, both the material and mental are preserved, but they are also transcended to reach a higher level of being. The infinite travels of the gaze between here where I am (but do not think) and there where I am not (but where my thought is) continually bridge the fragmented parts of my entire being, ending my spatial partition and alienation, and sublimating my being in the world.[16]

Still another line of interpretation is possible with Gaston Bachelard. To Bachelard, heterotopia would be the house, the first house representing not only the landscape of childhood, but also one's corner in the world, "in which we like to hide, or withdraw into ourselves" (Bachelard 1994, 136). That corner "is a symbol of solitude for the imagination" (Bachelard 1994, 136) and becomes "the space of our being" (Bachelard

1994, 137) or, to put it in the dialectical sense of Becoming, "a negation of the Universe" (Bachelard 1994, 136). The corner of solitude as the home of our being for which we forever long is best expressed by the poetic statement of Nietzsche's Zarathustra when he says, "O SOLITUDE! Solitude, my *home*! I have lived too long wildly in wild strange lands to come home to you without tears" (Nietzsche 1969, 202; italics in original). The corners in the first house of our being are rooted in the prelinguistic stage of engaging with existence, so our re-experience of them is "uncommunicative," to use Bachelard's word (1994, 137). Poetry, however, can break free from the restricting conventionalities of language and thus speak to and of that other space where childhood struggles to preserve itself in its embryonic silence of the first thoughts (Bachelard 1994, 6; 137).[17] That is precisely why Bachelard concentrates on poetry to unearth the "uncommunicative" spatial experiences of the house.

In more philosophical terms, the house is the space of the dialectics of fantasy and reality, where our dreams and memories are housed, where we can daydream peacefully. It is where the various, or one might add "contradictory," dimensions are integrated, and it is to this space of multidimensional integration and dialectical transcendence that we owe our existential depth (Bachelard 1994, 6; 8; 15). The house is heterotopia because it functions as a unique palette and set of subjective colors we use to "cover the universe with drawings we have lived" (Bachelard 1994, 12).

Now we can take this even further to claim that heterotopia, according to the above Bachelardian reading, can be set up as a direct contrast to the space of surveillance and control. In this sense, the Panopticon ultimately dehouses its inmates by sequestering them in a transparent space where they are continually trapped by the conditions of visibility and the power of the oppressive gaze. As Bachelard emphasizes, the walled, dark, and private corner of hiding is essential to the human imagination. He states, "We shall see the imagination build 'walls' of impalpable shadows, comfort itself with the illusion of protection—or, just the contrary, tremble behind thick walls, mistrust the staunchest ramparts" (Bachelard 1994, 5). Thus, the house, as the ultimate space of intimacy, simultaneously shelters the body and nests the imagination. The eye of power, so central to panopticism, specifically targets our being in this very fundamental sense by dehousing us, by penetrating our walls and caging our bodies within a one-dimensional space of control.

After all, our immediate and most essential space is the body. As Lefebvre states, "Each living body *is* space and *has* its space: it produces itself in space and it also produces that space" (1991, 170; italics in original [2000, 199]). Bachelard quotes Noël Arnaud, "I am the space where I am,"[18] and he adds, "This is a great line. But nowhere can it be better appreciated than in a corner" (Bachelard 1994, 137). The gaze of power tends to abolish that corner, one's very being. Targeting the body, which is the house of our imagination, and dehousing the body by placing it in a transparent space, amounts to more than just a symbolic death of the individual. It amounts to stripping the individual of an essential condition of her existential being. Furthermore, the politics of control becomes essentially totalitarian when it penetrates that poetic depth of our humanity. That is why the study of aura, as poetic it may sound qua a term, will put us in a position to know what exactly makes a space totalitarian.

In closing, heterotopia is the space that, when experienced actively and creatively (i.e., bridged to utopia), returns the gaze. Precisely because of that it can be called auratic space. Aura, which is the presence of the absent, is the presence of something that is real but absent in the sense of experiencing space (e.g., looking at the landscape of child-hood). However, the invoked does not have to be nostalgia, longing, sweet sorrow, reconnecting with what is lost through mourning, hopeless hope, or the combination of these. In fact, auratic experience of space is sublime and subliminally transcending precisely because it is not tangible or describable. It is not partly material and partly mental; rather, it is Becoming; it is the dialectical outcome of the clash between the two contradictory moments. Through providing access to the negative, to the aura of space, this Other space, heterotopia (as the opposite of the dominated space, disciplinary space, or space of control), will help us to reach a more developed theory of totalitarian space. "Totalitarian" is, after all, a political notion, whereas aura is highly poetic. It is precisely because of this contradiction that totalitarian space can be negatively defined through aura.[19]

4

Conceptualizing Aura

Though the etymology of "aura" is quite varied,[1] one of the more common historical applications of the word refers to the imagined halo surrounding a figure or object, as often used by theosophists. In his book *The Human Aura: A Study* (1896), Auguste Jean Baptiste Marques (1841–1929), a scientist, linguist, and leading theosophist, gives an extensive overview of the theosophist account of aura. In the introduction, he writes:

> While nothing can be found on the subject in scientific literature, in many of the early communications on Theosophy the idea was often hinted at, in a general but very guarded manner, that all objects in nature are surrounded by or exhale from their periphery a sort of vapor or cloud, constituting, as it were, their own localized atmosphere, which is more and more extended and complicated as we pass on to more complex organisms, from mineral up to man. Even artificial objects, made by man, emit auric manifestations, since they are formed of natural molecules, which, as such, possess their inherent auras. (Marques 1896, 2)[2]

Here and throughout the book, Marques tries to give a scientific account of aura, which seems to have been a common pursuit among late–nineteenth-century theosophists, obviously because of the dominance of positivistic paradigms. Helena Blavatsky, for example, defines aura as "a subtle invisible essence or fluid that emanates from human and animal bodies and even things. It is a psychic effluvium, partaking of both the mind and the body, as it is the electro-vital, and at the same time an electro-mental aura; called in Theosophy the âkâsic or magnetic aura" (Blavatsky 1892, 44).[3] The theosophist discourse, a representative example of which is Marques's book on aura, tries to sound confidently philosophical and, at the same time, submissively positivistic, with a fundamental religious belief hovering above, and pragmatically determining, the entire language. Therefore, the theosophist account could not have satisfied Benjamin.

However, it is not certain whether Benjamin was aware of these older theosophist definitions of aura, and it is possible that he associated the theosophist conception of aura mainly with the representations of aura in religious art.[4] Benjamin strongly rejects what he calls theosophist accounts of aura, and instead tries to secularize and philosophically problematize aura. In a piece on his hashish experiments originally written in 1930, Benjamin states, "Everything I said on the subject [of aura] was directed polemically against the theosophists, whose inexperience and ignorance I find highly repugnant" (Benjamin 2005a, 327). Then he goes on to list three main aspects of what he calls "genuine aura," in contrast to what he considers the theosophist/mystic notion of aura: "first, genuine aura appears in all things, not just in certain kinds of things, as people imagine"; second, aura changes when its subject undergoes changes; and "third, genuine aura can in no sense be thought of as a spruced-up version of the magic rays beloved of spiritualists and described and illustrated in vulgar works of mysticism" (Benjamin 2005a, 327–28). In contrast to these "magic rays," Benjamin defines aura as "an ornamental halo, in which the object or being is enclosed as in a case" (Benjamin 2005a, 328). So far, Benjamin's notion of aura does not diverge from the theosophist definitions of Blavatsky and Marques. However, when Benjamin mentions, "Perhaps nothing gives such a clear idea of aura as Van Gogh's late paintings, in which one could say that the aura appears to have been painted together with the various objects" (Benjamin 2005a, 328), it is clear that his understanding of aura is aesthetically oriented, perhaps as part of his attempt to reject any spiritual or even parapsychological approach. Going back to Benjamin's example of Van Gogh's paintings, one cannot help but wonder if he had Heidegger in mind, whose main example of a work of art that embodies the instrumentality or the Being of the object is also one of Van Gogh's paintings.[5,6] As I mention later, however, aura is by no means limited to works of art; in fact, aura is essentially a spatial phenomenon.[7]

The Indefinability of Aura

In his early writings, Benjamin used the term "aura" on several occasions outside the realm of aesthetics (yet still as a secular term), although none of those early uses of the term rises to the level of conceptual appropriation. For example, in his essay "Dostoevsky's *The Idiot*," written in 1917, he writes of the novel's protagonist, Prince Myshkin, that "he is surrounded in a quite unobtrusive way by an aura of complete isolation" (Benjamin 2004a, 79). Later, in "One-Way Street," written between 1923 and 1926, Benjamin posits the question: "And if an object dear to you has been lost, wasn't there—hours, days before—an aura of mockery or mourning about it that gave the secret away?" (Benjamin 2004c, 483). Finally, in a piece written in 1928 titled "Main Features of My Second Impression of Hashish," Benjamin invokes a slightly more physical dimension of aura when he writes of his own: "Bloch wanted to touch my knee gently. I could feel the contact long before it actually reached me. I felt it as a highly repugnant wound to my aura" (2005c, 87). In each of these examples, Benjamin's use of "aura" more or less follows the common use of the term to designate some kind of "ether or halo" (Hansen 2008, 340), but not in the mystical or religious sense.[8] Aura as a philosophical concept, however, is extremely challenging to define, and only in later writing does Benjamin undertake that challenge. As Adorno suggested, the near impossibility of defining aura as a concept only makes the task more philosophically interesting. In a letter to Benjamin dated February 29, 1940, Adorno writes, "The other matter concerns your chapter on the aura. I am convinced that our own best thoughts are invariably those that we cannot entirely think through. In this sense the concept of the aura still seems to me to be incompletely 'thought out.' One can argue about whether, indeed, it should be fully thought out as such" (Adorno and Benjamin 1999, 321). Following those words, and seemingly also caught up in the intrigue of aura (a project that would resurface throughout Adorno's work), Adorno even began attempting to think through the concept of aura.

As we learned from Bachelard in the previous chapter, experiencing spaces of intimacy, such as the home, is "uncommunicative" through the reified language of specialists, and so poetry is where Bachelard turns to grasp that experience. Similarly, aura resists conceptualization because it is something to be felt before it can be understood or theorized.[9] In other words, one could claim that in aura there exists the unique potential for a harmonious state of affairs that defies positivistic rational categorization, description, and definition. Indeed, if aura were easily classifiable, describable, and definable, it would lose this essential exceptionality. As Mariam Bratu Hansen states, "It is this conceptual fluidity that allows aura to become such a productive nodal point in Benjamin's thinking" (2008, 339). More than that, Benjamin's reconceptualization of aura has revolutionary significance. Again, in Hansen's words, "Aura's epistemic structure, secularized and modernized . . . , can also be seen at work in Benjamin's efforts to reconceptualize experience through the very conditions of its *im*possibility, as the only chance to counter the bungled (capitalist-imperialist) adaptation of technology that first exploded in World War One and was leading to the fascist conquest of Europe" (Hansen 2008, 338; italics in original). Thus, in the age of totalitarianism, Benjamin's acute insistence on problematizing individual experience and requestioning its possible and impossible limits seems to be in itself a profound act of resistance. Moreover, because the ultimate antipode of the totalitarian hegemony of human perception within all social and political arenas is auratic experience, conceptualizing aura is thus precisely the concretization of what has been demolished under the totalitarian system—a system that includes the totalitarian means of mass culture or the culture industry, instrumental rationalism, and ideological hegemony in general, ultimately amounting to the normalization of one-dimensionality not only in thinking, but also in everyday experience. As Benjamin wrote in his "Little History of Photography," originally published in 1931, aura "was being banished from reality by the deepening degeneration of the imperialist bourgeoisie" (Benjamin 2005b, 517). One could certainly claim this degeneration reached an unprecedented point in fascist totalitarianism, as Benjamin witnessed. The major challenge, then, is that the conceptualization of aura is basically equivalent to making the impossible condition of genuine individual experience comprehensible. At the same time, what makes this Benjaminian project even more difficult is that it must also undertake the emancipation of the concept of aura from its mythical and esoteric origins. Therefore, the question is: How can we philosophically reconceptualize aura (in a secular way) in a world that has already become more and more dominated by totalitarian norms (such as mass culture and instrumental rationality)?

Benjamin first hinted at the promising philosophical potentiality of aura in one of his early essays, "The Theory of Criticism" (1919–1920), where he states, "When we assert that everything beautiful somehow relates to the true and that its virtual place in philosophy is determinable, this means that a manifestation of the ideal of the philosophical problem can be discovered in every work of art. And we should add that such a manifestation may be assigned to every philosophical problem as its aura [*Strahlenkreis*], so to speak" (Benjamin 2004e, 218; brackets in original). Taking heed of the cadence of Benjamin's later writing on the subject, it is safe to say that with Benjamin one can stretch the poetic element of philosophy to go as close as possible to grasping and ultimately conceptualizing aura, despite aura's resistance to concrete conceptualization. After all, in the places where uniqueness obscures understanding, philosophy often seems to leap into the realms of poetry because only there can the hidden abilities of language truly be revealed. In Mallarmé's words, "Philosophically, verse makes up for what languages lack, completely superior as it is" (1982, 75). It is also this power of poetics, as opposed to "the positivity of psychological history and geography," that appeals to Bachelard and enables him to explore the intimacy of space (Bachelard 1994, 16).[10] Thus, my challenge is also how to conceptualize aura, along with its poetics, within a nonpositivistic yet critical project that enables us to illuminate what characterizes totalitarian space.

Aura as a Negative Notion

Admittedly, aura, in the best cases, is a vague term, and in that vagueness there exists major ambiguity, which in turn amounts to a fundamental contradiction. To show all this and move toward the concretization of the concept of aura, I start from this implicit vagueness and ambiguity. Aura does not designate a something that "is"; instead it refers to something that is absent. It is a negative notion that does not provide us with any positive knowledge; in Adorno's words, it is "the presence of that which is not present" (2006a, 102). Ultimately, aura reminds us that at least some part of truth lies beyond the virtual reality. Moving in this same direction, Benjamin, in "Some Motifs in Baudelaire," quotes Baudelaire from his "Salon of 1859" on the "useful illusion" of dioramas and the theater compared with landscape paintings: ". . . the majority of our landscape painters are liars, precisely because they fail to lie" (2006c, 341). By contrast, auratic works negate the dull reality; or rather the dull reality, inasmuch as it surrenders itself easily to the perception of the noncontemplative modern person, is the negation of the possibility of aura. That is why a great work of art, as far as it is a negation of the denatured and mechanized reality, the dullness of everydayness, or the entire immediate existential and historical human condition, is a rich locus of aura. In other words, art as the falsification of reality,[11] as the imaginative actualization of the impossible, or at least as the re-presentation of the absent by intensifying the depth of the trace of what is lost, is a rich locus for experiencing aura. Poetry as art also functions as the captor of what is absent. As Mallarmé writes, "I say: a flower! and outside the oblivion to which my voice relegates any shape, insofar as it is something other than the calyx, there arises musically, as the very idea and delicate, the one absent from every bouquet" (1982, 76). Aura is ultimately that negativity. Essential to art is this auratic negativity that simultaneously falsifies the appearance of reality and transcends the forms of intuition.

However, it is crucially important to note that aura is not unique to works of art, but rather that works of art are unique places for aura, which is why Benjamin so often refers to aura in relation to art. Benjamin, in "Little History of Photography" (1931), writes, "What is aura, actually? A strange weave of space and time: the unique appearance or semblance of distance, no matter how close it may be" (2005b, 518).[12] Later, in "The Work of Art in the Age of Its Technological Reproducibility" (1935–1936),[13] he makes the same statement again, almost identically: "What, then, is the aura? A strange tissue of space and time: the unique apparition of a distance, however near it may be" (Benjamin 2006b, 104–5). Despite the colon, the above quote can be interpreted as two distinct views on aura. First, aura can be understood as the unique atmosphere. On this account, a work of art in its original context could be analogized to a mushroom in its habitat: the air, the humidity, the temperature, the soil, and the light all contribute to the unique sense of the place where a mushroom grows. Thus, like mushrooms in a grocery store or in a can, severed completely from that sense of space, mechanically reproduced works of art are auraless. The second sense of aura, the "apparition of a distance," is more like what Adorno has in mind when he refers to "the presence of that which is not present." This notion of aura is that of the unintelligible sense that awakens a vague longing in us, a longing for something we cannot precisely fathom or name. Following the above quote from Benjamin, we read, "To follow with the eye—while resting on a summer afternoon—a mountain range on the horizon or a branch that casts its shadow on the beholder is to breathe the aura of those mountains, of that branch" (2006b, 105). Rodolphe Gasche thinks Benjamin's reference to a mountain range here might have been inspired by Goethe's line " 'and when during the day the distance of blue mountains longingly draws me' " (quoted in Gasche 1994, 188). In either case, aura in this sense constitutes the vague body of our nostalgia, of which distance is a key component.[14]

Gazing on a space of childhood is one example of an experience that can often generate the appearance of this nostalgia-inducing distance. In fact, the following words from Benjamin's "Berlin Childhood around 1900" (written in 1932) embody this idea perfectly: "For a long time, life deals with the still-tender memory of childhood like a mother who lays her newborn on her breast without waking it. Nothing has fortified my own memory so profoundly as gazing into courtyards, one of whose dark loggias, shaded by blinds in the summer, was for me the cradle in which the city laid its new citizen" (2006a, 345). In this sense, the phenomenological appearance of distance can be interpreted as sensing the presence of an absence.[15] Absence, however, is not the same as void or emptiness. On the contrary, absence always already bears a strong imprint of and reference to what is not there.

Aura then comes into play as the negativity that makes such intimacy possible, or, in other words, as the distance that renders the perception of the authenticity of the unreachable possible. Distance, as the experience of the flow of time, forces human mortality to center stage and thus makes present what there is not. Moreover, experience is individual only when it can be lived in relation to the individual memory because memory is the source of identity, of difference. Therefore, we cannot have auratic/individual experience without both absence and reappearance. For instance, the first gradual stage in reading a novel is the memory that the reader establishes within the world of the novel. Once a sense of past, that is, of the flow of time, of loss, of temporality, and of the mortality of the human way of being is established within the world of the novel and the world of the reader, reading becomes an appealing auratic (and thus individual) experience.[16] The same applies to the screening of a film; a film that succeeds in establishing a sense of the flow of time with an authentic texture, and can later stimulate evocations of the past within the past, tends to be the most haunting because it defictionalizes the fiction precisely through sculpting it within the viewer's memory via rendering the flow of time real and personal.

Eventually the viewer perceives this "appearance of a distance," which establishes her personal nostalgia. The closest we can get with regard to comprehending aura as nostalgia is what Hansen calls "the logic of the trace" (2008, 340).[17]

Aura as Trace

In this sense, aura can refer to the traces of a subject's past. Describing a famous photograph of Friedrich Schelling, Benjamin writes, "Just consider Schelling's coat. It will surely pass into immortality along with him: the shape it has borrowed from its wearer is not unworthy of the creases in his face" (2005b, 514).[18] The auratic object thus carries the traces of the passage of time in the subject's life and also speaks to what Heidegger calls "the being of the being" (2001, 35), but that being is necessarily rooted in the past, a past that reappears as a distance. As mentioned in chapter 2, perhaps this trace of the subject's past being is what fascinates Lefebvre when he refers to Provençal peasant houses as an example of appropriated space. By the same token, Bachelard's fascination with the house as the exemplary space of intimacy where the poetics of the subject's first world are preserved can also be interpreted in this same sense of aura, "the logic of trace."[19]

To understand aura as trace more concretely, we could look to Lee Jeong-hyang's film *The Way Home* (2002). Essentially, the film depicts the contradiction between two worlds: the young, modern, and metropolitan on the one hand, and the old and traditional on the other. It is the story of a boy's stay with his grandmother when his young single mother brings him to a remote village with some purported necessities, such as canned meat and mass-produced toys. Right from the beginning of the movie, in a prolonged scene on the bus to the village, we witness the contrast between the two travelers, who are bored and isolated, and the tired but still playful and cheerful villagers. This line of contrast continues between the child's world and the villagers' and especially his grandmother's, but what interests me here is the contrast between two sets of objects. The grandmother's objects, such as her hairpin, the functional yet beautiful chamber pot, the piece of wood that serves as a pillow for afternoon naps, her shoes, the wooden tool she uses for carrying pails of water, plates, spoons, and so forth, all carry the traces of both a deep familiarity and a continual history. Their instrumentality throughout long years has given them special touches and a unique location in the old woman's simple and authentic daily life. On the other hand, the little boy's treasured possessions are geometrical, soulless, and seminonfunctional objects, such as his electronic handheld game, shape puzzle blocks, and a toy robot, all of which never find a place or a distinct purpose, even in the child's daily life. Thus, when the child breaks his toy robot, we notice that it is a noteworthy event only insofar as the toy is a strange, and thus unique, object in that rural world. In another scene, we witness the sad moment when the child kicks the old woman's chamber pot and it shatters. Both objects, the toy robot and the chamber pot, have appeared in other scenes, so as viewers we have a history with both of them. However, the moment the chamber pot is smashed, a trace bearer ceases to exist; speaking in auratic terms, a distance disappears, unlike the accident of breaking the toy robot, which is meant to be comic in the context of the preceding events. In another scene, the child steals the old woman's hairpin and hopelessly tries to exchange it for batteries, reminiscent of the scene where the old woman is trying to make sense of the child's puzzle blocks as he is napping near her. In each case, one of the two characters is trying to make sense or a use of the strange object belonging to the other character. Thus, we see how out of place, dysfunctional even, the displaced objects are outside their actual context/world. What very obviously stands out in all these scenes is the auratic world of the old woman, including the path to her simple house, the house itself, and the objects in and around the house, as opposed to the dull world of the child and the original objects he brought with him from the city, which he gradually gives up, becoming more and more caught up in the intimacy and poetics of the space. Toward the end of the movie, when the child is beginning to embrace the intimacy of his relationship with his grandmother and is preparing to go see a young girl whom he hopes to woo, he chooses to wear his old pair of leather shoes that carry actual traces of time instead of the new pair his grandmother recently bought him from the town market. Whereas the opening scene introduces us to a child obviously coming from the world of mass production and extreme selfishness, the closing scene shows the same child a few months later leaving a world in which every face and everything has an aura of its own. In the beginning the child and mother are in a clear state of miscommunication and boredom. Each of them is stuck in his or her isolation to the degree that even when they converse, their gazes are out of place and lost in the kind of absentmindedness familiar to almost any lone bus rider or modern city dweller. In the final scene, however, as the bus that will take the child back to the city is pulling away from his grandmother, he finally and for the first time returns her gaze through the expanding distance of their departure.

Returning the Gaze

In "On Some Motifs in Baudelaire," Benjamin writes, "To experience the aura of an object we look at means to invest it with the ability to look back at us" (2006c, 338). This depiction of aura in terms of returning the gaze is one of Benjamin's most common attributions to aura. Normally, the subject perceives an object through her sensory perception, cognizes it, and categorizes it. However, the auratic object does not surrender itself so simply to categorization, or what Kant calls the determining (*bestimmend*) power of judgment (as opposed to the reflecting (*reflectirend*) power of judgment) (Kant 2000, 26–27 §20:224). As Yvonne Sherratt argues, "When we go over to the auratic image, instead of assimilating the meaning of the gaze into our language, we are *assimilated* into the image. This means we are assimilated into its 'vision.' When we look at it with our sight, our words, our vocabulary, it 'looks back' at us with its sight, its 'words,' its 'vocabulary.' This is how the auratic image returns our gaze" (Sherratt 1998, 36; italics in original). While the non-auratic object as a finitude has a limited and closed world, the auratic object does not offer itself as a finitude to our categories of understanding.[20] Perhaps the best way to clarify this is through a simple comparison between one's perception, to take an extreme example, of a flag, and one's experience of a painting by Monet, at the other extreme. In the first case, it is hard to imagine that any prolonged period of time pausing in front of a flag could foster a relationship between the flag and the subject, much less inspire an "experience" of some sort of reciprocity (even though in acts of pure performance people do pause to gaze at their flags). On the other hand, the example of the painting is much more than a simple representation; it has the capacity to haunt the subject, resisting her cognitive powers of representation and expression. Still, that is not to say the object always imposes the same power of assimilation on any observing subject. Of course, the subject has to give herself away to the experience. Perhaps, as a simpler example, while everyone passes by a traffic sign once its representation, its meaning, is cognized, no one can claim a definite understanding of any passing cloud. Good paintings, like clouds and mountains, resist purposive, utilitarian, pragmatist, and representational interpretations. In contrast to non-auratic objects, which are mere objects incapable of entering an open, subjective relationship with human beings, auratic objects can potentially penetrate the borders that define the subjectivity of the subject (Sherratt 1998). Thus, they are capable of returning our gaze, a notion of aura that can be delved into further by going back to Benjamin's reading of Baudelaire.

On that note, though Benjamin had many reasons to be fascinated by Baudelaire, undoubtedly one of the most appealing was that he saw in Baudelaire the poet of aura and its decay. In "Les Fleurs du Mal" in particular, Baudelaire is an observer standing at the edge of the era of mass production, eyes that have lost the ability to gaze, and ultimately the demolition of aura. Baudelaire is also, in a way, the model of poetic resistance for Benjamin. Baudelaire's poetry continually depicts the decay of aura with such masterful artistic falsification of reality and to such a degree that the poetry itself becomes an auratic locus, and that disintegration of aura is continually mourned by a voice that embodies the appearance of distance, which is the very condition of the poetry's creation. In spite of such decay, Baudelaire never gave up the noble search for the impossible auratic experience. He insisted on remaining faithful to the aura of space:

> Paris change! mais rien dans ma mélancolie
> N'a bougé! palais neufs, échafaudages, blocs,
> Vieux faubourgs, tout pour moi devient allégorie,
> Et mes chers souvenirs sont plus lourds que des rocs.
> (Baudelaire 2008, 174)

> Paris may change, but in my melancholy mood
> Nothing has budged! New palaces, blocks, scaffoldings,
> Old neighbourhoods, are allegorical for me,
> And my dear memories are heavier than stone.
> (Baudelaire 2008, 175)

If Benjamin is the solitary thinker who to the last day of his life struggled to maintain the ability to dream in fascist circumstances that rendered dreaming impossible, Baudelaire was the last poet in an age when poetry would become impossible.[21] Just as Baudelaire had insisted on preserving the allegorical in space (fighting the new reality of the metropolis with the poetic power to freeze the historical moment of ruins for the sake of the trace of the gaze), Benjamin, in works such as *The Arcades Project*, similarly tried to allegorize the ruins of the very cities (Berlin and Paris) that forever failed him as "the last European."[22] After all, neither Berlin nor Paris, nor the entire world for that matter, could secure Benjamin a corner. Ironically, in "The Return of the *Flâneur*" (1929), Benjamin wrote, "Landscape—this is what the city becomes for the *flâneur*. Or, more precisely, the city splits into its dialectical poles. It becomes a landscape that opens up to him and a parlor that encloses him" (2005e, 263). Then he adds, "The *flâneur* is the priest of the genius loci" (Benjamin 2005e, 264). Eventually, just as Athens sentenced Socrates to death, Europe sentenced Benjamin to death. Similar to Socrates's refusal to escape Athens to save his life, Benjamin turned down a number of his friends' pleadings and invitations for him to leave Europe.[23] At any rate, Benjamin's interest in Baudelaire is a philosopher's sorrowful pleasure in finding the last one of his species, a poet sending his gaze into a totalitarian age in which cities are collapsing into the sameness of fascist powers.

Lost Trace

Baudelaire, as the last city wanderer and last dreamer, searches for and gazes upon "singular beings with appalling charms" (Baudelaire 2008, 181). Above all, he thinks "of all those who have lost something they may not find / Ever, ever again" (Baudelaire 2008, 177). He goes on like "a double-visioned drunk" (2008, 181) in his "exiled soul" (2008, 177) to think of and depict the "haggard eye" (2008, 177), the eye that is "steeped in gall" (2008, 179), and many other eyes, including those of owls from under the protective wings of darkness insistently gazing at silence "up to the melancholy time" (2008, 137). Ultimately, his search is for the return of the gaze, like the experience of the mirror, or heterotopia, which restores one's fractioned self, as I discussed in chapter 3 in relation to Foucault. To Baudelaire, however, the problem is that the eyes in modernity are not capable of returning his gaze, and so the mirror experience becomes banal:

'. . . Car il ne sera fait que de pure lumière,
Puisée au foyer saint des rayons primitifs,
Et dont les yeux mortels, dans leur splendeur entière,
Ne sont que des miroirs obscurcis et plaintifs!'
(Baudelaire 2008, 14)

'. . . Since it is perfect luminosity
Drawn from the holy hearth of primal rays,
Of which men's eyes, for all their majesty,
Are only mournful mirrors, dark and crazed!'
(Baudelaire 2008, 15)

Yet, precisely because the gaze is no longer returned, Baudelaire becomes more obsessively and tragically devoted to the poetics of the lost gaze. It is presumably for this reason that Benjamin thinks Baudelaire's poetry is "unmistakably . . . marked by the disintegration of the aura" (Benjamin 2006c, 339) and "a rising up from the abyss" (Benjamin 2006f, 161). Wherever the human gaze is mentioned in *The Flowers of Evil*, Benjamin argues, the disintegration of aura is alluded to. "What happens here," Benjamin adds, "is that the expectation aroused by the gaze of the human eye is not fulfilled. Baudelaire describes eyes that could be said to have lost the ability to look" (2006c, 339).[24] But to Benjamin, Baudelaire also, perhaps more importantly, represents solidarity as an exiled soul who was able to have auratic experiences in the midst of so much auratic decay by negatively unfolding that decay of aura. Thus, Baudelaire is the very evidence of the actuality of what seems to be impossible; he is the voice coming right from the heart of modernity embodying the "Phoenix" (Baudelaire 2008, 181). Even though Baudelaire is the poet of ruins, the experience of his poetry is a testament to aura, as the appearance of distance. In other words, the true nightmare is not ruins themselves, but a situation in which ruins are not recognized as ruins. Retaining auratic experience, to Benjamin, is the only way to survive without being struck by "the plague," to use Camus's literary analogy for fascism in *The Plague*. As Camus writes, "The habit of despair is worse than despair itself" (1965, 149). This means the real hopeless misery is not living in misery itself, but rather losing the ability to recognize misery as such and lacking the language to express it. Extending this to its more political implications, the danger of totalitarian hegemony is that it prevents us from seeing what we have lost, such that even the trace of what has been lost is lost.

Politically, the implications of losing the trace of what has been lost (the disappearance of distance) is well expressed in Žižek's words: "Not only in 'totalitarian' conditions of censorship but, perhaps even more, in the more refined conditions of liberal censorship . . . we 'feel free' because we lack the very language to articulate our unfreedom" (2002, 2). Adorno similarly states, "Instead of solving the question of women's oppression, male society has so extended its own principle that the victims are no longer able even to pose the question" (2005, 92). In other words, one could say totalitarianism reaches its climax not through physical control, but through ideological hegemony: when people no longer have the imagination to imagine other possible worlds or the language to articulate their existing unfreedom. Whether one agrees with Žižek and/or Adorno regarding their attack on liberal capitalism or not, the point here is that when we cease to have the traces, the marks, of ruins, we will both ideologically and discursively normalize and internalize domination, oppression, and inequality. In an auraless world, we will cease to be utopic enough to challenge the existing order through the potential, the power to dream,[25] and the will to poetry. Hence, Benjamin's true fear is a world where even poetry is rendered impossible, and through conceptualizing aura he tries to arm us against the normalization of such a world.

Aura as Veil

In further developing aura as the return of the gaze by objects, Benjamin also refers to Proust (Benjamin 2006c, 338–39). For instance, according to Proust, works of art that have been gazed at with much appreciation obtain an aura, or, in Proust's own words, a " 'delicate veil,' " woven by those admiring perpetual gazes (quoted in Benjamin 2006c, 339). It is this "delicate veil" that captures our gaze, which explains why a great painting is one that our gaze "never gets its fill of" (Benjamin 2006c, 338). To explain the "delicate veil" as the returner of our gaze, and thus the auratic locus, we need to go back to an early work by Benjamin (written twenty-three years prior to "On the Some Motifs in Baudelaire"). Benjamin, in "Painting, or Signs and Marks" (written in 1917), differentiates between signs and marks, maintaining that signs function on the most material level. A sign as a graphic line drawn against a background gives the background an identity (different from its previous identity as a white/blank surface), and at the same time the background actualizes the graphic line as a sign. In the same way, the background also determines the relationship between two graphic lines that are drawn on it. Marks are active on a higher dialectical level, but alone they lack the transcending negation brought about by the composition as a whole (Benjamin 2004d, 85–86). Benjamin maintains that while signs are attached to objects, marks are almost always associated with living beings, and "the realm of the mark is a medium" (Benjamin 2004d, 84). Therefore, it seems that he suggests the medium of marks is the living interaction; that is, unlike the optical bareness of signs, marks involve a higher living interaction, because marks "emerge." As Benjamin writes, "The first basic difference is that the sign is printed on something, whereas the mark emerges from it" (2004d, 84). Then he argues that naming ultimately transcends the set of marks into a composition, the painting as we experience it.[26] The composition is thus the actual realm of the temporal diffusion and artistic falsification where the gaze of the viewer is simultaneously trapped and returned through the composition's falsifying muses, its veil, if you will. This process does not have to be hermeneutical because it is not always a conscious act of interpretation. Rather, the interaction between the viewer and the composition represents the possibility of living, experiencing, a discontinued and isolated moment not within the given reality, but in spite of it.[27]

This framework sets us up to more fully explore aura as the veil. Describing the beauty of the veiled object, Benjamin, in "The Significance of Beautiful Semblance" (a fragment written in 1935–1936), writes, "Through its veil, which is nothing other than the aura, the beautiful appears [scheint]. Wherever it ceases to appear, it ceases to be beautiful" (Benjamin 2006d, 137; brackets in original). Thus, the veil is the medium of beauty. Like the realm of marks, the realm of beauty is a living medium of dialectical (nonstop and multidimensional) interaction, and on the two poles of this aesthetic interaction are semblance and the play of the imagination (Benjamin 2006d, 137). Actually, in an essay that Benjamin wrote in 1919–1922, we can find the same connection between beauty and veil with regard to a character, Ottilie, from Goethe's Elective Affinities. The veil in this case is music: "affection, like the veiling of the image through tears in music, thus summons forth in conciliation the ruin of the semblance through emotion" (2004b, 348). Benjamin then adds:

> Neither humor nor tragedy can verbally grasp beauty; beauty cannot appear in an aura of transparent clarity. Its most exact opposite is emotion. Neither guilt nor innocence, neither nature nor the beyond, can be strictly differentiated for beauty. In this sphere Ottilie appears; this veil must lie over her beauty. For the tears of emotion, in which the gaze grows veiled, are at the same time the most authentic veil of beauty itself. (2004b, 248–49)

Embodying another conceptual dimension of aura, the veil is also the distance that renders the object both unreachable and autonomous in its authenticity, which in turn enables it to dialectically enter the realm of our subjectivity. In other words, as Hansen writes, "The veil defines both the condition of beauty and its essential unavailability, a symbolic integrity predicated on 'a distance however close the thing that calls it forth'" (2008, 353). This medium, whether we call it the veil or aura, is the distance that renders art at once both remote and appealing.[28]

The veil as remoteness, then, is a key to the aesthetic experience, but one could take this even further with examples in different realms other than that of art. Although it is true that Benjamin's work on aura ultimately secularizes the concept, it seems that we can go further than Benjamin and argue that it is the notion of aura, as distance, that makes up the quintessence of the theological image of God,[29] rather than vice versa. Simply put, inherent in the idea of God is this sense of remoteness and unreachability,[30] the belief that there is an infinite distance that separates the believer from her God. Because the distance is infinite, the muse that traps the mind's gaze is also infinite, meaning that the subject of worship becomes both indefinitely fascinating and unreachable. Accordingly, the power of the idea of God is ultimately rooted in the theological distribution of space (of course, this applies only to the believer, i.e., this sublime space is real only insofar as she believes in it). God in a sense is that imagined infinite distance itself, and that infinite distance basically constitutes a pure form of aura (aura without an actual object).[31] Moreover, the infinite remoteness associated with the monotheistic God (mainly in the three religions) is in fact a constituent of the power of God. Obviously, different religions follow different means of producing and maintaining this distance. For example, Islamic authorities have forbidden any depiction of God, assuming that an imagistic depiction of God would in some sense limit the imagined distance. In this same vein, God's communication, even with his messengers, including Muhammad, to humanity is through dreams, angels, and revelations, which presumes his spatial unreachability. As the religion strengthened its ideological and political apparatuses after the death of Muhammad, the orthodoxy did not even allow the depiction of Muhammad, in spite of the fact that Muhammad is not believed to have any divine aspect according to Islamic belief itself. The magic of this kind of imagined distance (for believers) is perhaps what later makes Benjamin turn his back on aura altogether, as I explain in the next chapter. However, I should note that my argument here regarding the role of the imagined distance and its role in the construction of the idea of God should not be confused with religious depictions of aura. On the contrary, the above argument is a rational formula capable of the demystification of some religious beliefs. That is to say, the power of the idea of God is not related to the actual aura of an entity called God; rather, the power of God (albeit in the psychological sense) is a play on the idea of aura. In other words, the formula of aura (as distance) explains the scheme according to which God has been created and sustained historically. The point is that through the conceptualization of aura, one can demystify the religious doctrine as opposed to allowing the religious doctrine to mystify the notion of aura.

A second example that embodies the power of aura as the appearance of distance is the dichotomy of home and exile. Home, as in Ovid's poetry, is typically poetic and irresistibly desirable from a place of exile, just as exile can be poetic and is characteristic of many archaic forms of tragic heroism from one's "home." In contrast, (the idea of) home is boring when at home, and exile is normally anything but poetic in exile. Further, when the exiled returns home, that is, when the veil covering home is removed, the magic of home all but disappears, and the subject then has to imagine the distance through reliving the experience of exile in order to re-create the appeal of home. In fact, from home, exile will gradually acquire the accoutrements of home. This conflict is depicted nicely in Milan Kundera's *Ignorance* (2002). During the day, the protagonist in the novel, Irena, has short and vivid nostalgic visions of her birthplace, Prague, but at night she frequently has what Kundera calls "the emigration-dream," which is basically the nightmare of being back in the so-called homeland (Kundera 2002, 15–16). Even the magical longing for "home" in the narrow sense of the word is strongly rooted in the appearance of distance. The best example can be found by going back to the philosopher of the poetics of home, Bachelard, who not once gives an example of the poetics of the first home, the first universe, from the point of view of the child. The nostalgic home in *The Poetics of Space* is always the home from which a distance separates the subject.[32]

Moreover, is the same power of distance not at work in the popular idea that we travel in order to miss (or better appreciate) home? That too shows the essentiality of distance for home to truly function as home. One such way to read Alain de Botton's *The Art of Travel* (2003) is that the other place where we want to be is so tempting precisely because we are not there, because there is a distance that lends a faraway, magical quality to it. He gives many examples from various biographies of artists and writers to demonstrate this point, but perhaps most telling are his personal stories. Writing about his own vacation to Barbados, de Botton remarks, "A momentous but until then overlooked fact was making its first appearance: that I had inadvertently brought myself with me to the island" (2003, 20). Because he brought himself to the island, the distance between him and the island disappeared, and because of that the magical attraction of the island at least partly disappeared as well.

According to this interpretation of aura, we can undertake a very different reading of Lacan's statement "I think where I am not, therefore I am where I do not think" (2001, 183). Clearly, in the first part of the statement Lacan is referring to the way the human psyche functions. Hence, the Other place, which is always separated by distance, is where human thought and fantasy is instinctively attracted. Further, as Camus and most existentialists believe, human beings do not have a nature because they always want to be something other than what they are. In Camus' words, "Man is the only creature who refuses to be what he is" (1960, 11). This lack of a fundamental nature actually amounts to the infusion of fantasy and daydreaming into the here and now, and at the far end of this distance between reality and fantasy is the desired image of the self. In another sense, it is the distance that separates us from the future that also makes life bearable and worth living. Yet even when the idea of the future does not hold such anticipation, there is always the past to send our thoughts to; even if hope becomes impossible, the realm of nostalgia remains as a safe refuge.

To give another example of the sublime that results from the experience of distance, central to the magic of narration in realistic literature is the creation of this auratic distance to reality. As such, it seems that we are normally more interested in stories of lives as opposed to the lives themselves because the story creates the distance necessary for the auratic experience to play out. Take, for instance, Dostoevsky's *The Idiot*: the protagonist, Prince Lev Nikolaevich Myshkin, is not an extraordinary person, and his surroundings are likewise quite ordinary. Moreover, unlike many works of fiction, as a great work of literature, the novel does not rely on cheap excitement or provoking superficial sensations in its reader. In fact, it stays faithful to the boring and alienating patterns of everydayness in Prince Myshkin's life. Not once does Dostoevsky attempt to philosophize Prince Myshkin's world, and it is precisely for this reason that the work shows Dostoevsky's brilliance. Ultimately, the art of Dostoevsky's storytelling is that he simply creates the auratic distance necessary for us to be able to gaze back at what is otherwise ordinary. As Adorno writes, "There is something emblematic in the *imago* of all books, waiting for the profound gaze into their external aspect that will awaken its language, a language other than the internal, printed one" (Adorno 1992, 30). The archetypal book, then, could be looked at as a window that bridges us to another space that is more like a temporal exile within reality than an actual part of reality, and from which we can also gaze back at reality through the created distance. This notion is actually ever present in our prolonged relationship with "the book." One can recall many commonplace sayings about how a book changed the reader's life, by which it is actually meant that it changed how the reader sees reality, from the other side of the window/book. Hence, the greatness of a book is actually measured by its power to sublimate ordinary everydayness, in other words, the book's transforming power to create the distance necessary to experience reality differently. Adorno's description in the above quote is an expression of the ontology of books gazed back at as potential bridges to negate and thus transcend the given in the ordinary mode of everydayness. It is this distance forged by the book as a window or bridge that both haunts and intrigues us.

Aura as Distance

Now, to return to examples from the realm of art, there is a basic question that illuminates this secret of aura as distance: Why is it that the painting of, say, a tree is more appealing than the tree itself? To quote an example from de Botton's book again, we can look to his description of Joris-Karl Huysman's character Duc Jean des Esseintes in À *rebours*. On Des Esseintes's disappointment with being in Holland as opposed to the Holland he had seen in great painters' works, de Botton writes, "Des Esseintes ended up in the paradoxical position of feeling more *in* Holland— that is, more intensely in contact with the elements he loved in Dutch culture—when looking at selected images of Holland in a museum than when travelling with sixteen pieces of luggage and two servants through the country itself" (2003, 16). Put in another way, my initial question aimed at revealing the exceptionality of aura can also be phrased to pit painting and photography against each other: why is that a painting of a tree (even if it is a realistic rendition) is incomparably more fascinating than a photograph of the same tree? As Benjamin puts it, "Photography is rather like food for the hungry or drink for the thirsty" (Benjamin 2006c, 338). Or perhaps one could say the experience of photography to the auratic experience of a great painting is like a sugar boost to the experience of wakefulness. In photography, it seems that the photograph of the familiar interests us only when the familiar is presented in such a way that it no longer resembles the familiar. Artistic photographers are especially good at plotting this twist, in creating a sense of distance from the actual object of the photo, and thereby providing an alternative mode of perception. The ability to create such a distance is perhaps what elevates some photography to the level of art.

The poetic experience is in a way about the acute awareness of this distance that separates the subject from the auratic object. Forugh Farrokhzad (who can be considered the Anna Akhmatova of Persian literature), in her poem "Let Us Believe in the Beginning of a Cold Season," writes, "Between the gaze and the window / there is always a distance / how come I haven't noticed?" (1967, 5–6; my translation).[33] Farrokhzad's lines about the distance between the gaze and the window perfectly embody the aura of space as well. Granted, the auratic experience is after all a subjective one, but this experience relies directly on the spatial characteristics surrounding the subject. That is to say, the distribution and production of space will unavoidably affect the aura of space. In terms of the auratic distance, then, space, whether appropriated or natural, does not guarantee auratic experience, but it allows it precisely because space presents itself through a distance capable of returning the gaze. In an endnote of his "On Some Motifs in Baudelaire" (originally published in 1940), Benjamin writes, "Whenever a human being, an animal, or an inanimate object thus endowed by the poet lifts up its eyes, it draws him into the distance. The gaze of nature, when thus awakened, dreams and pulls the poet after its dream. Words, too, can have an aura of their own. This is how Karl Kraus described it: 'The closer one looks at a word, the greater the distance from which it looks back' (Karl Kraus, *Pro domo et mundo* [Munich, 1912], 164) [Benjamin's note]" (Benjamin 2006c, 354). This also reminds us of Henry Barbusse's novel *Hell* (*L'enfer*), in which the entire premise of the story is a character who observes the world of others through a hole in the wall of his hotel room. This positioning and the poetic conclusions the character is able to make from his place of hiding suggest that perhaps the philosopher does indeed need to be in an ivory tower to see the world better. Without that distance, I would argue, philosophy itself does not seem possible. Maintaining a similar outlook, Žižek, unlike many other Marxist leftists, is against the common humanitarian call for urgent practical action, which implies some kind of anti-intellectualism, and insists on continually preserving the distance needed for reflecting on the world (Žižek 2008, 6–7; 2009, 11).

Conclusion

Finally, and perhaps most significantly, Benjamin describes aura as the return of the gaze and appearance of distance at the same time. In *The Arcades Project*, he writes, "A decisive value is to be accorded Baudelaire's efforts to capture the gaze in which the magic of distance is extinguished," and he continues, "Relevant here: my definition of the aura as the aura of distance opened up with the look that awakens in an object perceived" (1999, 314).[34] Now, if aura is the appearance of distance through which the gaze is returned, what would the elimination of aura entail? Aura itself is the negation of negation insofar as it is the appearance of distance (distance being the first negation and its appearance the second). The elimination of aura, then, is marked by the disappearance of distance, which directly implies not nearness, but rather the collapse of the multiplicity and multidimensionality of spatial experience. In fact, a world without aura amounts to the disintegration of all forms of the uniqueness in space. However, it should be noted that auraless space is not the same as ruins. In ruins, as I have argued, there are still the traces of what has been lost, but auraless space is a flat space of endless repetition, standardization, sameness, and total transparency. Ideologically, it is the space in which totalitarianism is so normalized that the masses lack even the ability to dream of a different world. Auraless space is the habitus not of despair (to paraphrase Camus again), but of the habit of despair, of one-dimensional thought that is incapable of articulating the living unfreedom. In such a space, there can be no "gaze," let alone the possibility of its return.

Reversibly, there is also the anti-auratic "gaze" that lacks or destructively negates the distance. In "On Some Motifs in Baudelaire," Benjamin states, "Glances may be all the more compelling, the more complete the viewer's absence that is overcome in them. In eyes that look at us with mirrorlike blankness, the remoteness remains complete. It is precisely for this reason that such eyes know nothing of distance" (Benjamin 2006c, 340).[35] Then, describing the "eye of the city dweller," he states, "In the protective eye, there is no daydreaming surrender to distance and to faraway things. The protective eye may bring with it something like pleasure in the degradation of such distance" (Benjamin 2006c, 341). Thus, in the latter quote, Benjamin is not only claiming that the protective eye in the age of reproduction is incapable of auratic gazing, but also that it destroys the auratic distance altogether. Accordingly, the banal stare of the masses that negates distance therefore also renders space flat and transparent. Combining this with my argument in chapter 3 on the destructive tendency of the panoptic gaze, one can claim that the gaze of power destroys the aura of space precisely by abolishing the auratic distance within and of any space it dominates.

Historically we have moved from the age of auratic perception to the age of mass reproduction (Benjamin 2006d, 137), and thus sameness, or auralessness, has become the rule wherever instrumental rationalism has prevailed. In Benjamin's words, "The stripping of the veil from the object, the destruction of the aura, is the signature of a perception whose 'sense for sameness in the world' has so increased that, by means of reproduction, it extracts sameness even from what is unique" (Benjamin 2006g, 255–56).[36] Thus, an auraless world not only destroys the dialectics of seeing, but it also destroys the spatial dialectics of experience altogether. Benjamin suggests the social roots of the destruction of aura are strongly linked to the modern phenomenon of the masses, whose desire for closeness tramples auratic distance (2006g, 255).[37] In the political dimension, however, the decay of the aura of space itself is more fully achieved by the gaze of power that is installed in such a way as to render space transparent. While Benjamin, quoting Georg Simmel, argues that "'interpersonal relationships in big cities are distinguished by a marked preponderance of visual activity over aural activity'" (Benjamin 2006c, 341), the spatial technologies of power, as I argued in the previous chapter, aim at the total exploitation of visual activity in order to produce a single transparent space structured around the power center for the purpose of the limitless exercise of power, and thus total control over all individual subjects.

Continuing this train of thought, the destruction of aura is then what deprives subjects of their individuality (Adorno 1992, 235)[38] and at the same time arranges the social world in such a way that totalitarianism will become the norm. Ultimately, totalitarianism is a system in which individual uniqueness is abolished in favor of the supreme uniformity of the whole. Because uniqueness is the source of difference, it is also the chief obstacle to assimilation. Therefore, because aura *is* uniqueness in its authentic sense, the annihilation of aura leads the way to totalitarianism. With all this in mind, I move to a critical discussion of Benjamin's article "The Work of Art in the Age of Its Technological Reproducibility," where we find important notes on aura in relation to mechanically reproduced works of art, and the political implications of the decay of spatial aura.

5

The Destruction of Aura and
Its Political Implications

Benjamin's "The Work of Art in the Age of Technological Reproducibility"[1] (written in 1935–1936) is his most well-known piece of writing
published before his death. Moreover, scholars have used this article as
the main, and often the only, source on Benjamin's concept of aura
among all his writings. After all, in The-Work-of-Art article Benjamin
does provide a relatively clear account of aura; however, he goes on to
show conflicting feelings toward its destruction. In this chapter, I critically review the relevant aspects of the article and advance my argument
regarding the spatial and political consequences of the destruction of
aura, which directly result from the mechanical/technological reproduction of artworks.

Benjamin begins by asserting that limited technological reproduction
(e.g., coins) has existed at least since the ancient Greeks. Later, through
the Middle Ages to the early 1800s, woodcutting, engraving, etching,
printing, and finally lithography were added to the Greek technology
of casting and stamping (2006g, 252). However, it was particularly
lithography—invented by Alois Senefelder in 1798[2]—that marked the
turning point in the technology of mechanical reproduction because it
allowed the reproduction of comparatively large numbers of copies of
graphic artwork at a pace that could keep up with everyday life (Benjamin 2006g, 252–53). From there, Benjamin, goes on, the invention of
photography ultimately allowed instantaneous pictorial depiction and thus
unprecedented reproducibility (Benjamin 2006g, 253). The question is no
longer the traditional aesthetic one—whether photography is art—rather,
it is whether photography, and even more so film, has not altered our

entire conception of art (Benjamin 2006g, 258). Having provided this backdrop, Benjamin then expresses his optimistic view regarding what he believed to be the political outcomes of the technological reproduction of works of art and the ensuing relationship between the masses and art. Benjamin maintained that when art becomes increasingly accessible to the masses, it stimulates progressive forces. What escaped him is the fact that the mechanical reproduction of artworks also can—and perhaps this is more likely—be seen as an access point to the mass mentality and thereby a manipulative means for ideological indoctrination. This is where Adorno, especially in his views on the culture industry, strongly objects to Benjamin's surprising shift in some parts of The-Work-of-Art article, where he betrays the concept of aura by nearly celebrating its destruction, as I explain in section 2. In this section, I build on the first five pages of Benjamin's article, in which his insights are aligned with his other works regarding the secularized concept of aura and his working-grief for its loss.

In his first allusion to the destruction of aura in The-Work-of-Art article, Benjamin states, "In even the most perfect reproduction, *one* thing is lacking: the here and now of the work of art—its unique existence in a particular place. It is this unique existence—and nothing else—that bears the mark of the history to which the work has been subject" (Benjamin 2006g, 253; italics in original). Then he adds, "One might encompass the eliminated element within the concept of the aura, and go on to say: what withers in the age of the technological reproducibility of the work of art is the latter's aura" (Benjamin 2006g, 254). Accordingly, aura is the missing element of the work of art that is reproduced or simply relocated or exhibited in a historical context different from its original one. As such, the technology of reproduction "*substitutes a mass existence for a unique existence*" (Benjamin 2006g, 254; italics in original). Technological mass reproduction thus fragments, recontextualizes, and reshapes the artwork, while at the same time liquidating its authentic context. Moreover, through the decay of aura, the medium of perception is altered, provided that there are different modes of perception in different historical eras (Benjamin 2006g, 255). The modern phenomenon of the "masses" is where the social basis of the decay of aura is rooted, and more specifically, as Benjamin writes, in their desire "to '*get-closer*' *to things spatially and humanly*" and "*equally passionate concern for overcoming each thing's uniqueness* . . ." (2006g, 255;

italics in original). In other words, this obsession with getting closer to objects (often manifested in demands to possess them or their mechanically reproduced copies) overcomes the auratic distance (destroying the veil) capable of returning our gaze, which amounts to the destruction of aura (Benjamin 2006g, 255–56).

The unprecedented decay of aura in the age of the masses and mass reproduction then directly implies the dominance of "a perception whose 'sense for sameness in the world'" tends to destroy all uniqueness (Benjamin 2006g, 256). The political implications of this are many. Although Benjamin, right from the introduction, states that the concepts he is about to introduce are *useful for the formulation of revolutionary demands in the politics of art [Kunstpolitik]* as opposed to those useful for fascism (Benjamin 2006g, 252; italics and brackets in original), the auratic destruction wrought by mass reproduction and the mass mode of perception (in their tendency to vanquish the gaze-capturing distance and uniqueness of objects) clearly signals the birth of fascism's spawn: totalitarianism. For totalitarianism, first and foremost, imposes "sameness" in its quest to smother difference as uniqueness, and authenticity as autonomy.

One could also say totalitarianism's spatial mode of production is "sameness" just as the dominant and dominating mode of perception in and behind it is "sameness." Notably, Benjamin associates aura directly with "uniqueness" (Benjamin 2006g, 256), and "sameness" directly with the decay of aura (Benjamin 2006g, 255–56). He also, as we have already established, associates aura with distance ("the unique apparition of distance"), and so the destruction of aura equates with the disappearance of distance. When this distance necessary for auratic experience is overcome by "the alignment of reality with the masses and of the masses with reality" (Benjamin 2006g, 256), the result is necessarily a space without topography, a flattened space, or what can be called totalitarian space. Therefore, "totalitarian space" designates the direct political and spatial outcome of the destruction of aura. In such a distance-less space of experience, where sameness is imposed by mass reproducibility, and where sameness is already the mode of perception, totalitarianism naturally finds its ideal space for growth. That is why such a space should be called totalitarian space, where "mass existence" takes the place of "unique existence." I reinforce this argument further as I continue this exploration of the spatio-political implications of the decay of aura.

Auralessness and New Absolutism

As can be inferred from arguably all Benjamin's writings where he mentions aura, he admires aura and, when relevant, mourns its decay. Indeed,
even in The-Work-of-Art article, before he shifts to his antagonistic
position toward aura, you can sense his admiration for it: "What, then,
is the aura? A strange tissue of space and time: the unique apparition
of a distance, however near it may be. To follow with the eye—while
resting on a summer afternoon—a mountain range on the horizon or a
branch that casts its shadow on the beholder is to breathe the aura of
those mountains, of that branch" (2006b, 104–5).[3] While in the first
three sections of The-Work-of-Art article his tone with regard to the
loss of aura remains one of mourning, in the fourth section, Benjamin
mentions the decay of aura for the first time as a progressive event that
he endorses. Did Benjamin change his political attitude toward the
concept of aura because at the end he feared it still clung to its mystic
origins, indivisible from the religious tradition? Was he reacting to the
cultic use of works of art in the era of fascism? These are questions to
be answered through a close reading of the rest of his article. However,
before I proceed to my critical analysis of Benjamin's article, it is worth
first quoting a passage from Adorno, who was one of the first to read
Benjamin's article prior to its publication. In a letter dated March 18,
1936, Adorno wrote to Benjamin:

> In your earlier writings, of which the present essay is a con-
> tinuation, you distinguished the idea of the work of art as
> a structure from the symbol of theology on the one hand,
> and from the taboo of magic on the other. But I now find
> it somewhat disturbing—and here I can see a sublimated
> remnant of certain Brechtian themes—that you have now
> rather casually transferred the concept of the magical aura to
> the "autonomous work of art" and flatly assigned a counter-
> revolutionary function to the latter. I do not need to assure
> you just how aware I am of the magical element that persists
> in the bourgeois work of art (especially since I constantly
> attempt to expose the bourgeois philosophy of idealism that
> is associated with the idea of aesthetic autonomy as some-
> thing mythical in the full sense). However, it seems to me
> that the heart of the autonomous work of art does not itself

belong to the dimension of myth—forgive my topical manner of speaking—but is inherently dialectical, that is, compounds within itself the magical element with the sign of freedom. (Adorno and Benjamin 1999, 128)

As Adorno mentioned, and as I explained in chapter 4, Benjamin insists on dissociating aura from its mystical, cultic, religious, and mythical uses right from the beginning of his work on aura. He then applies this secularized notion of aura to sublime experience not only in relation to artwork, but in general ("genuine aura appears in all things" [Benjamin 2005a, 328]). Yet in The-Work-of-Art article, to Adorno's and any critical reader's surprise, Benjamin reassociates aura with the cultic (ritual, magical, and religious) realm. As a result, he also associates the destruction of the aura of artworks through technological reproduction with the progressive socialization and politicization of art, and in doing so, he forced aura back into the mythical shackles from which he had up until this point tried to liberate it. Let us remember, for example, in "Hashish" (1930), where he wrote of aura, "Everything I said on the subject was directed polemically against the theosophists, whose inexperience and ignorance I find highly repugnant. And I contrasted three aspects of genuine aura . . . with the conventional and banal ideas of the theosophists" (Benjamin 2005a, 327). We can juxtapose this sentiment to the The-Work-of-Art article, where, starting from the sixth page (the fourth section on), Benjamin celebrates the destruction of aura as an emancipating and democratizing historical event because, he declares, "The artwork's auratic mode of existence is never entirely severed from its ritual function" (Benjamin 2006g, 256). Hence, Benjamin argues that the technological reproducibility of artworks, by eliminating the distance (aura) between the artwork and the recipient, by bringing artworks to the masses, emancipates art from the ritualistic, religious, mythical, and magical functions represented in cult value.[4] As I continue my analysis of Benjamin's article, the problem of this shift in his approach to aura will become clearer.

In The-Work-of-Art article, Benjamin claims that an artwork's use value, in antiquity, was one and the same with the work's cult value. He argues that cult value was shaped through various magical, ceremonial, and religious uses of what we would now call artwork and that in the Renaissance the secular form of aesthetics emerged, which brought with it exhibitions that emancipated artworks from their traditional entrenchments, ultimately leading exhibition value to supersede cult value. To Benjamin, this cult value was intrinsically linked to the distance that separated the artwork from the public. For example, he maintains that paintings and statues in cathedrals, monasteries, and churches are always deeply embedded in the broader traditions and value systems, and because of those ritualistic and hierarchical settings, there was and remains the convention "to keep the artwork out of sight: certain statues of gods are accessible only to the priest in the cella; certain images of the Madonna remain covered nearly all year round. . . ." (Benjamin 2006g, 257). On the general level, for Benjamin this meant the authenticity and uniqueness of art was shrouded in tradition (2006g, 256). More specifically, in an endnote he states, "The definition of the aura as the 'unique apparition of a distance, however near it may be,' represents nothing more than a formulation of the cult value of the work of art in categories of spatiotemporal perception" (2006g, 272). Expanding on that thought, Benjamin says the auratic distance is cultic in itself, and because exhibition is based on visibility, cult value must be based on invisibility (or limited visibility) (2006g, 272). This is the first time Benjamin takes this antagonistic stance toward the concept of aura. In fact, he goes on to argue that the destruction of the aura of works of art is progressive, stating, "Technological reproducibility emancipates the work of art from its parasitic subservience to ritual" (Benjamin 2006g, 256). In this sense, photography, as the most revolutionary and promising of the technologies of reproduction to Benjamin, did away with the idea of authenticity, and by doing so relocated artwork to social and political arenas instead of the traditional/ritual spheres that had caged art for so long. He writes, "In photography, exhibition value begins to drive back cult value on all fronts," earlier explaining, ". . . *with the emancipation of specific artistic practices from the service of ritual, the opportunities for exhibiting their products increase*" (Benjamin 2006g, 257; italics in original). Benjamin then explains that as a reaction to the revolutionary socialization of art, forms of the "theology of art" emerged (Benjamin 2006g, 256). He gives the example of the art-for-art movements in their advocacy of the purity of art and their rejection of the social and political contextualization of and representation in art. Yet Benjamin is confident in his response to such movements: "*As soon as the criterion of authenticity ceases to be applied to artistic production, the whole social function of art is revolutionized. Instead of being founded on ritual, it is based on a different practice: politics*" (Benjamin 2006g, 256–57; italics in original).

Now I turn to my critique of Benjamin's article, beginning with his presentation of exhibition value and cult value. Benjamin positions exhibition value and cult value as two extreme opposites: "The reception of works of art varies in character, but in general two polar types stand out: one accentuates the artwork's cult value; the other, its exhibition value" (Benjamin 2006g, 257). Yet, even if we accept this contrast, there is no reason to assume it is such a simple one (and, as any dialectician would say, there are no simple oppositions). The problem, then, with Benjamin's account is that it lacks dialectical understanding. For example, what if exhibition value and cult value, provided they are contradictory, transcend each other? What if the more an image is exhibited, the more cultic its function becomes? Of course, Benjamin would say the problem with this question is that it does not seem to take into account that exhibition, as nearness, as visibility, overcomes the auratic distance, which Benjamin at this point believed to be essential to cult value. However, cult value is not derived solely from auratic distance; a distance in terms of power relations can also have the same effect. In fact, Benjamin uses a similar notion of distance when he writes, "The magician maintains the natural distance between himself and the person treated; more precisely, he reduces it slightly by laying on his hands, but increases it greatly by his authority. The surgeon does exactly the reverse; he greatly diminishes the distance from the patient by penetrating the patient's body . . ." (Benjamin 2006g, 263). Benjamin then goes on to conclude, "Magician is to surgeon as painter is to cinematographer" (2006g, 263). However, he could, and should, have taken this further to argue that cult value relies (if not always, then sometimes) on a form of distance other than the auratic one, and that therefore the elevation of exhibition value does not necessarily amount to the decline of cult value. Had Benjamin taken this step, he could have avoided betraying his concept of aura in the The-Work-of-Art article.[5]

My next step is to contend that what is exhibited more (what is more visible) does, in fact, create greater cult value based not on auratic distance in the aesthetic sense, but rather on creating a space of power. A critical trait of power, as we have seen in the last chapter, is visibility. To quote Foucault again: "If Bentham's project aroused interest, this was because it provided a formula applicable to many domains, the formula of 'power through transparency,' subjection by 'illumination.' In the Panopticon, there is used a form close to that of the castle—a keep surrounded by walls—to paradoxically create a space of exact legibility"

(Foucault 1980, 154 [1977, 18]). To reiterate, vital to the technology of power is the principle of visibility in terms of not only instilling in the subject a conscious state of "being visible" to the eyes of power, but also making the eyes of power visible at all times to the subject. Now, would images of a fascist leader everywhere not function precisely in this sense (i.e., by creating the conscious sense that one is always visible to the omnipresent apparatuses of the leader/state)? Would that also not (precisely because of the overwhelming influx of exhibition) transcend cult value? This idea is embodied perfectly in a photograph of Saddam Hussein looking at images of himself in an official exhibition dedicated to his image. In effect, the image we see (of multiple Saddams on different levels of representation) situates the viewer in between two mirrors, the result of which is endless reflections, and thus an endless reproduction of the image to a point that the distance is indefinitely extended through the very act of negating every appearance of it. At least symbolically, an image of Saddam looking at images of Saddam shows that exhibition value is in fact indistinguishable from cult value: each feeds into the other proportionally, and each transcends the other dialectically. In the Kim Dynasty's North Korea, the regime has been relying heavily on unleashing limitless exhibition value precisely to render the cult value absolute. The requirement that every house have a picture of Kim Il Sung, Kim Jong Il, and now Kim Jong Un and that every citizen twelve and older wear a pin sporting their pictures has played an essential role in rendering them both omnipresent and omnipotent.

Only the cult can allow for countless images continually exhibited everywhere, and only exhibition can create such an image of the cult, and thus the cycle continues. That is to say, the modern cult relies on the principle of the reproduction of infinite patterns of visual ornament, drawing from Siegfried Kracauer's term (1995), which I expand on shortly. This should also remind us of a similar point in chapter 3 wherein I argued that the theological principle of the omnipresence of God has been transformed to the state, which tends to make its continual disciplinary presence part of every citizen's consciousness.

Ultimately, this emphasis on exhibition and the visual experience in modernity seems to have become the crucial condition for our notion of what is real. What is seen more is more real. Thus, if something is seen infinitely, it will gain infinite cultic power, a power that is not only real, but also capable of reshaping reality. It seems this has been one of the major shifts not just in our mode of perception, but also to the very basis of metaphysics. It was not until the Enlightenment that the demand for empirical proof emerged so profoundly, namely in response to the question of God's existence. The Enlightenment not only taught us that God is not real because he cannot be seen, but also that whatever is seen more is consequently more real. Accordingly, the infinitely visible has obtained the status of the absolute in modern consciousness. The Enlightenment did not abolish the idea of God; rather, it reversed the terms of such a being's existence, rendering the idea of God as a material being with spiritual influence, as opposed to the pre-Enlightenment God whose existence was spiritually grounded with an extended influence into the material world. When God fell from the spiritual into the material realm, creating god/s became a matter of visual industry.

Perhaps the best illustration of this rapid modernization of God can be found in a major Islamic paradox that, when interpreted within this framework, further illuminates my thesis. My argument is that the principle of infinite exhibition as the basis of constructing the image of the most powerful cult (God) is the modern equivalent of the lasting Islamic opposition to the depiction of religious figures (also known as aniconism).[6] What this means is that those Muslims who adhere to aniconism (most commonly Sunnis) are in essence wedged between their pre-Enlightenment concept of God (devoid of figural depictions) and the modern principle of more-visible-more-real. On the one hand, they have embraced modernity insofar as their lives are influenced by modern technology (such as the digital means of mass communication and reproduction); yet, on the other hand, nonvisibility remains the defining characteristic of their conception of God (which often represents the apex of their belief system). Islamists, thus, are in a war against their modern mode of perception. While they attribute divinity to an entity that has never and will never be seen, they have also internalized the principle that the most visible is inherently the most real. In the midst of this devastating contradiction between perception and belief, between the internalized principle of visibility and obeying the pre-Enlightenment metaphysical paradigm, they are torn apart. In other words, their crisis is the outcome of a fundamental inconsistency between epistemology and metaphysics. This churning conflict explains the apparent ease of provoking Islamists by using their epistemology to target their metaphysics, as demonstrated by a poorly produced video trailer on YouTube and coinciding magazine caricatures of Muhammad.[7] Ironically, each time, it seems it is extremist Islamists who initially disseminate the visual media piece to the masses, which then aggravates the existing epistemological-metaphysical crisis. These Islamists seem to have internalized the principle of visibility to the degree that they fail to understand that they can choose not to view the material in question. Instead, they struggle to prevent any visual media that insult the Islamic belief from being produced the world over. This campaign varies in scope from death threats to demands for international legislation that would criminalize any activity involving the (re)production of media pieces they consider insulting. If anything, this reaction (clearly demonstrating the vulnerability of God) speaks to the impending death of the invisible God and the unstoppable dominance of the paradigm of visibility as the main principle of cult industry.

Before returning to my critique of Benjamin's article, it is worth pausing again on Adorno's relevant thoughts on religion and art in modernism. In his "Theses Upon Art and Religion Today" (first published in English in 1945), Adorno writes:

> Any attempts to add spiritual meaning and thus greater objective validity to art by the reintroduction of religious content, for artistic treatment, are futile. Thus religion if treated in modern poetry and with the unavoidable means of modern poetical technique assumes an aspect of the "ornamental," of the decorative. It becomes a metaphorical circumscription for mundane, mostly psychological experiences of the individual. Religious symbolism deteriorates into an unctuous expression of a substance which is actually of this world. . . . And I must refer to the best-seller kind of religious novel of which we had some unpleasant examples during the last few years. This kind of literature has done away with any pretension to the ultimate validity of its religious theses. It glorifies religion because it would be so nice if one could believe again. Religion is on sale, as it were. It is cheaply marketed in order to provide one more so-called irrational stimulus among many others by which the members of a calculating society are calculatingly made to forget the calculation under which they suffer. This consumer's art is movie religion even before that industry takes hold of it. Against this sort of thing, art can keep faith to its true affinity with religion, the relationship with truth, only by an almost ascetic abstinence from any religious claim or any

touching upon religious subject matter. Religious art today is
nothing but blasphemy. (Adorno 1992, 293–94)

Religious art then proves the death of the monotheistic God precisely
through its appeal to means that are anything but spiritual to defend a
divinity that is supposed to be anything but material. Islamists, whose
religion is threatened by anything from a poorly directed and produced
YouTube video to a work of literature such as Salman Rushdie's *The
Satanic Verses* (1988), desperately appeal to the same means (the digital
reproduction of visual media and literature) to maintain their idea of
divinity. Thus, Adorno's insight shows not only the vulgarization of art
under the culture industry, but also the tasteless reification of religion
at its purest. His statement "This consumer's art is movie religion even
before that industry takes hold of it" is so accurate today that it is hardly
necessary to refer to incidents such as those that have resulted from otherwise valueless pieces of visual media, such as *Innocent Muslims* (2012).
The heavy reliance on imagery in political Islam is just the other side
of the same coin. Take, for example, how paradise is often depicted in
Islamist religious discourse as a Disneyland of sorts.[8] Hence, notwithstanding Benjamin's thesis in The-Work-of-Art article, religion and auraless
works of art are not the two extremes of the spectrum of mass culture;
rather, they feed into each other within the all-encompassing system of
the culture industry.

    This brings us back to Benjamin's new and troubling assertion in
The-Work-of-Art article that the politicization of art has inherently
revolutionary potentialities. As I mentioned briefly in the first section
of part 2, Benjamin's position ignores the fact that the politicization of
art opens the door not only to progressive functions of art, but also to
hegemonic purposes, as evident in the historical fascist regimes in Italy
and Germany and other forms of totalitarianism. Although Benjamin
did not live long enough to see how both photography and film, precisely through their power of exhibition, became the very engine of cult
value,[9] he did witness fascism's use of technologically reproduced images
to construct the cult leader. In fact, in the epilogue of The-Work-of-Art
article he draws very close to discovering this dialectical relationship
between cult value and exhibition value: "*The logical outcome of fascism
is an aestheticizing of political life.* The violation of the masses, whom fascism, with its *Führer* cult, forces to their knees, has its counterpart in the
violation of an apparatus which is pressed into serving the production

of ritual values" (Benjamin 2006g, 269; italics in original). Ultimately, by taking advantage of the more-visible-as-more-real phenomenon and forcing the revisualization of its idols, fascism was able to position itself above all other realities. Mechanical reproduction became the ideal method for creating endlessly repeated visual patterns that in turn led to manipulating realities and realities of manipulation. This is more compatible with Adorno, who thought the destruction of aura amounts to the destruction of art itself (1992, 296). This position, however, should not be mistaken as a defense of tradition. On the contrary, Adorno's position is unequivocally more progressive than Benjamin's. For example, in "Valéry's Deviations," Adorno writes:

> The dominance of the mechanical mass media often keeps even Valéry from asking whether advances in the rational domination of nature are not perverted to ideology when they distill magic in the form of art. Valéry too pays tribute to an age in which the positivist "given"—and his meditations show more than just a trace of the cult of that "given"—converges effortlessly with the enchantment of the world. The superior power of the status quo becomes a magical aura for the world. (Adorno 1991, 155)[10]

Hence, Adorno, in contrast with Benjamin, was adamant that the destruction of aura and the loss of the uniqueness of works of art are not only nonrevolutionary, but actually pave the way for the aestheticization of the existing order and the nullification of serious art's ability to falsify reality. Adorno's critical view situates the destruction of aura in its actual historical context, which is a context determined by capitalist modes of production embodied in the culture industry. Siegfried Kracauer, another major figure in the Frankfurt School, and a friend to both Benjamin and Adorno, introduced the idea of "the mass ornament" to argue, along Adorno's lines of criticism, that the capitalist mode of production abolishes "the natural organisms that it regards either as means or as resistance" (Kracauer 1995, 78). Essentially, Kracauer wanted to draw attention to the capitalist totality's reliance on "ornament," or a structure that resembles patterns of instrumentally organized bodies composed of deindividualized individuals whose sole function is to sustain the system without being aware of their role in doing so (1995, 78–79). Adorno, for his part, critically theorized the "calculative manipulation" (Adorno

1992, 296), that is, the industry behind mass culture, and within that theory he was able to provide a more inclusive and historical reading of the technological reproduction of artworks. Benjamin's account, on the other hand, lacks precisely that broader historical perspective capable of dialectically grounding the phenomenon of the destruction of aura, which he had so astutely problematized. I conclude with another look at auralessness from the point of view of the theory of the culture industry, and then renavigate.

Fetish vs. Aura

First, to review, the auralessness of mechanically reproduced objects amounts to the elimination of the space of individual-auratic experience by overcoming the appearance of distance necessary for any form of sublime experience. Auraless objects, by infecting the spaces they invade with sameness, impose the flatness necessary for totalitarianism to flourish. Thus, the destruction of aura eliminates auratic space only to replace it with a space of alienation presided over by the cult of power, which is installed in the form of the inspecting eye both literally (per Foucault) and ideologically (through the culture industry). Adorno, in his "Culture Industry Reconsidered," states, "Adopting Benjamin's designation of the traditional work of art by the concept of aura, the presence of that which is not present, the culture industry is defined by the fact that it does not strictly counterpose another principle to that of aura, but rather by the fact that it conserves the decaying aura as a foggy mist. By this means the culture industry betrays its own ideological abuses" (2006a, 101–2). In the same article, he writes, "Although the culture industry undeniably speculates on the conscious and unconscious state of the millions towards which it is directed, the masses are not primary, but secondary, they are an object of calculation; an appendage of the machinery" (2006a, 99). Therefore, to Adorno, the destruction of aura is again not only nonrevolutionary, but is indeed strongly linked to the eradication of even possibilities of resistance (to which the auratic distance of serious art is vital).

Works of art in the culture industry become mere cultural commodities that are so completely immersed in the system of exchange that their use value becomes indistinguishable from their exchange value. At the same time, because they are thus useless goods, they function as carriers for advertisement, that is, to sell other commodities (Horkheimer and Adorno 2002, 131). The bonus for tuning in to a TV channel or a radio station is, for example, viewing a movie or listening to a symphony, which masks the fact that the main media piece is not the movie or the symphony, but the advertisements that are interspersed within or in between the cultural goods. Eventually, the citizen is then no longer a recipient of artworks, but a consumer. Reshaping individuals as mere consumers by feeding them cultural commodities according to the scheme of the culture industry is arguably more effectively ideological than airing the fascist leader's speeches every day. The culture industry is, after all, an advanced method for ideological indoctrination. As such, the more opaque it becomes, the more efficiently it functions. The more remote it is from direct political slogans, the more political it becomes insofar as it is a tool for ideological diffusion and hegemony, a tool that strives for masses whose engagement in politics is essentially passive in leaving politics for politicians,[11] by blindly sustaining the existing order through extremely neutralized everyday collective behavior.[12] Even, or rather especially, when the cultural good is presented merely as a means of entertainment, the production of mass mentality that is essential for sustaining the dominant modes of production is the ultimate goal. In this regard, Adorno states, "Thus unfreedom is gradually annexing 'free time,' and the majority of unfree people are as unaware of this process as they are of the unfreedom itself" (2006b, 188).[13] The culture industry in its commodification of art and manipulation of mass mentality functions as an ideological tool to maintain monopoly capitalism.

The commodity character and the alienation inherent in it—as a fetish (Horkheimer and Adorno 2002, 128)—should not be mistaken for auratic appearance of distance (Witkin 2003, 54). As Robert Witkin states, "The concept of 'fetish' and that of 'aura' share in common the fact that both reflect (albeit in different ways) a disjunction and distance between subject and object. Both appear in quasi-magical guise and both demand from the subject an act of 'submission'" (2003, 54). Benjamin makes the obvious mistake of equating these two distinctly different forms of distance. Whereas auratic distance enriches individual experience and is empowering, the distance inflicted by the fetish is alienating and disempowering. In other words, the auratic distance is aesthetic and thus contemplative (Adorno associates it with serious art, and Benjamin in his other works associates it with art, natural space, and objects as well), while the distance between the fetish and the subject is objectifying and anticontemplative. Auratic distance captivates our gaze and the auratic object returns our gaze, which means the object will enter into a transformative subjective process;[14] on the contrary, the fetish dehumanizes the subject, and the distance it creates between the object and the subject tends to reify the subject. Therefore, the culture industry, precisely because of its destruction of aura and its creation of fetish-consciousness, forestalls possibilities of resistance and plays the role of the soft monopolizer to sustain the system of oppression. It continually reifies the consumer-subjects, deindividualizing their consciousness, and turning them into calculable, predictable, and governable entities.[15]

The culture industry is, in fact, "infecting everything with sameness" (Horkheimer and Adorno 2002, 94). Horkheimer and Adorno make the key point when they state, "The relentless unity of the culture industry bears witness to the emergent unity of politics" (2002, 96). The auralessness of cultural entities in the culture industry targets everyone as a passive consumer, whose desire for "uniqueness" would accordingly be fulfilled through the commodification of everything and, thus, the creation of the illusion of the reachability of everything through the principle of exchange. In the culture industry, under monopoly capitalism, "something is provided for everyone so that no one can escape; differences are hammered home and propagated" (Horkheimer and Adorno 2002, 97). Then, Horkheimer and Adorno add, "[t]he hierarchy of serial qualities purveyed to the public serves only to quantify it more completely" (2002, 97). The function of the culture industry, including its intolerance of uniqueness, difference, and autonomy, is inherently totalitarian. Horkheimer and Adorno sum up all these themes: "The universal repetition of the term denoting such measures makes the measures, too, familiar, just as, at the time of the free market, the brand name on everyone's lips increased sales. The blind and rapidly spreading repetition of designated words links advertising to the totalitarian slogan" (2002, 134–35).

To close with a final note on Benjamin, the move from auratic space to totalitarian space can be seen in The-Work-of-Art article. First Benjamin defines aura in terms of the special spatiotemporal weave that envelops a distant range of mountains or overhanging tree branches (Benjamin 2006g, 255). Then, by the end of the article, he moves to the technological society, writing that "in gas warfare it [society] has found a new means of abolishing the aura" (Benjamin 2006g, 270).[16] Except for his unjustified optimism about the progressive potentiality of photography and cinema as revolutionary tools of democratization (the demystification of art) and his simple dichotomy of cult-exhibition values, everything else he writes about aura and its destruction is consistent with the critical position Adorno takes toward mass culture under monopoly capitalism. In conclusion, everything has aura (Benjamin 2005a, 328; 2005b, 519; Jennings, Eiland, and Smith 2005, 827), but aura is essentially spatial (Benjamin 2006g, 255; van Reijen 2001, 36; Sherratt 1998, 27). Thus, its destruction inevitably has spatial consequences, which are in turn politically situated.

Renavigation

Once more, mechanically reproduced images are a main means for the production of totalitarian space in their rendering of the space they invade auraless. I started the journey by providing a critical account of totalitarianism with special focus on the thinkers of the Frankfurt School's helpful insights, including the theory of the culture industry. In the second chapter, I moved to the second main concept in the project's title, the production of space, which entailed providing a critical reading of Lefebvre's theory of space. Next, in the third chapter, I explained spatial technologies of power, which lent more specificity to the idea of the production of space, especially in the political sense of "totalitarian" space. In the fourth chapter, I problematized the concept of aura through my critical study of most of Benjamin's mentions of aura throughout his entire body of work. In this chapter, I have discussed the problem of the decay of aura in relation to mechanically reproduced works of art, with crucial references to Adorno's relevant criticism of some aspects of the culture industry, which is the main perpetrator of the destruction of aura. To make my main argument more concrete, I expand on a clear and distinct example of the culture industry and explain its spatial implications in a specific case of totalitarianism to show how totalitarian space is produced through the destruction of aura. Thus, in the next chapter, I show that mechanically reproduced images of the cult leader can produce and maintain totalitarian space precisely through the destruction of aura. We will see how, by infecting every place with sameness, the auraless images also become anti-aura, destroying the aura of any space they come in contact with, and thus producing a single flat space for the total exercise of power.

6

Images and the Production
of Totalitarian Space

The October revolution gave a magnificent impetus to all types of
Soviet art. The bureaucratic reaction, on the contrary, has stifled
artistic creation with a totalitarian hand. Nothing surprising here!
Art is basically a function of the nerves and demands complete
sincerity. Even the art of the court of absolute monarchies was
based on idealization but not on falsification. The official art of
the Soviet Union—and there is no other over there—resembles
totalitarian justice, that is to say, it is based on lies and deceit.
The goal of justice, as of art, is to exalt the "leader," to fabricate
an heroic myth. Human history has never seen anything to equal
this in scope and impudence

—Trotsky 1992, 106

In the first chapter I argued that crucial to totalitarianism is the totalitarian
world of the culture industry that, through its standardization, repetition,
predictability, and liquidation of individuality, prepares for mass mentality.
I explained that another equally important condition for totalitarianism is
instrumental rationality that allows social engineering and the reorganizing
of social relations on calculative bases. In turn, the culture industry and
instrumental rationality are at the heart of the ideological apparatuses
that impel the creation of the one-dimensional consciousness necessary
for mass society, which is subsequently the ideal social environment for
totalitarianism. The specific aspect of the culture industry that I want
to look at here is reproducibility in the form of the mass production of
images in relation to the production of totalitarian space.

Mechanically reproduced images, as auraless and anti-aura objects, produce and sustain the flattened space of totalitarianism. Under most classical totalitarian regimes, no public space is spared from the mechanically reproduced images of the leader or the leading party's symbols precisely to create a totalitarian space. That is not to say that only such images and symbols would produce totalitarian space, but the image of the totalitarian leader is a clear example of the immediate use of images and symbols in the production of totalitarian space. A dictatorial use of mechanically reproduced images is just a clear example of a mechanism that openly aims at the production of totalitarian space in the most nominal sense.

Mechanically reproduced images produce and reproduce totalitarian space by the systematic elimination of spatial aura. Corresponding to the multidimensionality of space, the destructive process is also active on more than one dimension. In what follows, I outline four *intertwined* ways in which mechanically reproduced images produce totalitarian space:

1. mechanically reproduced images as means of the creation of hyperreality;

2. mechanically reproduced images as means of panopticism;

3. mechanically reproduced images as means of producing and maintaining the omnipresent cult;

4. mechanically reproduced images as repetitive patterns simulating spatial sameness.

Before explaining each point separately, it is crucially important to note that they are in many ways inseparable. First of all, the fourth function is a vital condition for each of the other three. Moreover, the argument of the second point could not be sound without first taking into consideration the first point. Similarly, the third function is strongly dependent on the first and the second functions, as well as the fourth. In other words, the role of the mechanically reproduced images as anti-auratic loci, and thus producers of totalitarian space, is composed simultaneously of these four functions. After all, spatial aura is not a simple aspect of space: as I explained in detail in chapters 4 and 5, it is the uniqueness of space (already next to impossible to define by virtue of being unique to each particular space). It is the appearance of distance;

the presence of absence; the provoker of nostalgic longing for appropriated space based on natural human needs such as home, as the shelter for one's thoughts; and the poetic capacity to captivate the subject's gaze and return it aesthetically—all at the same time. Now, in terms of totalitarian space, prior to asking oneself what is missing, one would/should already sense that something crucial to the authentic experience of space is lost. If that missing spatial aspect is aura, as I argue, then it is essential to think of aura in all its complexity, or, more aptly, impossibility, before attempting to categorize or even define aura (at least in any positivistic fashion). Spatial aura is ultimately subject to one's own experience of space, and as such it is impossible to present a universal list of its characteristics. What we can do, however, is designate spaces in which aura is destroyed, as in totalitarian space. Because images are agents of auratic destruction in totalitarian space, they must be systematically active on more than one level to accomplish their destructive goal. This is precisely why it is so very important to note that only when all four of the aforementioned points are considered together can we see how they destroy the aura of space and thus produce totalitarian space.

Images as Means of Creating Hyperreality

The power of images does not originate in what they supposedly represent. By the same token, the power of the leader's images is not in their allusion to the person of the leader him- or herself. On the contrary, the power of the leader to a great extent is derived from these images. In essence, the leader created by mass-produced images is not a mortal among mortals, a human being who eats, sleeps, dreams, wishes, falls ill, and so on. He is rather a being who is above the laws of space and time, a being who is everywhere and nowhere, ageless and ever rising. The image is simulation, which is, in Baudrillard's words, "the generation by models of a real without origin or reality: a hyperreal" (2001, 169). Therefore, "the image can no longer imagine the real, because it is the real. It can no longer dream it, since it is its virtual reality" (Baudrillard 2002, 4).

"Simulation," Baudrillard writes, "threatens the difference between 'true' and 'false,' between 'real' and 'imaginary'" (2001, 171). It "transforms the real into hyperreal" (Baudrillard 1983, 50). Hence, the concept of simulation cannot be claimed by metaphysics (truth vs. untruth), ontology (existence vs. nonexistence), or epistemology (object vs. reflection, or essence vs. appearance); rather, simulation is the reproduction of signs reproducing signs indefinitely in a realm that is neither reality nor illusion, but hyperreality.

The resulting "hyperspace" (Baudrillard 2001, 170) can be associated with Lefebvre's representational, or lived, space, which is neither the real nor the imagined, but the dialectical negation of both. Lefebvre's representational space is "space as directly *lived* through its associated images and symbols, and hence the space of 'inhabitants' and 'users'" (Lefebvre 1991, 39; italics in original [2000, 49]). Yet it is also the space of creative forces, such as artists and philosophers who are against the dominant system (Lefebvre 1991, 39). In the case of totalitarian space, however, that force of creativity is targeted by besieging imagination itself, by creating a consciousness of being visible to the absolutism of the system. Thus, totalitarian space tends to liquefy spatial appropriation completely to the advantage of the one-dimensionality of domination, and images function as a means to that end.

The endless patterns of images at some point cease to refer to a mortal named, say, Mussolini, Stalin, Al-Assad, or Kim Jong Il, and that is the whole point; that is, "images become more real than the real" (Baudrillard 1993c, 195). Rather, these names refer to simulacra in a hyperreality stripped of auratic experience. Thus, as long as we think of images in terms of representation, we cannot comprehend the panoptic capacity of these images, for the concept of representation implies that the appearance is not real, or that it is real only insofar as it represents the real/object in the realm of sensory perception (appearance does not have spatiotemporal actuality in itself). With the collapse of the real-imaginary dichotomy, images construct a realm of experience independent of "reality," yet at the same time transforming reality. Then, at some advanced point of the process, images will no longer even carry the trace of reality, or what they have destroyed. Unlike ruins (which have aura by virtue of carrying the trace of absence), images qua simulation are always already reproductions (Baudrillard 1993b, 73), so they bear no resemblance to any entity outside the hyperreality. Baudrillard provides a schema for the process that takes us from representation to simulation. According to Baudrillard, an image functions in four successive stages:

1. It is the reflection of a basic reality.

2. It masks and perverts a basic reality.

3. It masks the *absence* of a basic reality.

4. It bears no relation to any reality whatever: it is its own pure simulacrum. (2001, 173; italics in original)

These stages correspond to the frequency of the repetition of images, which links this point to my fourth and final characterization of images as creators of totalitarian space: images as repetitive patterns. Central to Baudrillard's argument is the premise that mechanical reproducibility is "*that which is always already reproduced*: the hyperreal" (Baudrillard 1993b, 73; italics in original). Hence, in the process of being infinitely proliferated (for whatever hegemonic reasons), the image goes through the above four stages. The more the image is reproduced and spatially distributed, the more it evolves, and the more it functions as simulation. More importantly, this whole process, because of its intrinsic reliance on reproducibility,[1] amounts to the destruction of aura. Thus, the space that is transformed by simulation is auraless.

In their early stages, images of the leader claim an innocent function of direct reflection, and thus are initially nothing but a representation of an existing reality. Hence, a picture of the leader is simply a reference to the physical identity of the leader of the country or movement over which he or she presides. It is in Baudrillard's second stage that these images begin to interfere with the reality of reality, asserting some authority in the construction of reality. Ultimately, this intervention on the part of images then discounts the reality of the previous reality, before the intervention of images. In short, the images of the leader transform reality into the obscured foundation of an emerging reality.

The process, however, cannot continue so long as there are traces of the transformed reality, the absence of which implies the potentiality of its presence. Thus, to eliminate any trace of the original reality, images then mask its absence. Images of the leader are, after a certain point, no longer a reflection of the different phases of the life of an aging human being. Instead, the images portray a being that exists outside the bounds of time and space, not in reality. The leader becomes a divine being always in perfect condition, a figure whose immortal face that never ceases to gaze at our mortal reality is untouched by time, like the picture of Dorian Gray. Thus, the images of the leader do not allow the trapped viewer to trace them back to any specific time and place. In fact, all the faces of the leader and specific places in the images reflect no time or space whatsoever; they go so far as to deny even the absence of a reality based on time and space. The images themselves become the origin of reality (*precession of simulacra*)—another reality, but without any intimation of the murdered reality—rendering the hyperreal space flat with one and only one absolute. Essentially, this invented reality assassinates the original reality in a "*perfect crime*" (Baudrillard 2002). In fact, because reality cannot coexist with another of its kind, the process of inventing the new reality is one and the same with the murder of the original reality.

Once hyperreality has been crystallized, the cycle of images (simulacra) reproducing themselves becomes virtually endless, and thereby the rationality of the hyperreality becomes ever more hegemonic. Under dictatorial totalitarianism, the basic mechanism according to which images reproduce themselves through the human medium is fear. Given the sheer number of images of the leader, there is no need for a law obliging people to hang pictures of their leader. However, there are usually unspoken laws of fear to keep everything in the totalitarian order: to avoid drawing any doubtful attention about one's loyalty to the regime, everyone would "voluntarily" hang pictures of the leader. As Wedeen writes of Al-Assad's Syria, "No one actually demands that iconography be displayed on private property, and failing to do so rarely results in actual punishment, but as one university professor argued, 'People post the signs not because they love him [Hafiz Al-Assad], but because the system is self-enforcing and people are accustomed to it. People have internalized the control'" (1999, 76). And the more images are installed, the more normalized they become, which only means more pictures have to be presented to prove loyalty, leading to increasingly purer simulation and thus a one-dimensional hyper-reality. For instance, if an ordinary citizen hung up a picture of the leader, a member of the ruling party would be compelled to hang up more than one. If a member of the ruling party hung up two pictures, her neighbor would need to hang more than two in order to compensate for her not-being-a-party-member. Therefore, for the majority of those living in this hyperreality, the images only multiply their fear, and this fear, in turn, remultiplies the images constantly as proliferations of the damaged emotions stimulated by a damaging hyper-reality. Images thus become simulation, simulating still more images in the endless madness of reproduction.

As for the spatial implications of this, as Baudrillard writes, "Space is no longer even linear or one-dimensional: *cellular* space, indefinite generation of the same signals, like the tics of a prisoner gone crazy with solitude and repetition. Such is the genetic code: an erased record, unchangeable, of which we are no more than cells-for-reading. All aura of sign, of significance itself is resolved in this determination; all is resolved in the inscription and decodage" (1983, 105; italics in original). The above quote, especially with its indication of cells, prisoners, repetition, and the destruction of aura, can be read perfectly as a description of panopticism, whether Baudrillard meant to imply that or not. The difference is that the panopticism in this sense is not architectural, but rather symbolic, in the sense that Baudrillard uses the word.[2]

Images as Means of Panopticism

In chapter 3, I concluded that central to the production of totalitarian space is the organic role of the gaze of power. The most essential aim of the gaze of power in the panoptic technology is to create a space in which the subject lives and acts under the continual impression of the dominant presence of a disciplinary centralized power. Thus, the function of the Panopticon is not so much punishment as it is prevention, deterring any form of disobedience by locating the subject in a space where she feels she is constantly being watched. Tying this back to mechanically reproduced images at the stage of simulation, images of the leader, in their appropriation of the gaze of power, function perfectly as panoptic centers. With the image of the leader virtually everywhere, installing the gaze of power everywhere, the image functions as a symbolic panopticon and thus creates the spatial and psychological effects of a power center. The image of the leader is a constant reminder that you are not alone anywhere, that all spaces within the country belong to the regime, and that there is no limit to the power of the leader. In other words, the leader's image creates the same paranoia associated with Bentham's Panopticon, wherein self-censorship and a palpable mass effort to project oneself as the leader's loyal subject become the norm.

　　If the most crucial principles of the Panopticon are 1) the psychotechniques of creating the state of consciousness of being under the gaze of power, independent of what goes on inside the power center, and 2) the economic principle (minimal supervisors required to control the greatest number of subjects/inmates), then images of the leader function as perfect Panopticons by 1) activating the function of power at its purest symbolic level, and 2) reducing the number of supervisors to zero and inflating the space of control to include all spaces invaded by the image. Yet an image, or two, or a thousand of them on their own, of course, would not function as a panopticon. For images to function as panopticons, they must ultimately reach the stage of simulation. In other words, the patterns of repetition must be so numerous as to create a hyperreality, which is both sufficient and necessary for simulation. Additionally, even though the panoptic technology of images itself is entirely visual, from its earliest stages the image (as a representation) has to be associated with a power symbol (e.g., the face of the leader, or the eye of state).

Now, in terms of aura as distance,[3] Bentham's Panopticon was designed to overcome distance by subjugating all the cells around the power center to the gaze of power. However, this destruction of distance, this flattening of space through transparency, is still limited to the area within the specific architectural structure of the panoptic institution. As a formula of government, though, it is meant to be generalized all over the society.[4] Images of the leader do precisely that. In other words, instead of structuring all spaces in rings around singular power centers where a veiled gaze of power is positioned, the gaze of power as simulation is installed in all places, and the result is the destruction of all distance, the production of one flattened space, an auraless space. That is totalitarian space. Whereas Bentham's Panopticon, by spatially centralizing the inspecting gaze of power, was meant to be an economic formula efficiently rendering social space transparent for the purposes of control and discipline, the totalitarian leader transforms the panoptic formula by extracting the gaze of power and dispersing it in all places, turning an entire country into a prison (fostering the unlimited exercise of power). From schools, prisons, hospitals, factories, and government buildings to city squares and entrances to city limits, an image of the leader is positioned anywhere the gaze of the citizen may fall. In effect, the auraless images of the leader function as loci for destroying the aura of space as they render all spaces distanceless, exploiting the subjective gaze by the gaze of power, negating the presence of an absent, stimulating an entirely different state of consciousness within a reality constructed around deworlding the individual by entrapping her within a plane of control and total transparency.

Here I pause briefly on George Orwell's dystopian novel *1984*, in which images as all-seeing panopticons are a recurring motif. Orwell writes on the first page, "On each landing, opposite the lift-shaft, the poster with the enormous face gazed from the wall. It was one of those pictures which are so contrived that the eyes follow you about when you move. BIG BROTHER IS WATCHING YOU, the caption beneath it ran" (Orwell 2008, 3).[5] Notably, in the film adaptation directed by Michael Radford (1984), although these images are faithful to the novel's specifications, they appear without the foreboding caption. I would argue that this cinematic alteration speaks precisely to the inherent panoptic gaze of such images, to the fact that the picture of the totalitarian leader always already warns that it is watching the subject. In addition to these images of Big Brother, the novel also describes the telescreen that, besides televising the state propaganda, also functions more significantly as a constant source of potential surveillance. As Orwell describes it:

> There was of course no way of knowing whether you were being watched at any given moment. How often, or on what system, the Thought Police plugged in on any individual wire was guesswork. It was even conceivable that they watched everybody all the time. But at any rate they could plug in your wire whenever they wanted to. You had to live—did live, from habit that became instinct—in the assumption that every sound you made was overheard, and, except in darkness, every movement scrutinised. (Orwell 2008, 4–5)

In the film, another brilliant modification is combining the images of Big Brother with the telescreen, thereby perfectly executing my argument in a very literal way. As such, in the film the only places where Orwell's protagonist, Winston Smith, thinks it is safe to act freely are those where the image of Big Brother/the telescreen is markedly absent. Yet even when Winston rents a room above a secondhand shop to meet his lover, Julia, in apparent privacy, this too turns out to be just another extension of the same totalitarian space. One day as Winston and Julia are standing naked looking out the window of their secret hideaway, they hear a familiar "iron voice" (Orwell 2008, 230) echoing their conversation and turn around to see an old painting (familiar to them) fall off the wall, exposing the dreaded telescreen with the image of Big Brother gazing at them. The voice from the telescreen continues addressing them in a way that makes it clear they are being both watched and heard until they are both arrested a few moments later, naked and powerless, cowering before the gaze of Big Brother. It is then in the Ministry of Love, where thought criminals such as Winston are brought for rehabilitation via thought manipulation, that we learn the gaze of the authorities, in addition to surveilling every corner of public and private space, is even able to penetrate a citizen's dreams.[6] Basically, the images of Big Brother function as perfect panopticons, making all places totally transparent and rendering everything completely visible to the authorities. The ultimate result, as we see in both the novel and the film, is that the masses police themselves every moment to better blend in with the rationality of the totalitarian space.

The images of the leader enforce this exact same message: that he is watching everyone everywhere, at every moment. The gaze of the leader looking down on the subject creates a closeness that is devastating for the aura of the space, a closeness that negates the sense of distance, the perception of which is absolutely crucial for any auratic, and thus authentic, experience of space. The gaze of the leader simply assaults all spaces by depriving them of their capacity to hide us, and so contaminating our solitude and imagination by penetrating the space of our being, our home. As the gaze of power at its purest, the image of the fascist leader directly targets the subject's existential depths by deworlding her most intimate spaces in addition to her social space. Writing about Mussolini's images in public space, Falasca-Zamponi states, "Like God, Mussolini followed ordinary citizens in the fulfillment of their tasks and controlled them" (1997, 87). She also notes, "Mussolini's constant presence in people's everyday life, his supervising gaze that looked over pupils in schools, workers in factories, families at home, even passersby in the street, exercised a continuous authority over Italians" (Falasca-Zamponi 1997, 86). That is precisely the panoptic function of the images of the totalitarian leader: to induce the feeling of being at all times visible to the omnipresent power.

In addition to the vast number of images of the leader, which transform the images to simulation and thereby create a visual experience that overwhelms the possibility of auratic experience, the location of these images is crucial to their panoptic function. The images are often positioned in places that are visually impossible to avoid, enacting the panoptic principle of rendering the center of power overwhelmingly visible to the surveilled subjects. In Turkey, for example, the gaze of Ataturk looks down upon every user of space, in city squares, at the entrances of buildings, on the top of every blackboard in every single classroom, at the center of schoolyards, and in every public office space. This positioning above eye level is undoubtedly also influenced by the cultic function of such images, reinforcing their panoptic quality. Massive billboards and statues of Ataturk are strategically placed in such a way that his subjects must look up to meet his gaze, making them feel small and insignificant in the leader's towering presence. Ataturk's fascination with the use of his own images predated all European fascist leaders except Mussolini, who rose to power during the same years as Ataturk.

By the time Mussolini became the prime minister of Italy in 1922, Ataturk, who became the first president of the Republic of Turkey the following year, had already wiped out the Armenians of Anatolia. In doing so, he essentially introduced the notion of a "final solution" to twentieth-century Europe, and his genocidal campaigns made him an inspiring figure among the emerging fascist movements in Europe, especially in Germany (Ihrig 2014). The 1930s would then see Kemalism imitate Nazi racist sciences to propagate the claim that Turks were the world's superior race (Hanioglu 2011, 162–171). Ataturk also lifted the Islamic ban on statues and spoke of the importance of statues of the nation's heroes, by which he ultimately meant himself. Indeed, by the end of the 1920s, statues of Ataturk began to proliferate throughout Turkey (Hanioglu 2011, 185), and his photos as a commander, diplomat, educator, and national savior of Turks were so widely reproduced that they guaranteed his contextual penetration into all arenas of people's lives. Ataturk set the standard for invading space visually, and his tactics were imitated not only in Europe, but also in the Middle East. Saddam, for example, was notorious for disseminating images of himself, and Iraqi Baathists shrewdly selected images that fashioned Saddam in a particular light depending on the context.[7] In addition to mega-billboards and wall-length images, the leader would also be seen in mini-panopticons, such as on the face of watches, pins, coins, and stamps. These also mirror examples in Orwell's *1984*. The following excerpt, for example, would be equally applicable to the cases of Ataturk's Turkey, Al-Assad's Syria, Saddam's Iraq, Gaddafi's Libya, and the Kim Dynasty's North Korea:

> He took a twenty-five cent piece out of his pocket. There, too, in tiny clear lettering, the same slogans were inscribed, and on the other face of the coin the head of Big Brother. Even from the coin the eyes pursued you. On coins, on stamps, on the covers of books, on banners, on posters and on the wrappings of a cigarette packet—everywhere. Always the eyes

watching you and the voice enveloping you. Asleep or awake, working or eating, indoors or out of doors, in the bath or in bed—no escape. Nothing was your own except the few cubic centimetres inside your skull. (2008, 29)

However, the inside of one's skull is actually the ultimate target of these images, as is the case in Oceania, where Winston's entire cognitive system is eventually altered, and even his emotions are reshaped so that he can only love Big Brother (or at least he can say that he loves Big Brother and act accordingly). As opposed to fostering the possibility of an auratic return of one's gaze, the gaze of power manifested in images of the leader is always there to eliminate every sense of solitude, imposing a sense of total transparency under the eyes of this modern, materialized God, whose existence is above time and space, shaping everyone's life in every possible way.

Mechanically reproduced images provide the perfect means for making the cult of the totalitarian leader not only omnipresent, but also an unreachable subjugating gaze, akin to God watching everyone. While everyone displays pictures of the leader in the hope of warding off the arbitrary punishment of the regime, every new picture of the leader only means an additional gaze of power, which in turn contaminates the space even further in a vicious and infinite cycle. As Balaghi writes, "It was as if Saddam's picture became the political version of the 'evil eye' Arabs traditionally keep in their homes to ward off ill thoughts and deeds" (2006, 117). In other words, a resident of the totalitarian space is caught in the cycle of using pictures of the leader as a means of protection from the threat of the all-powerful leader, but at the same time making the leader ever more omnipresent and thus all-powerful. Totalitarianism in this sense functions as a machine continually repeating the same set of motions and endlessly reproducing sameness. By the same token, totalitarianism functions as a machine systematically destroying aura, and more specifically spatial aura.

Images as Means of Producing
and Maintaining the Omnipresent Cult

Before returning to the relationship between cult and exhibition value discussed in chapter 5, it is worth pausing on Baudrillard's thoughts regarding the idea of God. To Baudrillard, God is reproduced as simulation. As such, the metaphysics of true and false can no longer justifiably argue the existence or nonexistence of God simply because the question of God is categorically independent of such a judgment. God as simulation is a sign that reproduces itself and is exchanged within the realm of signs, endlessly circulating without need for an original reference. This, in fact, further supports an argument I put forth in chapter 5 that, in our age, what is seen more is more real and what is seen infinitely rises above reality itself, which leads us back to the claim that endless patterns of the same image create a godlike cult. After all, a cult is purely simulation; thus, we cannot make a truth claim about a cult so long as it continues to function as a cult. That is to say, because the cult essentially draws its power from hyperreality that is maintained by the reproduction of signs and symbols, the question of existence or nonexistence is not applicable to the cult. Rather, the cult is nothing more than a sign reproducing more signs, and, as such, its essence is its function. If it determines people's acts in a certain way, regardless of those people's "true" beliefs about the cult, then the cult is more real than reality itself.

In his *Simulacra and Simulation*, Baudrillard links images' capacity to murder reality with the death of God. Perhaps, he suggests, iconoclasts were aware images would kill the theological God: "Thus perhaps at stake has always been the murderous capacity of images: murderers of the real; murderers of their own model as the Byzantine icons could murder the divine identity" (Baudrillard 2001, 173). However, "God . . . can be simulated" (Baudrillard 2001, 173) by the same mechanisms that killed the pre-Enlightenment or invisible God, namely by means of infinite visualization, for example, the mechanical reproduction of images. Another way to look at this is that technological reproducibility can be used as a means to simulate an omnipresent power capable of rendering all spaces flat and transparent, a power that recognizes no limit to its oppressive operation: the ideal path to totalitarianism.

The first step toward idolizing leaders is (perhaps corresponding to Baudrillard's first stage in the process of simulation) abnormalizing them, because as long as they are thought of as normal human beings, they cannot be conceived of as omnipresent across space and time. Images are a main means toward this abnormalization. Not only do images of the leader give the impression that the leader is connected to all places (or, in other words, that his or her images convert all places to a single space); they also reduce all places to backdrops of the leader's domain. This image-driven version of the state then presents itself to the public in two opposing, yet linked, ways: the first is transparent and illuminated, while the second is invisible and dark. The first plane represents the leader's generous reward for the people, and the second, the leader's equivalent of God's hell, allows the leader to punish those who do not appreciate his or her kindness. These two worlds exist parallel to each other, with every citizen in danger of slipping into the underworld if s/he is not steadfastly fulfilling her/his responsibilities as a good member of the leader's populace.[8] In fact, this shadowy dimension of totalitarian space, the space for punishing those who are suspected of harboring dissent toward the system, is characteristic of terroristic totalitarianism. The fear of slipping into that other world is intended to make everyone living on the upper surface of totalitarian space grateful and, ultimately, obedient. Thus, just as the leader can select anyone to live or stay in his paradise of rewards, s/he can also doom anyone to the realm of torture (usually for disobeying the leader or expressing some kind of distaste for the leader's creation). In the meantime, the rest of the population must await their day of judgment.

Thus, the leader flattens the country into a single transparent surface where everyone's fate is supremely reliant on her show of love for the eternal leader (mirroring the Islamic doctrine about life in "this" world, in which an individual's obedience to God would determine the mortal's fate in the next world, where hell is in place to both punish and purify sinners). Recalling Orwell's 1984, Winston Smith experiences both layers of the totalitarian space in this same way. First, like any normal citizen of Oceania, he is living in the transparent space where he is continually under the gaze of telescreens, even in his home. Then, as the events of the story develop and he dares to dream of a different space than that of Big Brother, he suddenly finds himself in the underworld where they reshape his mind, releasing him only after "he had won the victory over himself. He loved Big Brother" (Orwell 2008, 311). If the religious doctrine is the product of this same despotic mentality in prehistoric times, the totalitarian state seems to be the embodiment of religious doctrine in modernity: another sign of the Enlightenment failing to overcome mythology and of modernity actualizing the darkest aspects of that mythology.

Along similar lines, the ancient function of art as magic has really only been modernized in totalitarian regimes. There, the leaders' images would have functioned perfectly as a magical icon, to be both feared and revered. Moreover, the reappearances of the same images again and again create a power that is as real as any traditionally established power. In fact, the magical power of an idol that appears in all places at once may even exceed conventional forms of established power because the former, the power of the idol, imposes itself as a continual dimension of mythical traditions.[9]

The appeal of fascism has always been its capacity to provide despondent individuals with a readily accessible sense of idealist glory, which brings a mission-like quality into their otherwise boring lives. To join the glorious mission, they must simply submit to a set of symbolisms requiring no intellectual effort whatsoever. In fact, autonomous thought and reflection are discouraged among the followers of fascist movements. At the heart of this fascist symbolism are the leader, the flag, and the salutation that glue the brotherhood together. Here the fascist leader is the modern replacement for the dead God. He plays the same psychological role: the father figure in the shadow of whom the follower can be a child again, a child without any of the unsettling anxieties that come with making moral choices. The homeland, in turn, becomes as sacred as the family home. It becomes the embodiment of the womb, the mother, the vulnerable female in the chauvinistic male imagination. Everyone who is not a member of this family is therefore perceived as a potential rapist of the helpless mother that is the homeland, and the only way to protect her is to submit to the wisdom and power of the father figure. His images become the assurance of security, and his vigilant gaze is the guardian of the collective honor. By virtue of submitting to this figure, the follower immediately dispels whatever existential anxieties would otherwise result from being free, from being responsible for deliberating every single action and nonaction. The leader's image serves as the gate into the community of brothers and sisters whose present and future are taken care of by the all-knowing and all-powerful father figure. The more powerless the subject, the more strongly she identifies with the powerful.

Motivated by sympathy, some egalitarian philosophers and poets who have a sense of the tragic tend to romanticize the personality of the oppressed to the extent of elevating it to a metaphysical level. Unfortunately, oppression rarely results in anything that is not as disturbing as the oppression itself; the oppressed get caught up in the spell of power for generations. Thus, what is most disturbing in fascism is not the personality of the fascist leader, but the submission of the millions of "ordinary" people to his or her will. The bitter truth we tend to resist is that fascism would have never been possible without mass individuals prone to replacing existential anxiety and the sense of individual responsibility with a cult that they themselves contribute to creating. There is not a single fascist leader who is not narcissistically self-obsessed and preposterously imprudent, yet, thanks to the cultic persona acquired through mechanically reproduced images, the leader's sadistic discourse also acquires a sacred status.

Images as Repetitive Patterns Simulating Spatial Sameness

This point would apply to the production of any mass visual patterns, whether the reproduced is images of a fascist leader, advertisement, or religious symbolism. Early in this chapter and throughout the previous three points, I emphasized the importance of images as patterns of visual repetition as the basis for the anti-auratic function of images on all levels. Moreover, in the previous chapter, mainly by building on Benjamin and Adorno's work, I explained how the sameness induced by reproducibility amounts to the destruction of aura. Recall, for instance, Benjamin's statement "The peeling away of the object's shell, the destruction of the aura, is the signature of a perception whose sense for the sameness of things has grown to the point where even the singular, the unique, is divested of its uniqueness—by means of its reproduction" (Benjamin 2005b, 519). Thus, mechanical reproduction aimed at creating repetitive visual patterns replaces the auratic mode of existence with a mass mode of existence (Benjamin 2006g, 254). Moreover, I have discussed the effectiveness of the culture industry, especially through its ultimate reliance on standardization and repetition, in eliminating aura by enforcing uniformity masked by pseudoindividuality as the dominant norm. Horkheimer and Adorno clearly indicate that repetition is a common principle on which both free-market advertisement and crude totalitarian discourse rely to normalize their universal sameness (2002, 134–35). Lefebvre, too, notes that the repetition of the same visual patterns in different places produces spatial sameness. In Lefebvre's own words, "It is obvious, sad to say, that repetition has everywhere defeated uniqueness, that the artificial and contrived have driven all spontaneity and naturalness from the field" (1991, 75 [2000, 91]). He also adds, "A further important aspect of spaces of this kind is their increasingly pronounced visual character. They are made with the visible in mind: the visibility of people and things, of spaces and of whatever is contained in them. The predominance of visualization . . . serves to conceal repetitiveness" (Lefebvre 1991, 75 [2000, 91]). By replacing "uniqueness" and "spontaneity and naturalness" in the first quote with aura, Lefebvre's statements can also be read to claim that visual patterns produce an auraless space of uniformity.

By reappearing in all places and thus creating a sense of endless repetition, images effectively function as transformers and unifiers of various spaces, thereby assassinating their uniqueness. Precisely by destroying the aura of particular places, these troops of images (mass ornaments) steamroll all the uniqueness of space to force it into the standardized and flat homogeneity required for totalitarianism. In other words, images, when infinitely reproduced and spatially distributed according to the centrality of the cult of power, necessarily affect the production of space in its three dialectical moments: perceived, conceived, and lived, to use Lefebvre again. This is so because they function as oppressive visual patterns swaying our mode of perception (i.e., affecting the perceived space, and thus the entire spatial experience) by producing the sameness sufficient for spatial standardization.

The fatality of the endless visual patterns of mechanically reproduced images is not just the immediate one (the destruction of the uniqueness of space in the present moment of history); at some point, they also begin to assassinate uniqueness qua singularity, even in the form of creative thought and authentic imagination. Once normalized, mechanical reproducibility produces its own rationality, a rationality that is inherently *mechanical*, and as such, capable of continually converting everything into the schema of mechanical reproducibility.[10] This alludes to the historicality of the problem of the destruction of spatial aura through mechanical reproducibility. Tying the historicality and the politicality of space to the question of the destruction of aura is of prime importance in any critical theory of space.

In short, infinitely reproduced images function as a visual network that connects all spaces that are violated by the image together and simultaneously feeds the subject's perception endless repetition, which essentially paralyzes her auratic experience. At the end of this process there will be no aura, no ruins, no trace of a murdered reality, no sense of loss (which is more dangerous than any loss itself), and hence no nostalgic longing triggered by the homeness of space, no appearance of distance between the gaze and an aesthetic return of it. Essentially, it will be a world devoid not only of the topography of space, but also of the poetics of space and spatial intimacy. These endless patterns of simulated, panoptic, and cultic images force space to betray its dwellers by rendering them naked with no corner left to hide in from the deindividuating gaze of power.

The Commodity and the Spectacle

In terms of spatial aura, the mass advertisement of commodities and mass-produced commodities can be just as damaging as images of a totalitarian leader, if not more so. In addition to their function as agents of sameness, the anti-auratic effect of which is discussed above, commodities develop a fetish character incomparably more appealing than the cult of the totalitarian leader. The images of a totalitarian leader work on the principle of inciting fear to guarantee obedience, which is more or less an advanced form of God-industry using modernity's means of the hegemony of vision, as discussed in chapter 5. Essentially, the leader is a father figure who is the source of both terror and mercy, cruelty and authority, life and death, rage and remorse, crime and guilt. The fetishism of commodities, on the other hand, directly correlates to an impulsive desire. Whereas the father is an intruder in the spaces of his suppressed children, including their dreams, the commodity compels consumers to invite it into their social space and fantasy world. The sight of the father remains nightmarish because of the crude power it represents, so the leader's images scare away vision, causing some to turn to nature where the gaze of the leader is not inescapably in their face. The commodity's gaze, on the other hand, is irresistibly seductive. It attracts with the promise of fulfilling desires that are sometimes not even known to the consumer-citizen, for it provides a glimpse of a pleasure that is only one small step away. In fact, in terms of vision, there is no distance between the commodity's nudity and the consumer's lust. The pleasure is already imagined before the commodity is purchased, and the commodity is such a welcome invader that no one would even notice the quiet death of aura.

The space of commodities is a prostituted and prostituting space of hypervisibility, as evidenced by the compulsive obsession with absolute transparency. Light and glass are the two defining elements of commodity-dominated spaces, where we roam absentmindedly wondering which commodity would bring more happiness. This is our everyday behavior in the totalitarian space that is best exemplified by a North American shopping center. Each commodity calls the consumer toward it to be gazed upon, creating desires and ruling the consumer through those desires. There is nothing more central to the creation of social space under capitalism than commodity fetishism. Even art that is intended only to have aesthetic value is often erected as another visual attraction to allure the citizen into the centralized space of commodities. The user of space, who is atomized by the relations of production and the frenzied competition at the heart of those relations, is isolated, but the commodities continue to multiply. In spaces of consumption, the nice manners, shiny floors, bright lights, and glass empires are structured around targeting the individual purely as a consumer. For the user of this space, the only dream she can have must include commodities. The dreams she has belong to commodities insofar as they instigate them.

Under a classical totalitarian regime, a typical user of space knows she is made to feel fear, so she must concentrate on resistance of some sort, be it through mere psychological means or, less often, through political action. In the commodity land, the user of space is promised happiness, so she must wipe out whatever negativity might come in the way of fulfilling that promise. Mental resistance to happiness is the only reason behind her unhappiness, she is constantly told, and so she reminds herself to appreciate the small things. After all, there are only small things anyway in the world of commodities. Happiness itself is small for the average citizen. Big happiness is reserved for those whose smiles, hairstyles, and clothes have the capacity to travel through millions of screens, those who are inseparable from the spectacle. The essence of happiness is associated with commodities, not just in the sense that the commodity is supposed to bring about happiness, but also in the sense that happiness is only attainable within the spectacle of the commodity. As a commodity, the celebrity is inseparable from the placeless spectacle. Her cult value is completely driven by her exhibition value, and therefore the celebrity exhibits everything. Her love life, children, mental health, and body are to be exhibited to the public, who only have small things to appreciate.

In the celebrity's commodification, what is conceived as the ultimate happiness is exhibited to the public in a way that the act of exhibition itself becomes essence. Thus, the ultimate rule becomes that the more you exhibit yourself, the happier you become. Everything must be brought out to the universally transparent space of the exhibition of all for all. Even the most mundane things, such as updates on eating or sleeping habits, are to be announced to all those who might be interested worldwide. The amount of happiness this exhibition yields is dependent on the number of reactions and comments received. Facebook and Instagram have become the ideal spaces for the spectacle wherein feelings can be exhibited at the moment of their emergence. Love and mourning are put on display for all to see, and even God is addressed on social media. In short, the spectacle has created a space large enough for everyone. Often the advertisement is itself the commodity. We see this especially in the case of social media, which has normalized the over-sharing of personal information. Personal pieces of information can be disclosed even before the person is born, as the spectacle's rays reach inside the womb and commodify the embryo. So much is exhibited that those who care about their privacy can only hope to hide in the light, surrounded or buried beneath the mounting information. In Byung-Chul Han's words, "Whenever information is very easy to obtain, as is the case today, the social system switches from trust to control" (2014, 40). Control is made easier than ever because of the enormous amount of information available on everyone. Precisely because a contemporary person lives in deep isolation as a bare individual removed from organic societal and ecological nets, communication has become her obsession, which in turn creates the ideal transparent condition for unlimited control. Communication not only does not cure isolation, but further fragments the subject's world, making her ever more dependent on the spectacle. The spectacle is, after all, the social relations, as Guy Debord argues (1983, §4). When commodities take the center of social relations, communication only intensifies alienation. Just as digital communication renders unlimited control attainable for systems of domination, commodity fetishism results in normalizing submission, as Debord argues (1983, §67), thereby completing the cycle of totalitarianism.

Debord also states, "In societies where modern conditions of production prevail, life is presented as an immense accumulation of spectacles. Everything that was directly lived is now merely represented in the distance" (1983, §1). Fifty years since the publication of Debord's *Society of the Spectacle*, the hegemony of the spectacle has reached a point where representation only makes sense inversely. That is to say, the living subjects represent their exhibited images much more effectively than the images represent them. The reference point has become the spectacle and nothing besides. Beyond the Facebook persona, there is only the creator gazing at the Facebook character. The authenticity of feelings is tested by their presence in the universal exhibition. The spectacle in effect creates a world of its image with no space for anything that is not transparent through and through. Under classical totalitarianism, distance is overcome through fear, but it can still be experienced in principle. The spectacle's world of commodification, in contrast, eliminates the very idea of distance. Indeed, the mass individual loathes distance because it translates to solitude for which she is not equipped. The fetishized commodity allows for one form of spatial experience and that is of the spectacle, which obliterates every sense of distance. Reflection, meditation, recollection, mourning, longing, and nostalgia are the kinds of experiences that entail distance, and in the commodifying world of the spectacle, even if they emerge, they are subjected to penetrating light in the same way that certain skin imperfections are treated with lasers.

Through its totalitarian abstraction of space, capitalism obliterates all the conditions of auratic experience. Debord was acutely aware of the spatial unifying power of capitalist relations of production that ultimately results in the creation of a single extended space, in which individuals have isolation in common (1983, §167). He unambiguously states,

> Capitalist production has unified space, which is no longer bounded by external societies. This unification is at the same time an extensive and intensive process of *banalization*. The accumulation of commodities produced in mass for the abstract space of the market, which had to break down all regional and legal barriers . . . also had to destroy the autonomy and quality of spaces. This power of homogenization is the heavy artillery which brought down all the Chinese walls. (Debord 1983, §165; italics in original)

"Autonomy and quality of space" cannot survive the invasion of commodities that eliminate every trace of aura. This systematic destruction is inherent in the capitalist pursuit of total domination. To again quote Debord: "[D]eveloping logically into absolute domination, capitalism can and must now remake the totality of space into *its own setting*" (1983, §169; italics in original). Capitalism is essentially expansionist, and it continually seeks cheaper labor and raw materials to exploit, so its globalizing tendency is inherent. As such, it eliminates geographical distance within formulas of mechanization and simultaneously alienates people by placing them in its reifying relations. The immediate result of the elimination of distance is the unity of space, which amounts to the impossibility of auratic experience. Capitalist spatial distribution is inseparable from social engineering, which is among the most exemplary applications of instrumental rationality. Thus, capitalist urbanism certainly entails and persistently increases the domination of capitalism, contributing to the production of a capitalist totalitarian space in which aura is the first victim. There is nothing about space that is more fragile than aura. It could disappear with the first noise of the construction machinery long before the cement and glass towers are erected under the sacred rule of profit and in the name of development, investment, and so forth. Aura is the last thing to have market value, so its destruction will always be the first in the production of totalitarian space.

7

In the Absence of Aura

Spatial Dialectics of Despair and Hope

From natural resources to works of art, from land to music, capitalism translates everything to one globalized language, and that language is capital. It is capital alone that determines the worthiness of things, including non-things such as memories, desires, and space. As a result, today's space is neither public nor social. Under the pretexts of security (conducted by the policing institutions of the state and its private partners) and the free market (manipulated by corporations), totalitarian space has been erected on the ruins of public space. This depublicization of space (Sennett 1974; Mitchell 1995) and its negative effects on democracy (Parkinson 2012) have not been perceived as a crisis or a social and political loss because of the death of "the public" itself. The body is no longer political, but just a physical body that unthinkingly follows the rules. Millions of people fill subways and busy streets every day as they move between spaces of production and consumption, but when could a public cause bring together so many individuals?

Even when a collective cause does bring a crowd together to protest the existing order or simply to demonstrate for a political demand, the system immediately responds by rendering the police presence visible. Indeed, police are increasingly on hand to proactively prevent protests, as we saw in the lead-up to the 2015 Climate Change Summit, when the French government banned demonstrations in Paris on the pretext of preventing further terrorist attacks following a series of attacks claimed by the Islamic State. As a result, a climate march that had long been planned for November 29 was canceled. In lieu of the march, would-be demonstrators formed a human chain and left some 20,000 shoes in the Place de la République in "silent protest" (CBC News 2015). With little to report on other than the rows of neatly arranged pairs of shoes, news agencies and social media devoted special attention to shoes representing public figures, such as those of the pope. Precisely by virtue of representing the bodies of would-be protesters, the shoes designated the absence of those bodies. The same human body that worked for more than two centuries to create public space suddenly found itself exiled from the public space by the Republic, highlighting the fact that the body is a political space in itself and one that the state continues to view as a threat.

There was something surrealistic about those 20,000 shoes left under that gloomy November sky. The act simultaneously invoked the absence of demonstration and demonstration of absence. Absence, when made present, forces one to think of the absent, and that which makes absence present has the power to determine the way in which one thinks of the absent. The aura of the demonstrators negatively emanated from those shoes, emphasizing the banality of power. Despite their inability to do much policing as they patrolled thousands of still, empty shoes, riot police stood guard throughout the day and later clashed with about 200 people who defied the ban, some chanting "a state of emergency is a police state" (PBS NewsHour 2015). By making the absence of the public so unmistakably present, the shoes demonstrated the death of the public space in a theatrical but very palpable way. They sculpted out the ruins of the public space, as a space without its users, an empty space guarded against the public. As ruins, the space gained an aura that no state power could destroy. In fact, the irony of the police presence only further emphasized the tragic element of the ruins, in turn making the place only more auratic.

Here it is worth revisiting Van Gogh's famous *Shoes*, which is arguably the most auratic of all his self-portraits in that it defied the traditional way of portraying the self. It is a portrait that invokes the image of the self through its traces. The shoes summon Van Gogh as a living body, a life with a past and a future. In the wrinkles of the shoes, one sees the traces of journeys and the passages of time, forcing one to imagine far more than would be conjured by a face gazing blankly at the viewer. A self-portrait is meant to make present the absence of the portrayed self. An excellent self-portrait, however, is one that makes the painter's absence present merely by portraying traces that refer to the absence of the painter. In other words, painting the traces, as opposed to the body, takes the dialectics of absence a degree higher by making present the absence of presence. By not referring to any part of the subject's body, her absence is made supremely present. Shoes can do this especially well because they hold traces of all the paths the subject has traveled. The older the shoes are, the more complete this coded biography becomes. Thus, Van Gogh's portrait of his shoes tells us more about him than any portrait of his face ever could because his shoes, especially when portrayed, have the negative power that can give rise to aura.

The shoes at the Shoe March transformed the space into a heterotopia comparable to a cemetery. A grave or gravestone is a sign of a represented absence of a person who was once living. In a somewhat similar fashion, every pair of shoes in the Shoe March referred to a person, but to a person whose body was deprived of its last political weapon: to be visible. For bodies in a crowd gathered to protest could still garner some visibility, drawing attention to their dissent, which is the nightmare of all governments, however democratic they claim to be. The rows of empty pairs of shoes all facing in the same direction denoted something about death. However, it was not the death of the absent bodies, but the death of public space as a space for free expression. The Shoe March amounted to an obituary for the public space in, of all places, Paris. In that sense, November 29, 2015, could be seen as the symbolic end of the era of public space and of the body as a political actor.

Auratic Negativity and Space

The indication of ruins can be very significant if perceived by progressive actors capable of reflecting on those ruins and transforming the space. In the case of the Paris Shoe March, regaining aura was accidental, but an accident can often lead to a revelation of an entirely new mode of knowledge. Progressive transformation is an attempt to push the boundaries of the possible, to remap norms, normalcy, and normality in such a way that what is imaginable can be actualized. In miserable times, however, the main problem is the lack of imagination itself. It is imagination itself that must be revolutionized so that a world in which exploitation is not the norm can be conceived as both rational and actualizable.

We must reach the point of imagining auratic life in auratic spaces. For that to happen, the conditions of dullness must be broken, even if only for a short time. The dullness of our imagination, which has far exceeded mere alienation, has paralyzed us for decades. Totalitarianism has flattened geography to the degree that even the corners located outside the zones of panoptic transparency are de-charged of dissent, of a language capable of articulating dissent. Standardization has reached such a point that boredom has become more universal than any ideal progressive movements have ever sought to be, including, or perhaps especially, those premised on equality. Boredom, then, is where we must start. For boredom is not a legitimate or excusable reason to join an army or a gang, but it certainly is a legitimate reason to join a progressive movement, to revolt against a system that has made boredom a norm. Standardization, predictability, and repetition, which characterize both the culture industry and totalitarian space, must be replaced with auratic modes of life. Yet that cannot and will not happen or even be imagined as long as we live in totalitarian space.

In a world in which totalitarianism is not normalized, aura is not abnormal. Aura is the first place's unity of space and time, the spatial poetics, the sweet sorrow of forgetfulness enveloped in nostalgia, the curves of a house that musically corresponds to the curves of the body, the traces of the hands that have grabbed the same teapot or the same door handle for thousands of unique moments in passing lives. Aura is randomness engraved by arbitrary happenings that create a locus of traces unique onto themselves. Because such randomness requires unique individual lives, regaining aura will not simply happen as a by-product of undoing totalitarian space.

Consciousness must be pushed to its limits to rediscover paths that lead to unexperienced modes of living. For to accomplish an auratic, and at the same time egalitarian, world in which everyone can enjoy a meaningful life, we must first imagine its conditions. To imagine those conditions, we need to emancipate ourselves from totalitarian space. In more restrictive words, only if we, dreamers of a free world, stop com-promising about the conditions that reproduce oppression can a move-ment capable of conceiving our auratic dreams and even housing them be possible. We need to wildly free ourselves from the normal limits of imagination or we will continue to orbit in a Hobbesian universe where the war of all against all can only be stopped by a sovereign that sup-presses all by ranking all, stationing all as oppressors of some sort. In terms of philosophy, we need to reread Nietzsche with a Marxian eye. The only power that can re-create aura is human will. Metaphysical claims that deny the absolute human responsibility for the historical conditions in which we all live are but components of a discourse that aims to sustain the existing order.

I

Movements that ideologically orbit within the positive and submissive modes of consciousness are incapable of breaking free from totalitarian space. This feat requires modes of consciousness that are both negative and utopic enough to realize another way of existence that is not based on bureaucratic and hierarchical management. In other words, truly emancipatory movements must recognize that the state inherently strives to reach unlimited control over space, and capitalist states have been especially successful in this production of totalitarian space. Socialist movements that aim to replace the capitalist system with a socialist one implicitly accept the rule of the state, but a fair one. Yet from an anarchist point of view, there is no such thing as a fair or good state, just as from a feminist perspective there can be no fair or good form of patriarchy. It is inconceivable that any state structure would abstain from imposing spatial uniformity in turn alienating and oppressing those it rules.

The state's administration of space through various ideological and police apparatuses inevitably creates anti-auratic conditions throughout the territory of its rule. First and foremost, the state signifies a territorial claim of authority, and as a master institution it parents subsidiaries that ensure its authority over every possible spatial structure and dimension. With the advancement of instrumental rationality, social and spatial engineering became part of the most normalized tasks of state bureaucracy. In fact, all state agencies are in one way or another agencies of spatial production. While the most obvious of these agencies are the executives of the police apparatuses, agencies such as those comprising the culture industry also have a role to play. According to more nuanced readings of state power, all state agencies serve a policing function, acting in various predetermined ways in accordance with the spatial tasks to which they have been assigned. In an advanced totalitarian state, citizens become the carriers of the gaze of power, continually inspecting each other and the deteriorating social space in the name of upholding law, order, civility, culture, and morality.

Too often, philosophy functions as just another safeguard of the totalitarian modes of spatial production, but, at least in principle, it can be emancipatory. The philosophical imagination should be capable of freeing consciousness from the limits of totalitarian space. Of course, the question then becomes what kind of philosophy can achieve this. In a world of falsehood, any form of conformity, no matter how critical in spirit, amounts to falsehood. Thus, in a world managed by oppressive states, any philosophical project that does not aim to negate the existing order contributes to the falsehood. Most often, it does so by further masking the falsehood and rendering it more sophisticated through mental muses that, in the best cases, only further normalize what is there and, in the worst cases, make students of philosophy lose their "common sense" without replacing it with a higher sense. This then results in an absurd form of conformist nihilism and absolute relativism.

By contrast, a philosophy that embraces negativity in terms of rejection rather than denial has the potential to dialectically sublimate itself to the point of imagining a realizable world in which auratic experience is not an exceptional possibility. Because aura is inherently negative, auratic space cannot be constructed through a plan. That said, because totalitarian space necessarily amounts to the destruction of aura, the abolishment of totalitarian space and its institutional production, embodied most clearly in the normal functioning of state institutions, is a necessary condition for regaining a space in which auratic experience is possible. While aura-driven philosophy is hardly possible under the existing order, it is necessary to make a different order of things possible. Accordingly, an aura-driven philosophy must make the conditions of its own existence possible through a critical conception of the totality of instrumental rationality and the conscious negation of it as a political act, thereby redefining the very limits of the possible. The pressing question is, how can that negativity be triggered? A totalitarian space is totalitarian precisely because it has already negated the power of the negative; it has positivized our modes of perception and spatial practices. Although there is no longer a social class intent on changing the ownership of the means of production, perhaps what could happen is the negation of the most symbolic by the least symbolic. This could eventually lead to a grand change in the ownership of the means of material and knowledge production, and thus all relations of production/power.

II

The body of the condemned, as the ultimate site of exploitation, has the potential to negate the existing order from within its most sanctified space. By virtue of carrying the traces of its historical oppression, the body of the condemned retains the codes for undoing the perfect order of the normalized mechanization of domination. The condemned is situated at the bottom of the system, and her spatial rebellion could therefore negate the sacred space that is at the very top of the existing order. This negation of the sacred space could then trigger a dialectical storm that, down the road, might lead to the negation of the other material and mental conditions that sustain the dominant mode of spatial production.

Given that space cannot, in itself, free us and that freedom cannot be realized within an abstract totalitarian space, it only makes sense to finally give back political spatiality to the body and social politicality to space. Buying into the dominant discourses that, consciously or unconsciously, separate the emancipation of social space from the emancipation of the body will only continue to hinder social movements of protest. Any form of philosophy, art, or activism that does not reconcretize these two conceptual dialectics in their negativity will have no choice but to operate within the existing order, making it prone to being positivized and commodified by the culture industry.

As much as it is the primary target and, thus, the main historical site of oppression, the body remains the only space of unlimited possibilities.[1] Unlike any other space, it carries within itself an inextricable will. The body can be and is used, exploited, reshaped, and commodified like other spaces, but it has not been completely colonized. It is precisely the fear of the body as the retainer of the indestructible will to freedom that provokes impulses of rape, torture, stoning, amputation, lynching, flagging, beheading, and so forth. Notably, all of these crimes continue to be committed by highly organized fascist movements and states. Such systems of oppression realize that it is impossible to truly defeat a living human body. The frustrated rage that results from this realization lies at the root of the brutality committed against the bodies of freedom fighters, women, and other oppressed individuals, often even after they have been murdered. As the only locus of freedom, the body has a negative power waiting to be tapped. The more oppressed the body, the more powerful its potential negativity. Every scar on the body of the oppressed is a secret path toward the realization of some lost freedom. Normally, the body of the condemned is confined to spaces relegated to the bottom of the hierarchy of power, meaning that even when the condemned rebels, it often goes unnoticed. However, when this positioning is reversed, the negating impact is immediate and indisputable.

The condemned enters the space of the sacred and renders the source of her own condemnation most visible. This move is revolutionary in two intertwined senses: first, it negates the condemnation by trans-forming it into a source of political force drawing from the visibility of the sacred space, and second, it sends shock waves all the way down to the base of the spatial pyramid of power. It liberates the body by way of confronting the highest manifestation of the establishment, voiding the spell of power through actualizing what the oppressed masses believe to be impossible. As Pussy Riot wrote of its performance of "Virgin Mary, Put Putin Away," they "needed to sing it not on the street in front of the temple, but at the altar—that is, in a place where women are strictly forbidden" (2013, 15). How, one might ask, can condemnation be immediately negated in a single act? The answer lies in the spatial context. Social space is abstracted and segregated in such ways that it is fundamentally totalitarian in its guarantee of the unlimited exercise of power. The only way out of the totalitarianism is to use the body as the locus of spatial freedom to negate the apex of the spatial power pyramid.

Let us call the most symbolic spaces of the concentration of power the sacred, which, materially and symbolically, has extracted all its value from the condemned. Only by occupying the sacred space can the con-demned make her own presence undeniably visible and thereby reclaim the stolen value. By doing so, the body of the condemned, the untouch-able, breaks an essential double-sided spatial rule that has perpetuated the marginalization of the condemned and rendered the sacred powerful. This, of course, will not change the relations of oppression including the dominant relations of spatial production, but it will certainly rupture something heretofore considered unbreakable. Thus, the move has the potential to trigger a change in representational space, which could in turn eventually lead to a change in people's spatial practices. Additionally, it could simultaneously disrupt the dominant modes of perception, giving rise to the beginning of a historical change in power relations.[2] Ideally, to change the modes of the production of space, people would change their spatial practice, which would gradually alter the representational (lived) space. However, such a process would necessarily involve chang-ing the relations of production by the majority, and such a revolutionary majority does not exist in today's world.

Strategically, the idea comes down to using the transparency of the totalitarian space and the hegemony of vision to create a sudden disturbance in the dominant mode of perception. This strategy could be called reverse shock therapy, subverting the techniques of the strate-gists of neoliberalism that have used "shock therapy" to implement an unregulated market to totalize the global domination of capitalism, as Naomi Klein has famously argued (2007). It only makes sense to use reverse shock therapy to denormalize the dominant mode of perception, provoking people to question that which is deemed unquestionable. The power symbolism of every dominant or sacred entity masks its underly-ing fragility. As such, merely breaking the spatial boundaries drawn to segregate the condemned from the sacred is often sufficient to unmask these hidden weaknesses of the established order and instigate a gradual collapse of oppressive hierarchy. Particularly insofar as the ideological hegemony that perpetuates domination essentially relies on indoctrina-tion, reverse shock therapy has the potential power to immediately falsify the internalized worldview. The secret of any ideological hegemony is that it is no longer perceived as an ideology; it is rather ingrained in the modes of perception as truth. Reverse shock therapy can negate the metaphysical status of the dominant truth, leading to the deindoctrination of the ideological regime behind the truth industry, ultimately exposing its falsehood. Normally, changing the modes of production must precede any profound change in the modes of perception. In hopeless times, however, the modes of perception should be disrupted in the hope of instigating the spark needed to prompt a shift in the popular sensibil-ity, which could then usher in more complete material and intellectual emancipation.

III

In principle, it is possible to overcome the cultic distance and occupy the sacred spaces of power in the hope of changing the modes of spa-tial production. It is also possible to undo the totalitarian transparency that is largely a product of the masses' own submission to the tyranny of commodities. What is less certain is whether auratic spaces can ever again be possible. For art alone is not enough to revive aura in every-day life. In fact, the very idea of art, at least in its abstracted, separate form that is the norm in the Western canon and Westernized societies, is already post-auratic. Art, at its finest, is either a protest against the impossibility of living beautifully or a form of mourning a loss of sorts. Only when living becomes impossible does (abstracted) art find come to the fore and open a window to another space that is neither physical nor mental. In other words, art is not an alternative to life but rather an alternative to death. When death is the only logical way out, art may negate the banality of life by creating another space, as opposed to exiting existence as such. From the point of view of the artist, the way the world is, or has become, is a fallacy that can no longer be tolerated. Death is the only answer to an unfixable life, but at that very moment the artist decides to protest, to re-create the world in a space that falls outside the bounds of geography.

Art, in its abstracted from, is historically and metaphysically impossible, so it cannot be a sufficient political answer to anything. For true art to be created, an awareness of the state of being is essential. However, such awareness renders art qua creation, qua action, impossible. In other words, the necessary condition of art is also what makes it impossible. Of course, there are "works of art" out there, but most of them are at best products that have been produced for exhibitional and/or cultic purposes within the dominant modes of production. A false life can be decorated with "works of art," but that often only further normalizes and aestheticizes the existing relations of domination. Fascism was never short of "works of art." In fact, the aesthetics of fascism made it ever more intriguing to the masses. Of course, there is great art, but its existence does not make the act of creating art any less impossible. Great art is born in fleeting moments of absolute negativity/madness in the face of the dominant rationality and the conventions of living in such a world. The fact that great works of art cannot be reproduced speaks to the impossibility of art. Art is a negative idea, not a product. When it occurs and takes a linguistic or material shape, it is an event as opposed to a process of production. The artist does engage in a process of crafting, but that is the artistic labor rather than the essential existential occurrence.

Works of art could, and sometimes do, invoke auratic moments, but even filling an entire city with great works of art would not make life in it auratic. The space of art galleries and museums is usually just as abstract as any other dominated space, even when the exhibited pieces are embodiments of true art. Indeed, the commodification of art would not have been possible in the first place had there not been a fundamental split between life and aura, between living and art. Even if we assume that most so-called works of art are indeed embodiments of art, their proliferation would be a sign of widespread alienation. An auratic life is inherently artistic, so art would be inseparable from the act of living itself, and every article of daily life would be or would become a work of art. Dwelling, as an ontological mode of being, would simultaneously be an auratic state of being. The artistic essence of the house would be inseparable from its function, its usefulness. In a beautiful life, no space would be wasted for articles that only have an aesthetic value, for beauty should be experienced in all things that have a use value as well as things that simply exist, such as mountains, stones, trees, and clouds. And just as an instrument becomes more beautiful as it accumulates the traces left by its users, the natural world attributes more auratic value to the mortal's life by leaving traces on her being.

For an auratic life to be possible, the conditions that separated art from living must be negated. Abstracted art may be able to allude to the loss, to the ruins, but it cannot actively change the world. The same thing applies to space. There can be no beautiful space without beautiful life, just as there can be no free space without free human beings. In an oppressive society, our experience of space is inevitably oppressive. That said, our spatiality need not amount to a passive form of reproduction. With an awareness of the scope of the unfreedom and a will to freedom, we can re-create the conditions of a world in which the question of alternative would not be necessary.

IV

To know what is wrong and reject it, we need not know what is right. Given the most fundamental materialist premise—that thought is directly correlated with the material conditions of life—we cannot perceive the (right) alternative as long as we live under these (wrong) conditions. The necessary alternative that is intrinsic in the idea of revolution is the negation of what is wrong. Is this not the most fundamental premise of progressive movements that have actually proven to be effective in terms of societal progress? Does feminism not struggle for a world in which feminism would not be necessary? We may not know what true equality is like, but we know too well what inequality is like and that it must be stopped. Rejecting inequality is not a matter of bargaining; rather, it is a matter of absolute and unconditional negation.

Although none of the causes of the normalized inequality, oppression, and violence are unavoidable, they may well be unavoidable outcomes of the existing global system. Adorno, in a lecture on May 7, 1963, said:

> We may not know what absolute good is or the absolute norm, we may not even know what man is or the human or humanity—but what the inhuman is we know very well indeed. I would say that the place of moral philosophy today lies more in the concrete denunciation of the inhuman, than in vague and abstract attempts to situate man in his existence. (Qtd. in Freyenhagen 2013, 10)

The absolute negation of the conditions that produce and reproduce inequality, oppression, and violence are the obvious course of action that we should take regardless of whether or not we can establish a perfectly just world. According to Freyenhagen's analysis, Adorno claims that we can only know what is wrong; we are not in the position to know the human potential. Freyenhagen calls this position epistemic negativism. He argues that Adorno was a substantive negativist as well, which amounts to adopting as a starting premise that the world is fundamentally wrong. This position could lead to nihilism, but the fact that Adorno calls for the negation of the existing world intrinsically makes his position revolutionary.

The Frankfurt School's first generation were in the position to experience what can only be called evil in the human project and the tragic failure of the Enlightenment project. Their despair as both philosophers and Europeans was such that not negating domination was not an option. As is always the case with outsiders whose very impossibility of life gives them creative perspectives that would otherwise be impossible, the path to despair was one and the same as the path to revolution. For them, the question was not the possibility of a rational and just alternative, but the impossibility of rationalizing and justifying the existing world. It was not a matter of whether another world is possible, but whether living at all can be possible without negating the existing order.

There is no statement that can express my argument better than Walter Benjamin's assertion that "only for the sake of the hopeless ones have we been given hope" (Qtd. in Arendt 1972). This is what I call the dialectics of hope. The complete absence of hope is precisely what transcends it. Hope is, thus, most meaningful when and where its presence is impossible, because only then can it reshape the world negatively. In hopeless situations, the existing world must be actively rejected for other possibilities to crystalize. Benjamin's statement is premised on the fundamental hopelessness of the world, yet it leaves no space between the perception of absolute despair and living the negative power of hope.

Likewise, there must be no distance between the realization of a reality that is inherently unjust and the act of negating it. Only through such negation can we go beyond nihilism, while not reaching nihilism simply amounts to living in the pre-philosophical stage of human intelligence. Any hesitation to reject absolute injustice marks the beginning of normalizing the infinite reproduction of the conditions of injustice. Falling into the abyss of the normalization of evil begins with accepting the world one is born into as somewhat irreplaceable. When reality negates the horizon of possibilities, a negative revolution is more than simply a way of life; it is the only way to live. There can be no meaningful way of speaking of emancipation if we do not first realize the degree to which and they ways in which we are unfree. Prior to that realization, we will, at best, continue to take paths that end at the wrong place and continue to grow more frustrated. As Adorno states, a "wrong life cannot be lived rightly" (2005, 39). Negation is not a mere method, but rather a way of creating the space for possibilities that are inconceivable otherwise. The alternative will not emerge prior to the negation of the established order that is structured to generate totalitarian reason.

One of the most devastating mistakes of the twentieth-century revolutions was that they were translations of prethought formulas. Moreover, those who theorized the revolutions often were not the same as those who enacted them. The division of labor that was supposed to be negated through the revolution was reproduced by the very act of revolution. To make revolution, we must live it from the first moment. The creation of the revolutionary space on the basis of negating the division of labor is the first step of a progressive revolution. Revolution is not a formula to be discovered theoretically, realized physically, and then left as the new grounds for a new world. Rather, it must be a world lived and thought every day, or it will be destined to fail from day one. When revolution is seen as the concern of a certain time in our history or a certain age of our lives, it will inevitably end up displaced in forgotten diaries, lecture rooms, poetry, or fiction in the best cases.

The necessary condition for negating totalitarian space is not the prior realization of an alternative, but awareness of the totality of the existing order, the scope of the crisis. Once that happens, acting in ways aimed at the negation of totalitarianism becomes an inevitable way of life. Of course, some fundamental principles are imperative in order not to relapse into the reproduction of relations of domination. Those principles are nothing mysterious, but they must be adopted faithfully.

The principles of universal equality and freedom will not become old no matter how many more attempts to realize them fail. We are repeatedly told that they are unrealizable utopic ideals, but often those who accuse revolutionaries of being utopic are the same people who find believing in heaven or some other afterlife to be realistic. Equality and freedom might never be realized, mainly because of the lack of popular belief in the possibility of their realization, but on all accounts, their realization is logically more probable than the existence of an afterlife of any form. Imagine for a minute how much more possible the realization of equality and freedom would be if the hundreds of millions who gather every Friday or Sunday on the basis of religious beliefs gathered for the purpose of realizing their own emancipation in the here and now. However, the assumption that the mass individual would want freedom in the first place is a flawed one. In fact, the mass individual has always been the force that made fascism possible. Because the mass individual was never defeated, fascism has continued to operate in various veins of society.

V

Capitalism, at the same time, has reached a degree of global domination to which no other totalitarian system has ever aspired. The visual techniques now used to idolize commodities have developed immensely since 1935, when Leni Riefenstahl's *Triumph of the Will* was released to idolize Hitler and celebrate Nazi Germany. Every advertisement in today's capitalist world is nothing but an article of the culture industry, which can be called the "Triumph of the Commodity." The target is still the mass individual, but qua a consumer whose role is as crucial for sustaining the capitalist domination as the role of the soldier was in the Nazi project. Just as there is no trace of suffering of the Jews and Gypsies in Riefenstahl's film, today's advertisements show nothing of ecological, social, and political horrors entailed in the capitalist modes of production. Like the neatly packaged meat we see in the grocery store, the suffering involved in the production of commodities is never made visible. The culture industry has used all the available technological means to awe the mass individual and stimulate obsessive desires, making her complaint in the irreversible ecological destruction, promising ultimate happiness in a world drained of all that is not sensual, in the world of the spectacle.

In an age of widespread social isolation and alienation, hedonism becomes the most sought-after form of salvation, which only worsens the situation. The same ideology both fetishizes happiness and pathologizes melancholy, disarming the individual in the face of inevitable phases of sadness, longing, anguish, and grief. Such bouts of melancholy are habitually diagnosed as clinical depression, with formulaic treatment plans to restore patients to a happy state. In fact, except in select societies where a sense of the tragic has survived, such as in Portugal, where *sodade* is still appreciated, wherever capitalism is dominant, the individual is expected to feel continually happy. Rooted in the maximization of the productivity of the labor force, this ideology attempts to mask the fact that unhappiness is a direct result of dull everyday life in totalitarian space. It treats unhappiness as a purely psychological problem that needs to be targeted and fixed on individual bases, as if it is not the most natural reaction to living in the unnatural space that is defined by total domination. Moreover, the culture of happiness is immensely suppressive if for no other reason than the fact that it forces the individual to deny some of her most existential feelings and thoughts, not to mention imposing an implicit submission to the totalitarian norms.

Boredom has similarly been targeted, leading to thriving industries of entertainment. While historically a fertile ground of creativity and even dissent, under capitalism, boredom has been transformed into a major source of capital accumulation. Under the tyranny of positivity, boredom must be obliterated and replaced with the pursuit of happiness within preordained channels, which basically comes down to any experience that can distract the subject from her unbearable lived space. The moment boredom strikes, there are readily available exits to the world of the spectacle through countless screens. Even during the few hours in which a traveler can now traverse entire continents, airlines must keep their passengers entertained. The goal is zero boredom, zero distance. Any opening of distance could prove fatal for the bare individual.

The more unbearable the lived reality becomes, the easier it must be made to escape spatial experience, to take refuge in a virtual or digital space. Religion promises the oppressed just such a space, provided that she accepts her unfreedom in this life. According to the monotheistic religious doctrines, the world is irredeemable, so the only hope is to cling to the promise of a utopic afterlife, a world outside the limits of physics. The price for that freedom from worldly misery, however, is submission to the divine rules, which are always the rules of the oppressors. In capitalist totalitarian space, submission is likewise a necessary condition for joining the happy class. To make it all bearable, various ways of escaping the moment- to-moment experience of the unbearable space is offered. The spectacle is the space to dwell in perpetually, and the commodity is the flying mythical creature one can ride to reach the spectacle. It seems the path to heaven crosses directly through the spaces of production and spaces of consumption.

Even art has made the enjoyment of the mass individual its ultimate goal. In fact, there is nothing left to distinguish works of art from advertisement in everyday life. The worker plugs into a stream of popular music or videos to create a feeling of enjoyment during her dreaded working hours. In order not to think where she is, the worker subjects herself to never-ending articles of mass culture. When she goes home, she then gives herself up to the real entertainment time, whether in the form of binge watching her latest obsession on Netflix or constructing her virtual reality via social media. All along, she is bombarded with advertisements targeted to her tastes and desires, signaling the ultimate triumph of commodities. Every single commodity is presented to her as an absolute necessity for the realization of true happiness, and images of commodities continually flow into her life, conditioning her to believe that happiness is only one purchase away.

In the morning, on the way to work, whether on the bus or in the subway, the worker ensures she is connected to the spectacle, most often through her smartphone. The smartphone is the mobile life-machine essential for overcoming the potential experience of distances that separate spaces of consumption from spaces of labor. It is the irresistible call of the commodity that lures millions of individuals to sell their future labor in exchange for consumption experiences. The frenzy of Black Friday, when millions of people wait long hours in lines to storm the stores to purchase more stuff or crash websites with their online shopping, is an illustrating example of the triumph of commodities. Humans come and go, but the commodity stays as shiny as ever. As long as no time or space is left to experience the mounting misery, as long as the spectacle creates a different sensation, then moments, hours, days, and years can pass without notice. Space too can be used absentmindedly without being experienced. In fact, the goal is not to experience space because space signifies the abyss in its entirety. The totalitarianism of the system comes together in its totality in space, and so everything is done to deny spatial experience.

Subway commuters look the spatial abyss in the face when they travel to their prescribed spaces of production each day. It is a space that does not fit perfectly into the totalitarian division of spaces of production and consumption, representing a journey into a sort of circumscribed underworld, as it were. Time spent commuting is wasted because it is neither devoted to labor nor to recharging the labor force. Despite all the Soviet totalitarian politics, Moscow subways played classical music and the walls were decorated with good works of art. In North American subways, however, dull advertisements intensify the alienating spatial experience. Caught between human gazes incapable of returning one's gaze and the prostituted gaze of the commodity, the individual is thrown into a world of complete objectification. The horror that results is the horror of soberness, when the loose individual, stripped of her existential experiences, is left alone at the edge of the abyss.

The dark mouth of the tunnel through which millions of strangers endlessly pass is one of the most bizarre scenes of life under capitalism, a life that is separated from death by a thin yellow caution line, a space that has escaped the colonization of advertisement. Is it any wonder that subways have become such a common site for suicide? Like a screeching snake connecting two chambers of hell, the train is a massive charging beast that offers a way out. Predictably, the system has responded with posters advertising suicide prevention hotlines and, more recently, by extending mobile networks and pubic broadband to this underground realm. By way of ensuring that the mass individual will no longer be forced to disconnect from the spectacle, the domination of totalitarian space has become even more absolute. The contemporary individual in the land of individuality has become so fragile, so vulnerable, that she can no longer be trusted to live her own life as an autonomous agent. The yellow caution line marks the end of our totalitarian world, and like an open wound between fantasy and reality, it is where the abyss looks back at the alienated pseudo-happy individual.

The individual is too isolated, too dependent on the new opium of the masses, too weak, to be a revolutionary subject. The first step toward emancipation must be to face the misery. Comprehending the scale of the hopelessness alone necessitates a revolution in our philosophical perspectives, and without comprehending the scale of the hopelessness, it is futile to talk about emancipation. Hope can only be born from the womb of the existing hopelessness, but as long as that hopelessness is masked, denied, and suppressed by the tyranny of positivity, there can be no chance for hope to become an emancipatory force of change. Thus far, the dialectics of hope has not been triggered because its first moment, the realization of hopelessness, has not taken place in the popular awareness. The misery and alienation that is the norm in the mass individual's everydayness must be faced as a necessary condition for negating hopelessness and thus triggering the dialectics of hope. By the same token, the contemporary individual must realize that she is an inmate in a totalitarian space sustained by her own passive everyday life. She must put an end to the commodity fetishism, tyranny of positivity, and mythic promise of consumerist happiness, and for this to happen, voicing the negativity of critical theory is imperative.

The new revolutionary is a person who has realized the ultimate hopelessness inherent in the existing order and reached the existential nihilism that follows any such awareness. Negating the hopelessness, which is the second moment in the dialectics of hope, can be triggered by identifying with the silenced victims of systems of oppression, such as the Yezidi women and girls enslaved by the Islamic State. The power of this negation will be dependent on the degree and the depth of our awareness of the hopelessness. In this sense, the revolutionary is a post-nihilist for whom motives, utopias, alternatives, and promises are not needed to make revolution the only way to live. The Frankfurt School critical theorists who escaped Nazism lived revolution in this way, knowing that there is always another way that is neither fetishism of an unfree life nor religious glorification of death. There is always a way to take the side of the hopeless ones without the need for myths, promises, masses, and collective identities. There is no hope and that is sufficient to power a negative revolution led by dialectical realization at every step.

The new revolution, unlike the formulaic revolutions of the twentieth century, cannot be theorized first by some and then carried out by the masses, just as it cannot replace one ruling elite with another. Instead, it must negate the division of labor that assigns theorization to some and action to others. We do not know, and we are not supposed to know, how the emerging world should or could look because we do not live under circumstances that would allow us to imagine a predetermined model. The new horizon should emerge bit by bit with each step of the negation of the existing hopeless order.[3] Human societies have already invented so many forms of oppression that the mere negation of those forms should put us well on our way to the realization of a world that would be fair and just by all conceivable standards. By climbing atop the heap of garbage that has accumulated over the course of civilization, we should begin to see a horizon never before seen.

Notes

Introduction

1. As Hannah Arendt reminds us, in addition to the fact that "the results of men's actions are beyond the actors' control, violence harbors within itself an additional element of arbitrariness" (1970, 4).

Chapter 1

1. This, of course, does not apply to anarchists, who took pride in fighting fascism, particularly in Italy and Spain, but also opposed communists.

2. Regarding the case of liberal compliance with fascism in Italy, Traverso writes, "In the classic homeland of liberalism, Great Britain, Winston Churchill had saluted the victorious struggle of Italian fascism against the 'bestial passions of Leninism' " (2016, 270).

3. See Wolin's discussion of "managed democracy," which he describes as "democracy systematized" (2010, 47; see also chapter 8).

4. As Havel writes, individuals "must live within a lie. They need not accept the lie. It is enough for them to have accepted their life with it and in it" (1990, 31; italics in original).

5. Although we will never know the full extent of the systematic horrors Armenian women and girls endured during the Armenian genocide, works such as Suzanne Khardalian's documentary Grandma's Tattoos (2011) have brought some of those stories to light. The persecution and systematic sexual abuse of women at the hands of the Turkish state also continue against Kurds and other minorities, as documented in Roj Women's report, A Woman's Struggle: Using Gender Lenses to Understand the Plight of Women Human Rights Defenders in Kurdish Regions of Turkey (2012). In Baathist Iraq as well, tens of thousands of women disappeared during the 1988 genocidal campaign against Kurds known as Anfal (Human Rights Watch 1993; Makiya 1993, 151–99).

6. Adorno also states, "Cultural entities typical of the culture industry are no longer also commodities, they are commodities through and through" (2006a, 100; italics in original).

7. That said, all of this could quickly change when today's youth start to become the majority of voters in liberal democracies and if unapologetic figures calling for social justice appear as candidates for the top offices. In the United States specifically, millennials have been found to be the most politically progressive of all generations. However, as Karen Fox warns, millennials "have been successful rule-followers since childhood" (2012, 8), making their day-to-day habits fundamentally at odds with their sense of social responsibility.

8. In the early 1970s, Lefebvre theorized that if not for the struggle led by the proletariat, capitalist abstract space would wipe out all differences. In his *The Production of Space*, to which I return in the next chapter, Lefebvre writes, "Today more than ever, the class struggle is inscribed in space. Indeed, it is that struggle alone which prevents abstract space from taking over the whole planet and papering over all differences" (1991, 55). However, with the death of the proletariat as a revolutionary subject, Lefebvre would likely now conclude that abstract space has taken over the planet, steamrolling all differences.

9. In capitalist market language, the credit one is granted by banks is literary called how much one is worth.

10. "Women take up prostitution for the same reason as they may take up any other livelihood option available to them. Our stories are not fundamentally different from the labourer from Bihar who pulls a rickshaw in Calcutta, or the worker from Calcutta who works part time in a factory in Bombay" (Sex Workers' Manifesto, Calcutta, 1997).

11. On the level of mass culture, this is exactly what Adorno was talking about. Standardization, repetition, and predictability are, for Adorno, the main characteristics of popular music, which is his representative model of mass culture (2006b).

12. Baudrillard's concept of "hyperreality" appears again in the last chapter.

13. "For consumers the use value of art, its essence, is a fetish, and the fetish—the social valuation which they mistake for the merit of works of art—becomes its only use value, the only quality they enjoy. In this way the commodity character of art disintegrates just as it is fully realized. Art becomes a species of commodity, worked up and adapted to industrial production, saleable and exchangeable" (Horkheimer and Adorno 2002, 128).

14. About this, Žižek writes:

Up to a decade or two ago, the system production-nature (man's productive-exploitative relationship with nature and its resources) was perceived as a constant, whereas everybody was busy imagining different forms of the social organization of production and commerce (Fascism or Communism as alternatives to liberal capitalism); today, as Fredric Jameson perspicaciously remarked, nobody seriously considers possible alternatives to capitalism any longer, whereas popular imagination is persecuted by the visions of the forthcoming "breakdown of nature," of the stoppage of all life on earth—it seems easier to imagine the "end of the world" than a far more modest change in the mode of production, as if liberal capitalism is the "real" that will somehow survive even under conditions of a global ecological catastrophe. (Žižek 1994, 1)

Chapter 2

1. Many thought the movement that began in Tunisia would bring an end to despotism in the North Africa and the Middle East, but in the absence of a popular progressive ideology, Islamist forces swiftly rode the wave halting any hope for democracy in most countries of the region. Nonetheless, it is worth revisiting the spatial practices of the initial secular pro-democracy movements in Tunisia and Egypt.

2. We can only speculate, for instance, what would have become of the Tiananmen Square protests of 1989 in China had they had the digital dimension of the Tahrir Square protests of 2011–2012 in Egypt.

3. Diana Boros and Haley Smith (2014) give a critical account of how the movement's goals were deemed utopic by many and were subjected to mockery by segments of the mass media, in large part because of the movement's commodification and the fact that it did not fit into the cognitive limitations of mass culture. I come to Boros and Smith's argument shortly.

4. The limited American support they have managed to secure is grounded on temporary pragmatic tactics tied to the fight against a common enemy, the Islamic State.

5. This claim is expanded in chapter 6.

Chapter 3

1. Stefan Ihrig has demonstrated with detailed historical evidence that Ataturk was the main inspiration of Hitler and the Nazi movement in general (2014).

2. Even some groups that identify themselves in spiritual or religious terms are obsessed with exhibitionism. For instance, collective praying in public, often as a form of political demonstration, is now a common phenomenon.

3. Horkheimer and Adorno (2002, 4).

4. While Bentham, too, wrote of the need for state officials to be transparent and accountable, what Foucault criticizes is transparency based on power-population, as embodied in the Panopticon.

5. In the context of his defense of Rousseau and to facilitate a better understanding of Rousseau's work, Philip J. Kain refers to an important distinction that is made in German philosophy, particularly Hegel, between two forms of morality: 1) Moralität: "individual, rational, and reflective morality . . . based on individual autonomy and personal conviction," and 2) Sittlichkeit: "ethical behavior grounded in natural custom, tradition, and religion . . . based on habit and imitation in accordance with the objective laws and traditions of the community" (1990, 323).

6. Lefebvre writes:

> The relationship between institutions other than the state itself (for instance, university, tax authority, judiciary) and the effectiveness of those institutions has no need of the mediation of the concept of space to achieve self-representation, for the space in which they function is governed by statutes (and regulations for their enforcement) which fall *within* the political space of the state. By contrast the state framework, and the state *as* framework, cannot be conceived of without reference to the *instrumental* space that they make use of. (1991a, 281; italics in original [2000, 324])

7. Lefebvre also states, "We are speaking of a space where centralized power sets itself above other power and eliminates it; where a self-proclaimed 'sovereign' nation pushes aside any other nationality, often crushing it in the process; where a state religion bars all other religions; and where a class in power claims to have suppressed all class differences" (1991a, 281 [2000, 324]).

8. There has been a substantial amount of debate over the scope and significance of panopticism in the context of contemporary surveillance. There are those who believe that panopticism remains extremely relevant to today's regimes of surveillance (Mathiesen 1997, Boyne 2000, Simon 2005, Caluya 2010, Gane 2012), while others argue that it no longer plays a noteworthy role (Bauman 1992, Lyon 1993, Bogard 2006, Smith, Bellier, and Altick 2011). The divide over the applicability of the methods manifest in the Panopticon has widened as technologies have grown more sophisticated. With the proliferation of CCTV, panoptic analyses of technologies of power saw a resurgence, especially in surveillance studies (see, for example, Davis 1990, Fyfe and Bannister 1996, Lyon 1994, Reeve 1998, Norris 2003, and Dobson and Fisher 2007). However, with the rapid advancement of technologies of power in recent years, the bulk of surveillance studies scholars have shifted away from the Foucauldian approach to

understanding the nature of power. Of course, the Panopticon is not a universal model on which all surveillance technologies have been built. However, even Foucault acknowledged that "[i]t would be wrong to say that the principle of visibility governs all technologies of power used since the nineteenth century" (1980, 148). The question, then, is whether panopticism as a formula can explain some important aspects of contemporary surveillance, rather than demanding that it account for all aspects in order to be valuable. As Foucault emphasizes, "[T]he Panopticon must not be understood as a dream building: it is the diagram of a mechanism of power reduced to its ideal form; its functioning, abstracted from any obstacle, resistance or friction . . . it is in fact a figure of political technology that may and must be detached from any specific use" (1995, 205). Although a panoptic analysis is not sufficient to comprehend all the determining principles of surveillance technologies, I argue that it is instrumental in the production of what I call totalitarian space. "The panoptic mechanism," Foucault writes, "is a way of making power relations function in a function, and of making a function function through these power relations" (1995, 204–5).

9. Robert Conquest in his *Reflections on a Ravaged Century* defines a totalitarian regime as a state that "recognize[s] no limits to its authority in any sphere, and in practice extend[s] that authority wherever remotely feasible" (2000, 74). Like Conquest (2000), Michael Curtis (1979) argues that the most defining feature of totalitarian regimes is that the state recognizes no limit to its power.

10. According to a 2012 report, an average Londoner is recorded on more than 300 different surveillance cameras on a normal day (Big Brother Watch 2012, 5).

11. See Greenwald (2014), especially the chapter titled "Collect it all."

12. Deleuze similarly states, "At the same time power individualizes and masses together, that is, constitutes those over whom it exercises power into a body and molds the individuality of each member of that body" (1992, 5).

13. Recall the panoptic principle of maximizing the utility of power.

14. Freud (2008) made a similar argument regarding the nature of dreams, that is, dream as the space of releasing what has been repressed.

15. Foucault does not develop this concept philosophically enough even though this quoted passage, and largely the first two pages of his six-page article, open up great potential avenues for further problematizing the concept. Thus, instead of a textual analysis of the last four pages of the article, I touch on some possible ways of reappropriating the concept of heterotopia with the aid of other thinkers.

16. Another way to go about this is through a Buddhist interpretation. In most Buddhist philosophies, "the self" is merely an illusion, but of course it is a real illusion. That is to say, it exists only insofar as one has not reached the absolute Truth. The moment one reaches the absolute Truth, and thereby leaves

the level of conventional truths, one realizes the truth of her selflessness. This realization is a significant step toward the final state of truthfulness: Nirvana. In Nāgārjuna's words, "Without approaching the absolute truth, *nirvana* cannot be attained" (1970, 146). Now that also means the true enlightenment, that is, discovering that there is only emptiness, entails the end of self-alienation not through completing the self, but through overcoming it in the sense of abolishing it. Accordingly, perhaps for the Buddhist, the equivalent of auratic space, heterotopia, is the space of meditation, where the mind overcomes itself. For more on the two truths, see also Sprung (1973).

17. Two points by Bachelard are worth mentioning here. First, he writes, "The positivity of psychological history and geography cannot serve as a touchstone for determining *the real being* of our childhood, for childhood is certainly greater than reality" (Bachelard 1994, 16; italics in original). He also states, "When we recall the hours we have spent in our corners, we remember above of all silence, the silence of our thoughts. This being the case, why describe the geometry of such indigent solitude?" (Bachelard 1994, 136–37).

18. "Je suis l'espace où je suis" (Arnaud 1950, 127).

19. Foucault never returned to the concept of heterotopia to develop it further beyond his lecture in 1967. However, more than two decades after that lecture, Paul Rabinow interviewed Foucault on the topic of space, and there Foucault sounds less than enthusiastic about his concept of "heterotopia" (1984). He tells a story that took place in 1966, the point of which is to show how unusual it was for a Sarterean to focus on spatiality, as opposed to historically. He says, "I recall having been invited . . . to do a study of space, of something that I called at that time 'heterotopias,'" and he goes on to define "heterotopias" as "those singular spaces to be found in some given social spaces whose functions are different or even the opposite of others" (1984, 252). In fact, that is the only time he mentions the concept throughout the interview. Perhaps Foucault realized that "heterotopia" is too narrow a concept to function as a paradigm in spatial studies. In the article, Foucault lists six principles of heterotopias, but, as Peter Johnson says, the concept "remain[s] briefly sketched and somewhat confusing" (2006, 75). In fact, only the first two pages are philosophically invoking, and I have exhausted those two pages in the above passages, insofar as they are relevant to this project.

Chapter 4

1. See, for instance, Lardreau, "The Difference Between Epileptic Auras and Migrainous Auras in the 19th Century" (2007) for a discussion of the etymology of "aura" and its use in the medical field.

2. Particularly notable in this passage is Marques's use of the word "exhale," which suggests something other than visual about the theosophist account of aura. In fact, in one of his definitions of aura, Benjamin uses the verb breathe (*atmen*): "While at rest on a summer's noon, to trace a range of mountains on the horizon, or a branch that throws its shadow on the observer, until the moment or the hour become part of their appearance—this is what it means to breathe the aura of those mountains, that branch" (Benjamin 2005b, 518–19 [1977, 378]) (This quote by Benjamin is an earlier version (1931) of the same statement I mention in endnote 6. The quote in its later version (as in endnote 6) reappears throughout the rest of this chapter). For more on aura and breathing, see van Reijen, "Breathing the Aura—The Holy, the Sober Breath" (2001). Also, Giorgio Agamben, in a piece on Benjamin's aura, mentions that olfaction is related to the representation of aura more than any other sense (1993, 45).

3. Marques also quotes this definition and closely studied Blavatsky (b. 1831–d. 1891), who arguably is considered the most important figure in theosophy. He even wrote a book on the scientific importance of Blavatsky's *Secret Doctrine* titled *Scientific Corroborations of Theosophy* (1908).

4. One can consider Raphael's last painting, *Transfiguration* (1518–1520), which features a transfigured Christ encircled in light, as such a religious depiction of aura in art.

5. Van Gogh has eight shoe paintings. In a letter dated 1965, Meyer Schapiro asked Heidegger to identify which of Van Gogh's paintings he refers to in "The Origin of the Work of Art." Heidegger, in his response, refers to a painting he had seen at an exhibition in March 1930 in Amsterdam. According to Schapiro's research, the painting is the one known as no. 255, or "Shoes." Schapiro explains that the actual subject of that painting is Van Gogh's own shoes, not a peasant's shoes as Heidegger thought. See Schapiro's *Theory and Philosophy of Art: Style, Artist, and Society* (1994, 136–41).

6. In "Origin of the Work of Art," Heidegger focuses on the historical context or place of the work of art as the crucial foundation of the truth of that work of art (2001, 41). By introducing the idea of "aura," Benjamin conceptualizes the original context or place of works of art (2006g, 253). Later I illustrate more on aura in relation to the original context of works of art, but for now I continue presenting and analyzing Benjamin's various accounts of aura.

7. The spatiality of aura can be seen from Benjamin's earliest works up to his latest. For example, in "Painting, or Signs and Marks" (written in 1917), Benjamin writes: "Marks in space. The realm of the mark also occurs in spatial structures, just as the sign in a certain function of the line can without doubt acquire architectonic (and hence also spatial) significance. Such marks in space are visibly connected with the realm of the mark in general, but we need further investigation in order to say in what way" (Benjamin 2004d, 86). Andrew Benjamin (2009) argues that the "mark" is an early conception of what

later becomes "aura" in Walter Benjamin's writing. As for a late example, in "The Work of Art in the Age of Its Technological Reproducibility" (written 1935–1936), Benjamin writes, "What, then, is the aura? A strange tissue of space and time: the unique apparition of a distance, however near it may be. To follow with the eye—while resting on a summer afternoon—a mountain range on the horizon or a branch that casts its shadow on the beholder is to breathe the aura of those mountains, of that branch" (Benjamin 2006b, 104–5). Commenting on Benjamin's above statement, Willem van Reijen writes, "Only readers of Goethe can probably make sense of this variation on 'closeness in distance' and 'distance in closeness.' The reference to Goethe is but one part of what Benjamin wants us to understand. As in Goethe, the 'phenomenon of a distance' clearly evokes a spatial dimension, but its continuation ('until the moment or the hour becomes part of their appearance') introduces a temporal dimension" (van Reijen 2001, 36).

8. For similar examples from Benjamin's letters, see *The Correspondence of Walter Benjamin 1910–1940* (1994, 22; 173; 358).

9. Or, as Konstantinos Vassiliou puts it, "Aura denotes an affinity, a feeling, and even an existential flow that can be less thought and more possibly *enacted*" (2010, 158; italics in original).

10. Along similar lines, Žižek writes, "Adorno's famous saying, it seems, needs correction: it is not poetry that is impossible after Auschwitz, but rather *prose*. Realistic prose fails, where the poetic evocation of the unbearable atmosphere of a camp succeeds. That is to say, when Adorno declares poetry impossible (or, rather, barbaric) after Auschwitz, this impossibility is an enabling impossibility: poetry is always, by definition, 'about' something that cannot be addressed directly, only alluded to" (Žižek 2008, 4–5; italics in original).

11. Pablo Picasso makes a similar claim in his "Statement to Marius de Zayas" (1923): "We all know that Art is not truth. Art is a lie that makes us realize truth, at least the truth that is given us to understand" (1988, 3).

12. This statement is frequently quoted and discussed in the literature on Benjamin. See, for example, McCole, *Walter Benjamin and the Antinomies of Tradition* (1993, 4); and Goebel, "Introduction: Benjamin's Actuality" (2009, 10–11).

13. I mainly use the third version of this article (2006g). However, I also occasionally refer to the other two versions as well. The second version (2006b) differs slightly from the third one, and so in some places the wording in it is more appropriate for my purposes. Last, the first version is included in *Illuminations*, edited by Hannah Arendt and translated by Harry Zohn (1969), and is the one mostly used in the secondary literature written prior to 2006. The year indicates the version I refer to: 1969 for the first version, 2006b for the second version, and 2006g for the third version.

14. Benjamin hints at the connection between aura and nostalgia in his "Paris Diary." See *Walter Benjamin: Selected Writings, Volume 2, Part 1, 1927–1930* (2005d, 341).

15. Indeed, Benjamin specifically mentions ". . . the aura of the habitual. In memory, childhood, and dream" (Benjamin 1999, 461).

16. Benjamin, in fact, wrote an essay titled "The Storyteller: Observations on the Works of Nikolai Leskov" (originally published in *Orient und Occident*, October 1936). In this essay, Benjamin writes, "The storyteller: he is the man who could let the wick of his life be consumed completely by the gentle flame of his story. This is the basis of the incomparable aura that surrounds the storyteller, in Leskov as in Hauff, in Poe as in Stevenson. The storyteller is the figure in which the righteous man encounters himself" (Benjamin 2006e, 162).

17. These examples of establishing an auratic relationship with a novel and a film are just meant to further clarify the idea of auratic distance in terms of nostalgia.

18. This again reminds us of Heidegger's approach to works of art and especially his interpretation of Van Gogh's "Shoes." To Heidegger, the now-famous painting reveals the truth of the shoes, their being in the world, their equipmentality. As he states, "In the work of art the truth of an entity has set itself to work. 'To set' means here: to bring to a stand. Some particular entity, a pair of peasant shoes, comes in the work to stand in the light of its being. The being of the being comes into the steadiness of its shining" (2001, 35).

19. In *The Arcades Project*, Benjamin also used "trace" in direct opposition to aura: "Trace and aura. The trace is appearance of a nearness, however far removed the thing that left it behind may be. The aura is appearance of a distance, however close the thing that calls it forth. In the trace, we gain possession of the thing; in the aura, it takes possession of us" (Benjamin 1999, 447). However, as Hansen shows, Benjamin's more consistent accounts of aura link it to the continuation of tradition, which implies the notion of trace (2008, 340–41).

20. This view is strongly associated with Kant's account of the beautiful and sublime (Kant 2000). For example, on the beautiful, Kant says, "In order to decide whether or not something is beautiful, we do not relate the representation by means of understanding to the object for cognition, but rather relate it by means of the imagination (perhaps combined with the understanding) to the subject and its feeling of pleasure or displeasure. The judgment of taste is therefore not a cognitive judgment, hence not a logical one, but is rather aesthetic, by which is understood one whose determining ground cannot be other than subjective" (Kant 2000, 5: 204; 89). On the sublime, he says, "That is sublime which even to be able to think of demonstrates a faculty of the mind that surpasses every measure of the senses" (Kant 2000, 5: 250; 134).

21. Adorno writes, "Cultural criticism finds itself faced with the final stage of the dialectic of culture and barbarism. To write poetry after Auschwitz is barbaric. And this corrodes even the knowledge of why it has become impossible to write poetry today" (Adorno 1983, 34). However, it seems Adorno realized how his claim regarding the impossibility of poetry after Auschwitz can be

oversimplified and misunderstood, so later in his *Negative Dialectics* he writes, "Perennial suffering has as much right to expression as a tortured man has to scream; hence it may have been wrong to say that after Auschwitz you could no longer write poems. But it is not wrong to raise the less cultural question whether after Auschwitz you can go on living—especially whether one who escaped by accident, one who by rights should have been killed, may go on living" (Adorno 2007, 362–63).

22. Benjamin sarcastically, and tragically, referred to himself as the "last European." On the subject of Benjamin's potential immigration to America, Arendt wrote, "Nothing drew him to America, where, as he used to say, people would probably find no other use for him than to cart him up and down the country to exhibit him as the 'last European'" (Arendt 1969, 17–18). For more detailed references to Benjamin's own coining of the term, see the Chronology section in *Walter Benjamin: Selected Writings, Volume 4, 1938–1940* (Eiland and Jennings 2006, 441).

23. Arendt, among others, mentions that some of Benjamin's close friends tried to help him to escape Europe, but he was reluctant to do so, to say the least (Arendt 1969, 17–18).

24. Herder's following statement can be read as a description of auratic gaze, "The human being *gazes in wonder* at everything before he *sees*, only arrives at the *clear idea* of the true and the beautiful through *amazement*, only at the first possession of the good through *submission* and *obedience*—and certainly likewise the *human species*" (2002b, 279; italics in original).

25. Regarding the literal meaning of dreams, Benjamin quotes Paul Valéry's words, "the things I look at [in dreams] see me just as much as I see them" (Benjamin 2006c, 339), which essentially defines the mode of perception in dreams as auratic. However, Benjamin does not develop this line of thinking further. Perhaps he just means to provide us with another approximation of what auratic experience is like, especially knowing that in the space of dreams, the play of the imagination is shaped partly by unconsciousness, and the things envisioned are shaped and located within the boundaries of the subject, who in turn is transformed by them according to symbolism that is more or less free from the laws of physics.

26. For more on the importance of naming to Benjamin, see Andrew Benjamin, "Framing Pictures, Transcending Marks: Walter Benjamin's 'Paintings, or Signs and Marks'" (2009).

27. Later, in "The Work of Art in the Age of Its Technological Reproducibility," Benjamin returns to the idea of the absorption of the recipient by the work of art as opposed to auraless, or technologically reproduced works of art, that are readily absorbed by the masses. This is also the basis for his distinction between distraction (by auraless works) and concentration (before an auratic work) (Benjamin 2006g, 268).

28. Benjamin also writes of the essential relationship between distance and the psychology of hope in "On Some Motifs in Baudelaire": ". . . A wish fulfilled is the crowning of experience. In folk symbolism, distance in space can take the place of distance in time; that is why the shooting star, which plunges into infinite space, has become the symbol of a fulfilled wish" (Benjamin 2006c, 331).

29. Here and in every other mention of the word "God," I am referring to the notion of God in the monotheistic religions unless otherwise specified.

30. I have not found any literature on this topic, making the connection I am suggesting between aura as distance and the theological notion of God. However, I think this connection is implicit in monotheistic notions of God. That said, Ryan Stark, in the context of his discussion of "entelechy," writes, "Entelechy is a concept from a world long since displaced and made unfamiliar by modern skepticism. The concept requires as a presupposition the belief that purposeful auras, powers, cosmic signs, angels, and devils populate and cosmos and influence human affairs in the sublunary region, and furthermore are evidenced in the shapes of things" (2001, 324). Then, referring to a passage in Benjamin's "The Work of Art in the Age of Mechanical Reproduction" (from *Illuminations*), Stark adds, "Walter Benjamin suggests that some art is hidden out of view in the nooks of these cathedrals in order to create an aura of aesthetic exclusivity, but Benjamin places too little emphasis upon the entelechial nature of cathedrals (221–23). The hidden art speaks to the *mysterium tremendum et fascinans*, and illustrates by inaccessibility the wisdom that God's ways are mysterious" (2001, 325). Obviously, Stark's argument is different from mine, but his definition of entelechy and criticism of Benjamin show that the ideas of unreachability and distance are crucial to the construction of the notion of God.

31. This should not be mistaken for theologizing aura. On the contrary, it is my attempt to demystify the idea of God (by offering an explanation for its successful construction).

32. As Henry Seidan explains, the theme of longing for the lost home goes back at least to Odysseus and Gilgamesh and continues to run through folk tales, literature, cinema and so on (2009, 197). He even ties the Judeo-Christian notion of paradise to this idea of longing for the *lost* home (2009, 195).

33. In Farrokhzad's poetry, the "window" is a repeating theme that, I think, also refers to the distance that captures the gaze of the poet. In fact, she wrote a poem titled "Window," the opening of which reads:

A window for seeing.
A window for hearing.
A window like a well
that plunges to the heart of the earth
and opens to the vast unceasing love in blue.

A window lavishing the tiny hands of loneliness (. . . .)
One window is enough for me. (Farrokhzad 2007, 97)

In another poem titled "The Gift," she writes:

O kind friend, if you visit my house,
bring me a lamp, cut me a window,
so I can gaze at the swarming alley of the fortunate. (Farrokhzad,
    2007, 57)

34. Both Hansen (2008, 339–40) and Susan Buck-Morss (1991, 194) also mention Benjamin combining the definition of aura as returning the gaze and the appearance of distance specifically in *The Arcades Project*.

35. In *The Arcades Project*, Benjamin says that to Baudelaire the masses, and particularly the crowds in Paris, represent the veil or the distance through which Paris is transformed. He writes, "The masses in Baudelaire. They stretch before the flâneur as a veil: they are the newest drug for the solitary.—Second, they efface all traces of the individual: they are the newest asylum for the reprobate and the postscript.—Finally, within the labyrinth of the city, the masses are the newest and most inscrutable labyrinth. Through them, previously unknown chthonic traits are imprinted on the image of the city" (Benjamin 1999, 446). In the same manuscript, he says, "Baudelaire's genius, which feeds on melancholy, is an allegorical genius. With Baudelaire, Paris becomes for the first time the subject of lyric poetry. This poetry of place is the opposite of all poetry of the soil. The gaze which the allegorical genius turns on the city betrays, instead, a profound alienation. It is the gaze of the flâneur, whose way of life conceals behind a beneficent mirage the anxiety of the future inhabitants of our metropolises. The flâneur seeks refuge in the crowd. The crowd is the veil through which the familiar city is transformed for the flâneur into phantasmagoria" (Benjamin 1999, 21).

36. In "Little History of Photography" (originally published in 1931), Benjamin makes an almost identical statement: "The peeling away of the object's shell, the destruction of the aura, is the signature of a perception whose sense for the sameness of things has grown to the point where even the singular, the unique, is divested of its uniqueness—by means of its reproduction" (Benjamin 2005b, 519).

37. In Benjamin's words (from "The Work of Art in the Age of its Technological Reproducibility"), it is *the desire of the present-day masses to 'get closer' to things spatially and humanly, and their equally passionate concern for overcoming each thing's uniqueness [Überwindung des Einmaligen jeder Gegebenheit] by assimilating it as a reproduction*" (2006g, 255; italics and brackets in original). Also, in "A Little History of Photography," Benjamin states, "Now, to bring things

closer to us, or rather to the masses, is just as passionate an inclination in our day as the overcoming of whatever is unique in every situation by means of its reproduction. Every day the need to possess the object in close-up in the form of a picture, or rather a copy, becomes more imperative" (Benjamin 2005b, 519; italics in original).

38. Jay Bernstein states, "For both Adorno and Benjamin, the destruction of experience is always connected with the destruction of aura . . ." (Bernstein 2001, 111).

Chapter 5

1. Throughout this chapter I use the third version of the article, the English translation of which appears in *Selected Writings, Volume 4, 1938–1940*. Henceforth the title is also abbreviated as The-Work-of-Art-Article.

2. For more on the invention of lithography and a brief account of its historical development, see Griffiths, *Prints and Printmaking: An Introduction to the History and Techniques* (1996, 100–9).

3. Admittedly, as I have mentioned previously, Benjamin originally wrote this passage for "Little History of Photography" in 1931, but its recurrence is significant (Benjamin 2005b, 518–19). In the third version, Benjamin qualifies the definition as that of the aura of natural objects, and it reads, "The concept of aura which was proposed above with reference to historical objects can be usefully illustrated with reference to an aura of natural objects. We define aura of the latter as the unique apparition of a distance, however near it may be . . ." (2006c, 255).

4. Adorno thought the opposite of this is true, that is, that the collectivization of art as it happens in the culture industry is in fact a regression into religious traditions. Thus, his criticism of mechanically reproduced works of art, prominent in the culture industry, shows both the remystification and vulgarization of art (rather than its secularization and democratization). The following passage is representative of Adorno's criticism:

> Today, the obsolescence of individualistic art and its replacement by collectivism are taken for granted. It is this formula which engenders the most passionate attempts to mobilize once again the artistic forms of past religious ages. It is highly characteristic, however, that none of the attempts made in this direction has as its basis a true and concrete reconciliation between subject and object, between individual and collectivity, but that they reach their collective character only at the expense of the individual whose freedom of expression is more or less curtailed. This is closely connected with

totalitarian tendencies in our society which I cannot discuss in these
brief remarks. Conversely, it should be acknowledged, however, that
there is no way back to individualistic art in the traditional sense
either. In its relationship with collectivism and individualism art
today faces a deadlock which we might try to overcome concretely
but which certainly cannot be mastered by any general recipe and
even less by "synthesis," by selecting the middle road. This deadlock
is a faithful expression of the crisis of our present society itself.
(Adorno 1992, 294–95)

5. Hansen uses the expression "Benjamin's betrayal of aura" and discusses
it in relation to Adorno's criticism of Benjamin (2008, 357).

6. It should be noted that aniconism (and iconoclasm—the destruction
of images) is not unique to Islam, nor is it embraced by all Islamic traditions.
In fact, both Judaism and Christianity have a long history of aniconism to
varying degrees based on different interpretations of the Bible and the Torah,
but it endured more prominently in Sunni Islam. Among Shiite Muslims, the
imagistic depiction of God is also religiously forbidden; however, imagery of Ali
(the defining character of Shiite Islam) is extremely popular. In fact, in post-
Saddam Iraq, where the Shiite majority are no longer deprived of their religious
freedom, mechanically reproduced images of Ali are arguably the most popular
of all images. For more on the long and complicated history of aniconism and
iconoclasm, see Assmann and Baumgarten, *Representation in Religion: Studies in
Honour of Moshe Barasch* (2001); Crone, "Islam, Judeo-Christianity and Byzantine
Iconoclasm" (1980); Allen, "Aniconism and Figural Representation in Islamic
Art" (1988); and Gaifman, *Aniconism in Greek Antiquity* (2012).

7. "Innocence of Muslims," as the video has been coined, was uploaded
in its fullest version (13:51 minutes long) onto YouTube as "Muhammad Movie
Trailer" on July 2, 2012 (http://www.youtube.com/watch?v=qmodVun16Q4).
Then, following a week of riots and protests against the video beginning on
September 11, 2012, the French satirical weekly *Charlie Hebdo* also printed a
series of caricatures purportedly mocking Muhummad in its September 19 edition.

8. There are countless examples of modern Islamist discourse that heavily
rely on imagery. In Tamara Albertini's article "Dreams, Visions, and Nightmares
in Islam: From the Prophet Muhammad to the Fundamentalist Mindset," in
addition to her own thesis regarding the role of dreams, one can see various
examples of imagery in Islamist discourse, examples of which are quoted in her
article (2010).

9. Benjamin did not address the cult of movie stars, but he did write,
"Film responds to the shriveling of the aura by artificially building up the 'personality' outside the studio. The cult of the movie star, fostered by the money
of the film industry, preserves that magic of the personality which has long been
no more than the putrid magic of its own commodity character" (2006c, 261).

10. Adorno also writes, "Art, and so-called classical art no less than its more anarchical expressions, always was, and is, a force of protest of the humane against the pressure of domineering institutions, religious and others, no less than it reflects their objective substance. Hence there is reason for the suspicion that wherever the battle cry is raised that art should go back to its religious sources there also prevails the wish that art should exercise a disciplinary, repressive function" (Adorno 1992, 293).

11. There is a repetitive theme in the discourse of officials in the United States pleading Americans to keep spending in times of crisis as an act of patriotism. The following passage by Andrew Bacevich touches on this theme and the passive role the masses are expected to play in politics in one of George W. Bush's speeches:

> From the very outset, the president described the "war on terror" as a vast undertaking of paramount importance. But he simultaneously urged Americans to carry on as if there were no war. "Get *down* to Disney World in Florida," he urged just over two weeks after 9/11. "Take your families and enjoy life, the way we want it to be enjoyed." Bush certainly wanted citizens to support his war—he just wasn't going to require them actually to do anything. The support he sought was not active but passive. It entailed not popular engagement but popular deference. Bush simply wanted citizens (and Congress) to go along without asking too many questions. (2008; italics in original)

12. Adorno, in an article titled "Transparencies on Film," writes:

> That, among its functions, film provides models for collective behaviour is not just an additional imposition of ideology. Such collectivity, rather, inheres in the innermost elements of film. The movements which the film presents are mimetic impulses which, prior to all content and meaning, incite the viewers and listeners to fall into step as if in a parade. In this respect, film resembles music just as, in the early days of radio, music resembled film strips. It would not be incorrect to describe the constitutive subject of film as a "we" in which the aesthetic and sociological aspects of the medium converge. *Anything Goes* was the title of a film from the 1930s with a popular English actress Gracie Fields; this "anything" captures the very substance of film's formal movement, prior to all content. As the eye is carried along, it joins the current of all those who are responding to the same appeal. The indeterminate nature of this collective "anything" (*Es*), however, which is linked to the formal character of film facilitates the ideological misuse of

the medium: the pseudo-revolutionary blurring in which the phrase "things must change" is conveyed by the gesture of banging one's fist on the table. (2006d, 183; italics in original)

13. Adorno argues that under capitalism, free time "is a continuation of the forms of profit-oriented social life" (2006b, 189).

14. Sherrat writes, "Auratic distance consists of the features of indeterminacy and transcendence. Putting this in ordinary language, we could say that auratic distance is a distance of the 'unfathomable.' Now Adorno claims that we cannot simply just ignore that which is 'unfathomable' because it leaves us with a sense of something lacking. He writes: 'the enigmatic quality is a deficiency, a condition of want' (Adorno, 1984, 186). The effect of this, he explains, is that it pulls us—draws us in. It exerts a fascination" (Sherratt 1998, 33).

15. Keith Tester addresses the decay of the aura of individuals in relation to politics. He writes, "During the 20th century then, the individual has come to mean and retain little more than what is present in the here and now. The individual has become disposable. Any semblance of an auratic distance about the individual has been destroyed and, instead, the individual has become identical with her or his body. But that body can also be made and destroyed through specifically contemporary techniques. In other words, even the body has been taken away from the individual and been transformed into something monstrous. All the individual can rely on now is the situation; after all there is nothing else" (1998, 33).

16. Tester notices this point too (1998, 20).

Chapter 6

1. Baudrillard states, "Walter Benjamin, in 'The Work of Art in the Age of Mechanical Reproduction,' was the first to draw out essential implications of the principle of reproduction. He shows that reproduction absorbs the process of production, changes its goals, and alters the status of the product and the producer" (1993b, 55).

2. "The symbolic is neither a concept, an agency, a category, nor a 'structure,' but an act of exchange and *a social relation which puts an end to the real*, which resolves the real, and, at the same time, puts an end to the opposition between the real and the imaginary" (Baudrillard 1993b, 133; italics in original).

3. Baudrillard states, "Because we are no longer capable today of coping with the symbolic mastery of absence, we are immersed in the opposite illusion, the disenchanted illusion of the proliferation of screens and images" (2002, 4). In other words, we conceal the appearance of absence (aura) with images: an illusionary presence. In fact, he adds, "We live in a world where the highest

function of the sign is to make reality disappear and, at the same time, to mask that disappearance. Art today does the same. The media today do the same" (2002, 5). The key phrase here is "to mask that disappearance," which amounts to the same thing: the destruction of aura. I have also explained aura in terms of distance. Without mentioning aura at all, Baudrillard in an interview makes this connection as well, when he claims that television overcomes the distance necessary for the play of the imagination, for returning the gaze: "a certain distance without which there can be no looking, no play of glances, and it is that play that makes things appear or disappear" (1993a, 69).

4. Foucault states, "Panopticism is not a regional mechanics limited to certain institutions; for Bentham, panopticism really is a general political formula that characterizes a type of government" (2008, 67).

5. Orwell's repeated references to the image of Big Brother continue through to the last chapter of the novel, where he again writes, "Winston sat in his usual corner, gazing into an empty glass. Now and again he glanced up at a vast face which eyed him from the opposite wall. BIG BROTHER IS WATCHING YOU, the caption said" (2008, 300).

6. For more on the connection between 1984 and panopticism, see Lyon, *Surveillance Studies: An Overview* (2007); and Lefait, *Surveillance On Screen: Monitoring Contemporary Films and Television Programs* (2012).

7. "Before the war [in 2003] there were giant photographs of Saddam on government buildings carrying bowls of rice (Saddam the Provider), brandishing rocket-propelled grenades (Saddam the Protector), eating bread with poor villagers (Saddam the Man of the People), and surrounded by adoring schoolchildren (Saddam the Father)" (Engel 2011, 8). Also see Balaghi, *Saddam Hussein: A Biography* (2006, 117).

8. In the 1990s in Syria, there were rumors, probably started by the secret police themselves, about underground prisons spanning the areas below many public areas in Damascus, literally under people's feet.

9. In reference to Saddam's construction of his cult of personality, Benjamin Isakhan writes, "This project was much more than the banality of tyrannical imagery that leered and watched as Iraqis went about their days" (2011, 261). Then Isakhan goes on to explain how Saddam used religious and historic symbolism to construct his cult figure. Significantly, in Iraq's totalitarian art, Saddam was analogized with the pre-Islamic King Nebuchadnezzar, who exiled the Jews from Mesopotamia; the Shiite's most important figure, Ali; the Sunni Islamic leader Al-Mansur; and Saladin, the conqueror of Jerusalem who fought against the crusaders (Isakhan 2011, 262–63). Also see Baram, *Culture, History and Ideology in the Formation of Ba'athist Iraq, 1968–89* (1991); Douglas and Malti-Douglas, *Arab Comic Strips: Politics of an Emerging Mass Culture* (1994, 59); Galbraith, *"Truth vs. Beauty"* (2003, 124); and Coughlin, *Saddam: The Secret Life* (2002, 183–84). For a similar discussion on Hafiz Al-Assad's cultivation of his

own cult, see Wedeen, *Ambiguities of Domination: Politics, Rhetoric, and Symbols in Contemporary Syria* (1999).

10. Horkheimer and Adorno write, "The routine translation of everything, even of what has not yet been thought, into the schema of mechanical reproducibility goes beyond the rigor and scope of any true style" (2002, 100).

Chapter 7

1. I am careful not to romanticize the character of the condemned, as has often been done in literature. On the contrary, I am aware that conditions of oppression almost always only produce more oppression and misery, making it difficult to imagine the condemned taking things into their own hands. As is more often the case, they will continue oppressing each other on all levels, from the institution of the family to that of the state. Had true solidarity among the oppressed existed on a substantial level, the state of the world would not have reached such a hopeless point in the first place. The source of agency in this theory is an individual or a group of individuals who somehow escape the total domination and concentrate on the ideal of liberation from the existing spatial economy.

2. Unfortunately, the condemned body's occupation of the sacred is most effective in situations where it is least tolerable, such as in societies that do not recognize bourgeois freedoms. For example, the rebellion of a woman in a sacred space within a conservative society could very well be deadly for her. It follows that this strategy is least effective when it is most tolerable in the dominant system, which speaks to the importance of choosing a space of protest that is the apex of the pyramid of power.

3. As Rudolf Rocker writes of his identification with anarchism, "There is never an end to the future. So it can have no final goal. I am an anarchist not because I believe Anarchism is the final goal, but because I believe there is no such thing as a final goal. Freedom will lead us to continually wider and expanding understanding and to new social forms of life. To think that we have reached the end of our progress is to enchain ourselves in dogmas, and that always leads to tyranny" (1956, 421–22).

References

Adorno, Theodor W. 1983. "Cultural Criticism and Society." In *Prisms*. Translated by Sherry Weber Nicholsen and Samuel Weber, 17–34. Cambridge, MA: MIT Press.

———. 1984. *Aesthetic Theory*. Translated by C. Lenhardt. Edited by Gretel Adorno and Rolf Tiedemann. London: Routledge & Kegan Paul plc.

———. 1991. *Notes to Literature, Volume 1*. Edited by Rolf Tiedemann. Translated by Shierry Weber Nicholsen. New York: Columbia University Press.

———. 1992. *Notes to Literature, Volume 2*. Edited by Rolf Tiedemann. Translated by Shierry Weber Nicholsen. New York: Columbia University Press.

———. 2005. *Minima Moralia: Reflections on a Damaged Life*. Translated by E. F. N. Jephcott. London: Verso.

———. 2006a. "Culture Industry Reconsidered." Originally translated by Anson G. Rabinbach. In *The Culture Industry: Selected Essays on Mass Culture*, edited by Jay M. Bernstein, 98–106. London: Routledge.

———. 2006b. "Free Time." Translated by Gordon Finlayson and Nicholas Walker. In *The Culture Industry: Selected Essays on Mass Culture*, edited by Jay M. Bernstein, 187–97. London: Routledge.

———. 2006c. "On the Fetish Character in Music and the Regression of Listening." Translated by Gordon Finlayson and Nicholas Walker. In *The Culture Industry: Selected Essays on Mass Culture*, edited by Jay M. Bernstein, 187–97. London: Routledge.

———. 2006d. "Transparencies on Film." Originally translated by Thomas Y. Levin. In *The Culture Industry: Selected Essays on Mass Culture*, edited by Jay M. Bernstein, 178–86. London: Routledge.

———. 2007. *Negative Dialectics*. Translated by E. B. Ashton. New York: Continuum.

Adorno, Theodor W., and Walter Benjamin. 1999. *The Complete Correspondence, 1928–1940*. Edited by Henri Lonitz. Translated by Nicholas Walker. Cambridge, MA: Harvard University Press.

Agamben, Giorgio. 1993. *Stanzas: Word and Phantasm in Western Culture.* Translated by Ronald L. Martinez. Minneapolis: University of Minnesota Press.

Albertini, Tamara. 2010. "Dreams, Visions, and Nightmares in Islam: From the Prophet Muhammad to the Fundamentalists Mindset." In *Dreams and Visions: An Interdisciplinary Enquiry,* edited by Nancy van Deusen, 167–82. Leiden, NL: Brill.

Arendt, Hannah, ed. 1969. "Introduction: Walter Benjamin: 1892–1940." In *Illuminations: Essays and Reflections,* by Walter Benjamin. Translated by Harry Zohn, 1–55. New York: Schocken Books.

Arendt, Hannah. 1970. *On Violence.* New York: Harcourt, Brace & World.

———. 1979. *The Origins of Totalitarianism,* new ed. San Diego, CA: Harcourt Brace & Company.

Arnaud, Noël. 1950. *L'état d'ébauche.* Paris: Le Messager Boiteux.

Bacevich, Andrew J. 2008. "He Told Us to Go Shopping. Now the Bill Is Due." *Washington Post.* http://www.washingtonpost.com/wp-dyn/content/article/2008/10/03/AR2008100301977.html.

Bachelard, Gaston. 1994. *The Poetics of Space.* Translated by Maria Jolas. Boston: Beacon Press.

Balaghi, Shiva. 2006. *Saddam Hussein: A Biography.* Westport, CT: Greenwood Press.

Baram, Amatzia. 1991. *Culture, History and Ideology in the Formation of Ba'athist Iraq, 1968–89.* New York: St. Martin's Press.

Barbusse, Henri. 1995. *Hell.* Translated by Robert Baldick. Reprint, New York: Turtle Point Press.

Baudelaire, Charles. 2008. *The Flowers of Evil.* Translated by James McGowan. Oxford: Oxford University Press.

Baudrillard, Jean. 1983. *Simulations.* Translated by Paul Foss, Paul Patton, and Philip Beitchman. New York: Semiotext(e).

———. 1993a. "Is an Image Not Fundamentally Immoral? Interview with Cinéma 84." Translated by Mike Gane and G. Salemohamed. In *Baudrillard Live: Selected Interviews,* edited by Mike Gane, 67–71. New York: Routledge.

———. 1993b. *Symbolic Exchange and Death.* Translated by Ian Hamilton Grant. London: Sage Publications.

———. 1993c. "The Evil Demon of Images and the Precession of Simulacra." In *Postmodernism: A Reader,* edited by Thomas Docherty, 194–99. New York: Columbia University Press.

———. 2001. "Simulacra and Simulations." Translated by Paul Foss, Paul Patton, and Philip Beitchman. In *Jean Baudrillard: Selected Writings,* 2nd ed., revised and expanded, edited by Mark Poster, 169–87. Stanford, CA: Stanford University Press.

———. 2002. *The Perfect Crime.* Translated by Chris Turner. Reprint, London: Verso.

Bauman, Zygmunt. 1992. *Intimations of Postmodernity*. London: Routledge.

Benjamin, Andrew E. 2009. "Framing Pictures, Transcending Marks: Walter Benjamin's 'Paintings, or Signs and Marks.'" In *Walter Benjamin and the Architecture of Modernity*, edited by Andrew Benjamin and Charles Rice, 129–42. Prahran, AU: re.press.

Benjamin, Walter. 1969. "The Work of Art in the Age of Mechanical Reproduction." Translated by Harry Zohn. In *Illuminations: Essays and Reflections*, edited by Hannah Arendt, 217–51. New York: Schocken Books. Originally published in 1936 as "L'œuvre d'art à l'époque de sa reproduction méchanisée," in *Zeitschrift für Sozialforschung* 5 (1): 40–68.

———. 1973. *Charles Baudelaire: A Lyric Poet in the Era of High Capitalism*. Translated by Harry Zohn. London: NLB.

———. 1977. *Gesammelte Schriften*, vol. 2.1. Edited by Rolf Tiedemann and Hermann Schweppenhäuser. Frankfurt am Main: Suhrkamp.

———. 1994. *The Correspondence of Walter Benjamin, 1910–1940*. Edited by Gershom Gerhard Scholem and Theodor W. Adorno. Translated by Manfred R. Jacobson and Evelyn M. Jacobson. Chicago: University of Chicago Press.

———. 1999. *The Arcades Project*. Translated by Howard Eiland and Kevin McLaughlin. Edited by Rolf Tiedemann. Cambridge, MA: Belknap Press.

———. 2004a. "Dostoevsky's *The Idiot*." Translated by Rodney Livingstone. In *Walter Benjamin: Selected Writings, Volume 1, 1913–1926*, edited by Marcus Bullock and Michael W. Jennings, 78–81. Cambridge, MA: Belknap Press of Harvard University Press. Originally published as "Der Idiot von Dostojewskij" in 1921; republished in 1977 in *Gesammelte Schriften*, vol. 2, 237–41 (Frankfurt am Main: Suhrkamp).

———. 2004b. "Goethe's Elective Affinities." Translated by Stanley Corngold. In *Walter Benjamin: Selected Writings, Volume 1, 1913–1926*, edited by Marcus Bullock and Michael W. Jennings, 297–360. Cambridge, MA: Belknap Press of Harvard University Press. Originally published as "Goethes Wahlverwandtschaften" in 1924–1925; republished in 1974 in *Gesammelte Schriften*, vol. 1, 123–201 (Frankfurt am Main: Suhrkamp).

———. 2004c. "One-Way Street." Translated by Edmund Jephcott. In *Walter Benjamin: Selected Writings, Volume 1, 1913–1926*, edited by Marcus Bullock and Michael W. Jennings, 444–88. Cambridge, MA: Belknap Press of Harvard University Press. Originally published as "Einbahnstraße" in 1928; republished in 1972 in *Gesammelte Schriften*, vol. 4, 83–148 (Frankfurt am Main: Suhrkamp).

———. 2004d. "Painting, or Signs and Marks." Translated by Rodney Livingstone. In *Walter Benjamin: Selected Writings, Volume 1, 1913–1926*, edited by Marcus Bullock and Michael W. Jennings, 83–86. Cambridge, MA: Belknap Press of Harvard University Press. Unpublished in Benjamin's

lifetime; published in 1977 as "Über die Malerei oder Zeichen und Mal,"
in *Gesammelte Schriften*, vol. 2, 603–7 (Frankfurt am Main: Suhrkamp).

———. 2004e. "The Theory of Criticism." Translated by Rodney Livingstone. In
Walter Benjamin: Selected Writings, Volume 1, 1913–1926, edited by Marcus
Bullock and Michael W. Jennings, 217–19. Cambridge, MA: Belknap Press
of Harvard University Press. Unpublished in Benjamin's lifetime.

———. 2005a. "Hashish, Beginning of March 1930." Translated by Rodney
Livingstone. In *Walter Benjamin: Selected Writings, Volume 2, Part 1,
1927–1930*, edited by Michael W. Jennings, Howard Eiland, and Gary
Smith, 327–30. Cambridge, MA: Belknap Press of Harvard University
Press. Unpublished in Benjamin's lifetime; published in 1985 as "Haschisch
Anfang März 1930," in *Gesammelte Schriften*, vol. 6, 587–91 (Frankfurt
am Main: Suhrkamp).

———. 2005b. "Little History of Photography." Translated by Edmund Jephcott
and Kingsley Shorter. In *Walter Benjamin: Selected Writings, Volume 2, Part
2, 1931–1934*, edited by Michael W. Jennings, Howard Eiland, and Gary
Smith, 507–30. Cambridge, MA: Belknap Press of Harvard University Press.
Originally published in September–October 1931 in *Die literarische Welt*;
republished in 1977 as "Kleine Geschichte Photographie," in *Gesammelte
Schriften*, vol. 2, 368–85 (Frankfurt am Main: Suhrkamp).

———. 2005c. "Main Features of My Second Impression of Hashish: Written
January 15, 1928, at 3:30 p.m." Translated by Rodney Livingstone. In
Walter Benjamin: Selected Writings, Volume 2, Part 1, 1927–1930, edited
by Michael W. Jennings, Howard Eiland, and Gary Smith, 85–90. Cam-
bridge, MA: Belknap Press of Harvard University Press. Unpublished in
Benjamin's lifetime; published in 1985 as "HAUPTZÜGE DER ZWEITEN
HASCHISCH-IMPRESSION: Geschrieben 15 Januar 1928 nachmittags ½
4," in *Gesammelte Schriften*, vol. 6, 560–66 (Frankfurt am Main: Suhrkamp).

———. 2005d. "Paris Diary." Translated by Rodney Livingstone. In *Walter Ben-
jamin: Selected Writings, Volume 2, Part 1, 1927–1930*, edited by Michael
W. Jennings, Howard Eiland, and Gary Smith, 337–54. Cambridge, MA:
Belknap Press of Harvard University Press. Originally published in April–
June 1930 in *Die literarische Welt*; republished in 1972 as "Pariser Tagebuch,"
in *Gesammelte Schriften*, vol. 4, 567–87 (Frankfurt am Main: Suhrkamp).

———. 2005e. "The Return of the Flâneur." Translated by Rodney Livingstone.
In *Walter Benjamin: Selected Writings, Volume 2, Part 1, 1927–1930*, edited
by Michael W. Jennings, Howard Eiland, and Gary Smith, 262–67. Cambridge, MA: Belknap Press of Harvard University Press. Originally published
in October 1929 in *Die literarische Welt*; republished in 1972 as "Berliner
Kindheit um neunzehnhundert," in *Gesammelte Schriften*, vol. 3, 194–99
(Frankfurt am Main: Suhrkamp).

———. 2006a. "Berlin Childhood Around 1900: Final Version." Translated by
Howard Eiland. In *Walter Benjamin: Selected Writings, Volume 3, 1935–1938*,

edited by Howard Eiland and Michael W. Jennings, 344–86. Cambridge, MA: Belknap Press of Harvard University Press. Unpublished in Benjamin's lifetime; published in 1989 as "Berliner Kindheit um neunzehnhundert," in *Gesammelte Schriften*, vol. 7, 385–433 (Frankfurt am Main: Suhrkamp).

———. 2006b. "The Work of Art in the Age of Its Technological Reproducibility: Second Version." Translated by Edmund Jephcott and Harry Zohn. In *Walter Benjamin: Selected Writings, Volume 3, 1935–1938*, edited by Howard Eiland and Michael W. Jennings, 101–33. Cambridge, MA: Belknap Press of Harvard University Press. Unpublished in Benjamin's lifetime; published in 1989 as "Das Kunstwerk im Zeitalter seiner technischen Reproduzierbarkeit: Zweite Fassung," in *Gesammelte Schriften*, vol. 7, 350–84 (Frankfurt am Main: Suhrkamp).

———. 2006c. "On Some Motifs in Baudelaire." Translated by Harry Zohn. In *Walter Benjamin: Selected Writings, Volume 4, 1938–1940*, edited by Howard Eiland and Michael W. Jennings, 313–55. Cambridge, MA: Belknap Press of Harvard University Press. Originally published in January 1940 in *Zeitschrift für Sozialforschung*; republished in 1974 as "über einige Motive bei Baudelaire," in *Gesammelte Schriften*, vol. 1, 605–53 (Frankfurt am Main: Suhrkamp).

———. 2006d. "The Significance of Beautiful Semblance." Translated by Edmund Jephcott. In *Walter Benjamin: Selected Writings, Volume 3, 1935–1938*, edited by Howard Eiland and Michael W. Jennings, 137–38. Cambridge, MA: Belknap Press of Harvard University Press. Unpublished in Benjamin's lifetime; published in 1989 as a fragment in *Gesammelte Schriften*, vol. 7, 667–68 (Frankfurt am Main: Suhrkamp).

———. 2006e. "The Storyteller: Observations on the Works of Nikolai Leskov." Translated by Harry Zohn. In *Walter Benjamin: Selected Writings, Volume 3, 1935–1938*, edited by Howard Eiland and Michael W. Jennings, 143–66. Cambridge, MA: Belknap Press of Harvard University Press. Originally published in 1936 in *Orient und Occident*; republished in 1977 as "Der Erzähler Betrachtungen zum Werk Nikolai Lesskows," in *Gesammelte Schriften*, vol. 2, 438–65 (Frankfurt am Main: Suhrkamp).

———. 2006f. "Central Park." Translated by Edmund Jephcott and Howard Eiland. In *Walter Benjamin: Selected Writings, Volume 4, 1938–1940*, edited by Howard Eiland and Michael W. Jennings, 161–99. Cambridge, MA: Belknap Press of Harvard University Press. Unpublished in Benjamin's lifetime; published in 1974 as "Zentralpark," in *Gesammelte Schriften*, vol. 1, 655–90 (Frankfurt am Main: Suhrkamp).

———. 2006g. "The Work of Art in the Ages of Its Technological Reproducibility: Third Version." Translated by Harry Zohn and Edmund Jephcott. In *Walter Benjamin: Selected Writings, Volume 4, 1938–1940*, edited by Howard Eiland and Michael W. Jennings, 251–83. Cambridge, MA: Belknap Press of Harvard University Press. This version was not published in Benjamin's lifetime; published in 1974 as "Das Kunstwerk im Zeitalter seiner technischen Reproduzierbarkeit: Dritte Fassung," in *Gesammelte Schriften*, vol. 1, 471–508 (Frankfurt am Main: Suhrkamp).

———. 2006. "Introduction." In *The Culture Industry: Selected Essays on Mass Culture*, by Theodor W. Adorno. Edited by Jay M. Bernstein, 1–28. London: Routledge.

Bentham, Jeremy. (1791) 2012. *Panopticon: Or, the Inspection-House*. Dublin: Thomas Byrne. *Eighteenth Century Collections Online*. Gale. 2012.

———. (1843) 2012. *The Works of Jeremy Bentham / Published Under the Superintendence of his Executor, John Bowring*, 11 vols. Edinburgh. *The Making of Modern Law*. Gale. 2012.

Berlin, Isaiah. 2000. *Three Critics of the Enlightenment: Vico, Hamann, Herder*. Edited by Henry Hardy. Princeton, NJ: Princeton University Press.

Bernstein, Jay M. 2001. *Adorno: Disenchantment and Ethics*. Cambridge: Cambridge University Press.

Blavatsky, Helena Petrovna. 1892. *The Theosophical Glossary*. London: The Theosophical Publishing Society.

———. 1978. *The Secret Doctrine: Collected Writings, 1888*. 3 vols. Adyar, India: The Theosophical Publishing House.

Big Brother Watch. 2012. "The Price of Privacy: How Local Authorities Spent £515m on CCTV in Four Years." https://www.bigbrotherwatch.org.uk/files/priceofprivacy/Price_of_privacy_2012.pdf#.T0OlbfI8Cd4.

Bogard, William. 2006. "Surveillance Assemblages and Lines of Flight." In *Theorizing Surveillance: The Panopticon and Beyond*, edited by David Lyon, 97–122. Uffculme, UK: Willan Publishing.

Boros, Diana, and Haley Smith. 2014. "#OccupyTheEstablishment: The Commodification of a 'New Sensibility' for Public Space and Public Life." In *Re-Imagining Public Space: The Frankfurt School in the 21st Century*, edited by Diana Boros and James M. Glass, 215–39. New York: Palgrave Macmillan.

Boyne, Roy. 2000. "Post-panopticism." *Economy and Society* 29 (2): 285–307.

Brown, Kevin. 1986. "Establishing Difference: Culture, 'Race,' Ethnicity and the Production of Ideology." *Journal of Sociology* 22 (2): 175–86.

Brunon-Ernst, Anne, ed. 2012. *Beyond Foucault: New Perspectives on Bentham's Panopticon*. Farnham, UK: Ashgate.

Buck-Morss, Susan. 1991. *The Dialectics of Seeing: Walter Benjamin and the Arcades Project*. Cambridge, MA: MIT Press.

Caluya, Gilbert. 2010. "The Post-panoptic Society? Reassessing Foucault in Surveillance Studies." *Social Identities* 16 (5): 621–33.

Cameron, James. 1997. *Titanic*. Los Angeles, CA: Paramount, 1999. DVD.

Camus, Albert. 1960. "Introduction." In *The Rebel: An Essay on Man in Revolt*, translated by Anthony Bower, 3–11. New York: Vintage Books.

———. 1965. *The Plague*. Translated by Stuart Gilbert. Harmondsworth, UK: Penguin Books Ltd.

CBC News. 2015. "Shoes Stand in Silent Protest at Paris Climate Conference." November 29. http://www.cbc.ca/news/world/climate-protest-paris-1.334 2384.

Chaplin, Charlie. 1936. *Modern Times*. MK2 Éditions; Burbank, CA: Warner Home Video, 2003. DVD.

Christofferson, Michael Scott. 2004. *French Intellectuals Against the Left: The Antitotalitarian Moment of the 1970s*. New York: Berghaln Books.

Colangelo, Jeremy. 2011. "Internet Activists: Occupy Wall Street." *The Brock Press*, September 20. http://www.brockpress.com/2011/09/internet-activists-occupy-wall-street/.

Conquest, Robert. 2000. *Reflections on a Ravaged Century*. New York: W. W. Norton & Company.

Conway, Kellyanne. 2017. "Conway: Press Secretary Gave 'Alternative Facts.'" *NBC News*, January 22. https://www.nbcnews.com/meet-the-press/video/conway-press-secretary-gave-alternative-facts-860142147643. Video, 3:39.

Coppola, Francis Ford. 1972. *The Godfather*. Los Angeles, CA: Paramount Pictures, 2001. DVD.

Coughlin, Con. 2002. *Saddam: The Secret Life*. London: Macmillan.

Curtis, Michael. 1979. *Totalitarianism*. New Brunswick, NJ: Transaction Books.

Dallas, Gregor. 2005. *1945: The War That Never Ended*. New Haven, CT: Yale University Press.

Davis, Mike. 1990. *City of Quartz*. London: Vintage Press.

de Botton, Alain. 2003. *The Art of Travel*. London: Penguin Books.

Debord, Guy. 1983. *Society of the Spectacle*. Translated by Ken Knabb. Detroit, MI: Black & Red.

———. 1990. *Comments on the Society of the Spectacle*. Translated by Malcolm Imrie. London: Verso.

Deleuze, Gilles. 1983. *Nietzsche and Philosophy*. Translated by Hugh Tomlinson. London: Continuum.

———. 1992. "Postscript on the Societies of Control." Translated by M. Joughin. *October* 59 (Winter): 3–7.

Deutch, Howard. 1995. *Grumpier Old Men*. Burbank, CA: Warner Home Video, 2002. DVD.

Dobson, Jerome E., and Peter F. Fisher. 2007. "The Panopticon's Changing Geography." *Geographical Review* 97 (3): 307–23.

Dostoevsky, Fyodor. 1998. *The Idiot*. Translated by Alan Myers. Oxford: Oxford University Press.

Douglas, Allen, and Fedwa Malti-Douglas. 1994. *Arab Comic Strips: Politics of an Emerging Mass Culture*. Bloomington: Indiana University Press.

Durbar Mahila Samanwaya Committee (DMSC), India. 1997. "Sex Workers' Manifesto, Calcutta, 1997." http://www.bayswan.org/manifest.html.

Eiland, Howard, and Michael W. Jennings, eds. 2006. "Chronology, 1938–1940." In *Walter Benjamin: Selected Writings, Volume 4, 1938–1940*, translated by Edmund Jephcott et al., 427–47. Cambridge, MA: Belknap Press of Harvard University Press.

Elden, Stuart. 2001. "Politics, Philosophy, Geography: Henri Lefebvre in Recent Anglo-American Scholarship." *Antipode* 33 (5): 809–25. doi: 10.1111/1467-8330.00218.

———. 2003. "Plague, Panopticon, Police." *Surveillance & Society* 1 (3): 240–53.

Ellul, Jacques. 1964. *The Technological Society*. Translated by John Wilkinson. New York: Vintage Books.

Engel, Richard. 2011. *War Journal: My Five Years in Iraq*. New York: Simon & Schuster.

Falasca-Zamponi, Simonetta. 1997. *Fascist Spectacle: The Aesthetics of Power in Mussolini's Italy*. Berkeley: University of California Press.

Farrokhzad, Furugh. 1967. ايمان بياوريم به آغازفصل سرد. ["Let us Believe in the Beginning of a Cold Season."] http://www.adabestanekave.com/book/iman_beyawarim_be_aghaz_fasl_%20sard.pdf.

———. 2007. *Sin: Selected Poems of Forugh Farrokhzad*. Translated by Sholeh Wolpé. Fayetteville: University of Arkansas Press.

Ferrara, Alessandro. 1993. *Modernity and Authenticity: A Study in the Social and Ethical Thought of Jean-Jacques Rousseau*. Albany: State University of New York.

Foucault, Michel. 1980. "The Eye of Power." Interview by Jean-Pierre Barou and Michelle Perrot. Translated by Colin Gordon. In *Power/Knowledge: Selected Interviews & Other Writings, 1972–1977*, edited by Colin Gordon, 146–65. New York: Pantheon Books. Originally published in 1977 as "L'Oeil du Pouvoir," in *Le Panoptique* by Jeremy Bentham, 9–31 (Paris: Pierre Belfond).

———. 1984. "Space, Knowledge, and Power." Interview by Paul Rabinow. Translated by Christian Hubert. In *Foucault Reader*, edited by Paul Rabinow, 239–56. New York: Pantheon Books. Originally published in March 1982, in *Skyline, the Architecture and Design Review*: 16–20.

———. 1986. "Of Other Spaces." Translated by Jay Miskowiec. *Diacritics* 16 (1): 22–7. Republished in 1984 as "Des espaces autres," in *Dits et écrits II, 1976–1988*, 1571–81 (Paris: Gallimard).

———. 1995. *Discipline and Punish: The Birth of Prison*. Translated by Alan Sheridan. New York: Vintage Books. Originally published in 1975 as *Surveiller et punir: Naissance de la prison* (Paris: Gallimard).

———. 2008. *Birth of Biopolitics: Lectures at the Collège de France, 1978–1979*. Edited by Michel Senellart. General editors: François Ewald and Alessandro Fontana. English series editor: Arnold I. Davidson. Translated by Graham

Burchell. Basingstoke, UK: Palgrave Macmillan. Originally published in 2004 as *Naissance de la biopolitique: Cours au Collège de France, 1978–1979* (Paris: Hautes Études).

———. 2010. "2 February 1983: Second Hour." In *Government of Self and Others: Lectures at the Collège de France 1982–1983*, edited by Frédéric Gros. General editors: François Ewald and Alessandro Fontana. English series editor: Arnold I. Davidson. Translated by Graham Burchell, 173–86. Basingstoke, UK: Palgrave Macmillan. Originally published in 2008 as "Leçon du 2 février 1983: Deuxiéme heure," in *Le gouvernement de soi et des autres: Cours au Collège de France, 1982–1983*, vol. 1, 157–69 (Paris: Hautes Études).

Fox, Karen. 2012. *Their Highest Vocation: Social Justice and the Millennial Generation*. New York: Peter Lang.

Freud, Sigmund. 2008. *The Interpretation of Dreams*. Translated by Joyce Crick. Edited by Ritchie Robertson. Oxford: Oxford University Press.

Freyenhagen, Fabian. 2013. *Adorno's Practical Philosophy: Living Less Wrongly*. Cambridge: Cambridge University Press.

Friedrich, Carl J., and Zbigniew Brzezinski. 1956. *Totalitarian Dictatorship and Autocracy*. Cambridge: Harvard University Press.

Fyfe, Nicholas R., and Judith T. Bannister. 1996. "City Watching: Closed Circuit Television Surveillance in Public Spaces." *Area* 28 (1): 37–46.

Gane, Nicholas. 2012. "The Governmentalities of Neoliberalism: Panopticism, Post-panopticism and Beyond." *The Sociological Review* 60 (4): 611–34.

Gasche, Rodolphe. 1994. "Objective Diversions: On Some Kantian Themes in Benjamin's 'The Work of Art in the Age of Mechanical Reproduction.'" In *Walter Benjamin's Philosophy: Destruction and Experience*, edited by Andrew E. Benjamin and Peter Osborne, 183–204. London: Routledge.

Giddens, Anthony. 1985. *The Nation-State and Violence*. Vol. 2 of *A Contemporary Critique of Historical Materialism*. Cambridge: Polity Press.

Gilloch, Graeme. 1996. *Myth and Metropolis: Walter Benjamin and the City*. Cambridge, UK: Polity.

Goebel, Rolf J. 2009. "Introduction: Benjamin's Actuality." In *A Companion to the Works of Walter Benjamin*, edited by Rolf. J. Goebel, 1–22. Rochester, NY: Camden House.

Greenwald, Glenn. 2014. *No Place to Hide: Edward Snowden, the NSA, and the U.S. Surveillance State*. London: Penguin Books.

Griffiths, Antony. 1996. *Prints and Printmaking: An Introduction to the History and Techniques*. Berkeley: University of California Press.

Griswold, Alison. 2017. "'The Origins of Totalitarianism,' Hannah Arendt's Definitive Guide to How Tyranny Begins, Has Sold Out on Amazon." *Quartz*, January 29. https://qz.com/897517/the-origins-of-totalitarianism-hannah-arendts-defining-work-on-tyranny-is-out-of-stock-on-amazon/.

Han, Byung-Chul. 2105. *The Transparency Society*. Stanford, CA: Stanford University Press. Kindle edition.

Hanioglu, Sukru. 2011. *Ataturk: An Intellectual Biography*. Princeton, NJ: Princeton University Press.

The Hannah Arendt Center. 2016. "American Politics and The Crystallization of Totalitarian Practices." *Medium*, August 5. https://medium.com/quote-of-the-week/american-politics-and-the-crystallization-of-totalitarian-practices-464e1f02f514.

Hansen, Miriam Bratu. 2008. "Benjamin's Aura." *Critical Inquiry* 34 (Winter): 336–75.

Harvey, David. 1982. *The Limits of Capital*. Oxford: Basil Blackwell.

Havel, Václav. 1990. "The Power of the Powerless." Translated by Paul Wilson. In *The Power of the Powerless: Citizens Against the State in Central-Eastern Europe*, by Václav Havel et. al. Edited by John Keane, 23–96. Armonk, NY: M.E. Sharpe.

Heidegger, Martin. 2001. *Poetry, Language, Thought*. Translated by Albert Hofstadter. New York: Perennial Classics.

Herder, Johann Gottfried Von. 2002a. "This Too a Philosophy of History for the Formation of Humanity." In *Philosophical Writings*, translated and edited by Michael N. Forster, 268–360. Cambridge: Cambridge University Press.

———. 2002b. "Letters for the Advancement of Humanity: (1793–7)—Tenth Collection." In *Philosophical Writings*, translated and edited by Michael N. Forster, 380–424. Cambridge: Cambridge University Press.

———. 2004. "Governments as Inherited Regimes." In *Another Philosophy of History and Selected Political Writings*, translated by Ioannis D. Evrigenis and Daniel Pellerin, 121–29. Indianapolis, IN: Hackett Pub.

Hobsbawm, Eric. 1995. *The Age of Extremes: The Short Twentieth Century 1914–1991*. London: Abacus.

Horkheimer, Max, and Theodor W. Adorno. 2002. *Dialectic of Enlightenment: Philosophical Fragments*. Translated by Edmund Jephcott. Edited by Gunzelin Schmid Noerr. Stanford, CA: Stanford University Press.

Human Rights Watch. 1993. *Genocide in Iraq: The Anfal Campaign Against the Kurds: A Middle East Watch Report*. New York: Human Rights Watch. Also available at https://www.hrw.org/reports/1993/iraqanfal/#Table of

Ihrig, Stefan. 2014. *Atatürk in the Nazi Imagination*. Cambridge, MA: The Belknap Press of Harvard University Press.

Isakhan, Benjamin. 2011. "Targeting the Symbolic Dimension of Baathist Iraq: Cultural Destruction, Historical Memory, and National Identity." *Middle East Journal of Culture and Communication* 4: 257–81. doi: 10.1163/187398611X590200.

Jameson, Frederic. 2003. "Future City." *New Left Review* 21: 65–79.

Jay, Martin. 1984. *Adorno*. Cambridge, MA: Harvard University Press.

Jennings, Michael W., Howard Eiland, and Gary Smith, eds. 2005. "Chronology, 1927–1934." In *Walter Benjamin: Selected Writings, Volume 2, Part 2, 1931–1934*, translated by Rodney Livingstone et al., 823–56. Cambridge, MA: Belknap Press of Harvard University Press.

Johnson, Peter. 2006. "Unravelling Foucault's 'Different Spaces.'" *History of the Human Sciences* 19 (4): 75–90.

Kant, Immanuel. 2000. *Critique of the Power of Judgment*. Translated by Paul Guyer. Cambridge: Cambridge University Press.

Kellner, Douglas. 2001. "Introduction: Herbert Marcuse and the Vicissitudes of Critical Theory." In *Towards a Critical Theory of Society*. London: Routledge.

Khardalian, Suzanne. 2011. *Grandma's Tattoos*. (Sweden: HB PeÅ Holmquist Film). https://www.youtube.com/watch?v=bwj4e_f_1DI.

Klein, Naomi. 2007. *The Shock Doctrine: The Rise of Disaster Capitalism*. New York: Metropolitan Book.

Koskela, Hille. 2003. "'Cam Era'—the Contemporary Urban Panopticon." *Surveillance & Society* 1 (3): 292–313.

Kracauer, Siegfried. 1995. *The Mass Ornament: Weimar Essays*. Translated and edited by Thomas Y. Levin. Cambridge, MA: Harvard University Press.

Kundera, Milan. 2002. *Ignorance*. Translated by Linda Asher. New York: Harper Collins Publishers.

Lacan, Jacques. 2001. "The Agency of the Letter in the Unconscious, or Reason Since Freud." In *Écrits: A Selection*, translated by Alan Sheridan, 161–97. London: Routledge Classics. Ebrary e-book.

Lardreau, Esther. 2007. "The Difference Between Epileptic Auras and Migrainous Auras in the 19th Century." *Cephalalgia* 27: 1378–85. doi: 10.1111/j.1468-2982.2007. 01447.x.

Lee, Jeong-hyang. 2002. *Jibeuro* [*The Way Home*]. Los Angeles: Paramount Classics, 2003. DVD.

Lefait, Sebastien. 2012. *Surveillance on Screen: Monitoring Contemporary Films and Television Programs*. Lanham, MD: Scarecrow Press.

Lefebvre, Henri. 1974. *Dialectical Materialism*. Translated by John Sturrock. London: Jonathan Cape. Republished in 1990 as *Le matérialisme dialectique* (Paris: Quadrige).

———. 1982. *The Sociology of Marx*. Translated by Norbert Guterman. New York: Columbia University Press. Reprinted in 1974 as *Sociologie de Marx*, 3rd ed. (Paris: Presses Universitaires de France).

———. 1991a. *The Production of Space*. Translated by Donald Nicholson-Smith. Malden, MA: Blackwell Publishing. Reprinted in 2000 as *La production de l'espace*, 4th ed. (Paris: Anthropos).

———. 1991b. *Critique of Everyday Life, Volume 1: Introduction*. Translated by John Moore. London: Verso. Republished in 1958 as *Critique de la vie quotidienne I: Introduction*, 2nd ed. (Paris: L'Arche Editeur).

———. 2002. *Critique of Everyday Life: Foundations for a Sociology of the Everyday.* Vol. 2. Translated by John Moore. London: Verso. Originally published in 1961 as *Critique de la vie quotidienne II: Fondements d'une sociologie de la quotidienneté* (Paris: L'Arche Editeur).

———. 2003a. "Hegel, Marx, Nietzsche." In *Henri Lefebvre: Key Writings*, edited by Stuart Elden, Elizabeth Lebas, and Eleonore Kofman, 42–49. New York: Continuum. Originally published in full in 1975 as *Hegel-Marx-Nietzsche ou le royaume des ombres*, 9–12; 46–52 (Paris: Casterman).

———. 2003b. "Preface to the New Edition: The Production of Space." In *Henri Lefebvre: Key Writings*, edited by Stuart Elden, Elizabeth Lebas, and Eleonore Kofman, 206–13. New York: Continuum. Originally published in 1986 as "Préface," in *La Production de l'espace*, 3rd ed., i–xii (Paris: Anthropos).

———. 2003c. "Triads and Dyads." In *Henri Lefebvre: Key Writings*, edited by Stuart Elden, Elizabeth Lebas, and Eleonore Kofman, 50–56. New York: Continuum. Originally published in full in 1980 as *La Présence et l'absence: Contribution à la théorie des représentations*, 143; 225–31 (Paris: Casterman).

———. 2004. *Rhythmanalysis: Space, Time, and Everyday Life.* Translated by Stuart Elden and Gerald Moore. New York: Continuum. Originally published in 1992 as *Éléments de rythmanalyse: Introduction à la connaissance des rythmes* (Paris: Éditions Syllepse).

———. 2005. *Critique of Everyday Life: From Modernity to Modernism (Towards a Metaphilosophy of Daily Life).* Vol. 3. Translated by Gregory Elliot. Originally published in 1981 as *Critique de la vie quotidienne, III: De la modernité au modernisme (Pour une métaphilosophie du quotidien)* (Paris: L'Arche).

———. 2009. "Space: Social Product and Use Value." In *State, Space, World: Selected Essays*, edited by Neil Brenner and Stuart Elden. Translated by Gerald Moore, Neil Brenner, and Stuart Elden, 185–95. Minneapolis: University of Minnesota Press. Originally published in 1976 as "L'espace: produit social et valeur d'usage," in La Nouvelle Revue socialiste no. 18.

Levin, David Michael. 1993. "Introduction." In *Modernity and the Hegemony of Vision*, edited by David Michael Levin, 1–29. Berkeley: University of California Press.

Long, Heather. 2017. "Trump Has Done a Big Flip-Flop on Wall Street." *CNN Money*, April 26. http://money.cnn.com/2017/04/26/investing/donald-trump-wall-street/index.html.

Lukács, Georg. 1971. *History and Class Consciousness: Studies in Marxist Dialectics.* Translated by Rodney Livingstone. London: Merlin Press.

Lyon, David. 1993 "An Electronic Panopticon? A Sociological Critique of Surveillance Theory." *The Sociological Review* 41 (4): 653–78.

———. 1994. *The Electronic Eye: The Rise of Surveillance Society.* Minneapolis: University of Minnesota Press.

———. 2007. *Surveillance Studies: An Overview.* Cambridge, UK: Polity.

MacLean, Nancy. 2017. *Democracy in Chains: The Deep History of the Radical Right's Stealth Plan for America*. New York: Viking.

Makiya, Kanan. 1993. *Cruelty and Silence: War, Tyranny, Uprising, and the Arab World*. New York: W. W. Norton & Company.

Mallarmé, Stéphane. 1982. "Variations on a Subject: Crisis in Poetry (Excerpts)." In *Stéphane Mallarmé: Selected Poetry and Prose*, edited by Mary Ann Caws. This section translated by Mary Ann Caws, 75–76. New York: New Directions.

Marcuse, Herbert. 1968. *One-Dimensional Man: Studies in the Ideology of Advanced Industrial Society*. 7th printing. Boston: Beacon Press.

———. 1997. *Reason and Revolution: Hegel and the Rise of Social Theory*. Atlantic Highlands, NJ: Humanities Press.

———. 2001. *Towards a Critical Theory of Society*. London: Routledge.

Marks, Jonathan. 2005. *Perfection and Disharmony in the Thought of Jean-Jacques Rousseau*. Cambridge: Cambridge University Press.

Marques, Auguste Jean Baptiste. 1896. *The Human Aura: A Study*. San Francisco, CA: Mercury. PDF e-book.

———. 1908. *Scientific Corroborations of Theosophy: A Vindication of the Secret Doctrine by the Latest Discoveries*. London: The Theosophical Publishing Society. PDF e-book.

Marx, Gary T. 1988. *Undercover: Police Surveillance in America*. Berkeley: University of California Press.

Marx, Karl. 1967. *Writings of the Young Marx on Philosophy and Society*. Edited and translated by Lloyd David Easton and Kurt H. Guddat. Garden City, NY: Anchor Books.

———. 1988. *Economic and Philosophic Manuscripts of 1844 and Communist Manifesto*. Translated by Martin Milligan. Amherst, NY: Prometheus Books.

———. 1990. *Capital: A Critique of Political Economy*. Vol. 1. Translated by Ben Fowkes. Reprint, London: Penguin Books.

Marx, Karl, and Fredric Engels. 1972. *The Marx-Engels Reader*. 2nd ed. Edited by Robert C. Tucker. New York: W. W. Norton & Company.

Mathiesen, Thomas. 1997. "The View Society: Michel Foucault's 'Panopticon' Revised." *Theoretical Criminology* 1 (2): 215–34.

McCole, John. 1993. *Walter Benjamin and the Antinomies of Tradition*. Ithaca, NY: Cornell University Press.

McKay, Adam. 2008. *Step Brothers*. Culver City, CA: Columbia Pictures Industries. DVD.

Miles, Malcolm. 2014. "Critical Spaces: Public Spaces, the Culture Industry, Critical Theory, and Urbanism." In *Re-Imagining Public Space: The Frankfurt School in the 21st Century*, edited by Diana Boros and James M. Glass, 107–23. New York: Palgrave Macmillan.

Mitchell, Don. 1995. "The End of Public Space? People's Park, Definitions of the Public, and Democracy." *Annals of the Association of American Geographers* 85 (1): 108–33.

Moggach, Douglas. 2005. "Failures of Autonomy: A Hegelian Diagnosis of Modern Tyranny." In *Confronting Tyranny: Ancient Lessons for Global Politics*, edited by Toivo Koivukoski and David Edward Tabachnick, 53–66. Lanham, MD: Rowan & Littlefield.

The Movement for Black Lives. 2016. "A Vision for Black Lives: Policy Demands for Black Power, Freedom, & Justice." https://policy.m4bl.org/wp-content/uploads/2016/07/20160726-m4bl-Vision-Booklet-V3.pdf.

Müller-Lauter, Wolfgang. 1999. *Nietzsche: His Philosophy of Contradictions and the Contradictions of his Philosophy*. Translated by David J. Parent. Urbana: University of Illinois Press.

Mussolini, Benito. 1932. "The Doctrine of Fascism." http://www.worldfuturefund.org/wffmaster/Reading/Germany/mussolini.htm.

Nāgārjuna. 1970. *Nāgārjuna: A Translation of His Mūlamadhyamakakārikā*. Translated by Kenneth K. Inada. Tokyo: Hokuseido.

NAACP. 2017. "Criminal Justice Fact Sheet." http://www.naacp.org/criminal-justice-fact-sheet/.

Newsweek Staff. 2008. "Military UAVs: Up in the Sky, an Unblinking Eye." *Newsweek*, May 31. http://www.newsweek.com/military-uavs-sky-unblinking-eye-89463.

Nietzsche, Friedrich. 1967. *The Birth of Tragedy and the Case of Wagner*. Translated by Walter Kaufmann. New York: Vintage Books.

———. 1969. *Thus Spoke Zarathustra*. Translated R. J. Hollingdale. London: Penguin Books.

Norris, Clive. 2003. "From Personal to Digital: CCTV, the Panopticon and the Technological Mediation of Suspicion and Social Control." In *Surveillance as Social Sorting: Privacy, Risk and Automated Discrimination*, edited by David Lyon, 249–81. London: Routledge.

O'Harrow, Robert. 2005. *No Place to Hide: Behind the Scenes of Our Emerging Surveillance Society*. New York: Free Press.

Orwell, George. 2008. *1984*. London: Penguin Books.

Pallasmaa, Juhani. 2005. *The Eyes of the Skin: Architecture and the Senses*. Chichester, UK: Wiley.

Parkinson, John. 2012. *Democracy and Public Space: The Physical Sites of Democratic Performance*. Oxford: Oxford University Press.

PBS NewsHour. 2015. "174 Detained as Climate Protesters Clash with Police in Paris." PBS, November 29. http://www.pbs.org/newshour/rundown/174-detained-as-climate-protesters-clash-with-police-in-paris/.

Phillips, Tod. 2009. *The Hangover*. Burbank, CA: Warner Bros, 2009. DVD.

Picasso, Pablo. 1988. "Two Statements by Picasso, 1923." In *Picasso on Art: A Selection of Views*, edited by Dore Ashton, 3–14. New York: Da Capo Press.

Podeh, Elie. 2010. "From Indifference to Obsession: The Role of National State Celebrations in Iraq, 1921–2003." *British Journal of Middle Eastern Studies* 37 (2): 179–206. doi: 10.1080/13530191003794731.

Pussy Riot. 2013. *Pussy Riot! A Punk Prayer for Freedom.* New York: Feminist Press at the City University of New York.

Radford, Michael. 1984. *1984.* London: Umbrella-Rosenblum Films Production. DVD.

Raphael. 1518–1520. *Transfiguration* [painting]. Oil on panel. 13 ft. 3 in. × 9 ft. 1 in. (4.05 × 2.78 m). Pinacoteca, Vatican Museums, Vatican State. Artwork in the public domain.

Reeve, Alan. 1998. "The Panopticisation of Shopping: CCTV and Leisure Consumption." In *Surveillance, Closed Circuit Television, and Social Control,* edited by Clive Norris and Jade Moran, 69–87. Aldershot, UK: Ashgate.

Rocker, Rudolf. 1972. "The Anarchist 'Melting Pot': The London Years." In *The Essential Works of Anarchism,* edited by Marshall S. Shatz. New York: Quadrangle Books.

Roj Women. 2012. *A Woman's Struggle: Using Gender Lenses to Understand the Plight of Women Human Rights Defenders in Kurdish Regions of Turkey.* London: Roj Women. https://rojwomen.files.wordpress.com/2010/05/a-womans-struggle.pdf.

Rousseau, Jean-Jacques. 1953. *The Confessions of Jean-Jacques Rousseau.* Translated by J. M. Cohen. London: Penguin Books.

———. 2008. *Discourse on Political Economy and The Social Contract.* Translated by Christopher Betts. Oxford: Oxford University Press.

Rushdie, Salman. 1988. *The Satanic Verses.* London: Viking.

Schaeffer, Frank. 2014. "My Horrible Right-Wing Past: Confessions of a One-time Religious Right Icon." *Salon,* December 24. https://www.salon.com/2014/12/24/my_horrible_right_wing_past_confessions_of_a_one_time_religious_right_icon/.

Schapiro, Meyer. 1994. *Theory and Philosophy of Art: Style, Artist, and Society.* Selected Papers. Vol. 4. New York: George Braziller.

Schmid, Christian. 2008. "Henri Lefebvre's Theory of Production of Space: Towards a Three-Dimensional Dialectic." In *Space, Difference, Everyday Life: Reading Henri Lefebvre,* edited by Kanishka Goonewardena, Stefan Kipfer, Richard Milgrom, and Christian Schmid, 27–45. New York: Routledge.

Seidan, Henry M. 2009. "On the Longing for Home." *Psychoanalytic Psychology* 26 (2): 191–205. doi: 10.1037/a0015539.

Sennett, Richard. 1974. *The Fall of the Public Man.* London: Penguin Books.

Sherratt, Yvonne. 1998. "Aura: The Aesthetic of Redemption?" *Philosophy & Social Criticism* 24 (1): 25–41.

Simon, Bart. 2005. "The Return of Panopticism: Supervision, Subjection and the New Surveillance." *Surveillance & Society* 3 (1): 1–20.

Smith, Charles Anthony, Thomas Bellier, and John Altick. 2011. "Ego-Panopticism: The Evolution of Individual Power." *New Political Science* 33 (1): 45–58.

Soja, Edward W. 1989. *Postmodern Geographies: The Reassertion of Space in Critical Social Theory*. London: Verso.

———. 1996. *Thirdspace: Journeys to Los Angeles and Other Real-and-Imagined Places*. Malden, MA: Blackwell.

Sprung, Mervyn, ed. 1973. *The Problem of Two Truths in Buddhism and Vadanta*. Boston: D. Reidel Publishing Company.

Stark, Ryan J. 2001. "From Mysticism to Skepticism: Stylistic Reform in Seventeenth-Century British Philosophy and Rhetoric." *Philosophy and Rhetoric* 34 (November 4): 322–34. doi: 10.1353/par.2001.0021.

Starobinski, Jean. 1988. *Jean-Jacques Rousseau: Transparency and Obstruction*. Translated by Arthur Goldhammer. Chicago: University of Chicago Press.

Steinert, Heinz. 2003. *Culture Industry*. Translated by Sally-Ann Spencer. Oxford: Polity.

Tester, Keith. 1998. "Aura, Armour and the Body." *Body & Society* 4 (1): 17–34.

Traverso, Enzo. 2016. *Fire and Blood: the European Civil War, 1914–1945*. Translated by David Fernbach. London: Verso.

Trotsky, Leon. 1992. *Art and Revolution: Writings on Literature, Politics, and Culture*. New York: Pathfinder.

van Dijk, Teun A., Stella Ting-Toomey, Geneva Smitherman, and Denise Troutman. 1997. "Discourse, Ethnicity, Culture and Racism." In *Discourse as Social Interaction*, edited by Teun A. van Dijk, 144–80. London: Sage.

van Reijen, Willem. 2001. "Breathing the Aura—The Holy, the Sober Breath." *Theory, Culture & Society* 18 (6): 31–50.

Vassiliou, Konstantinos. 2010. "The Aura of Art After the Advent of the Digital." In *Walter Benjamin and the Aesthetics of Change*, edited by Anca M. Pusca, 158–70. London: Palgrave Macmillan.

Wallerstein, Immanuel. 2005. *World-Systems Analysis: An Introduction*. Durham, NC: Duke University Press.

Wedeen, Lisa. 1999. *Ambiguities of Domination: Politics, Rhetoric, and Symbols in Contemporary Syria*. Chicago: University of Chicago Press.

Witkin, Robert W. 2003. *Adorno on Popular Culture*. London: Routledge.

Wolin, Sheldon S. 2010. *Democracy Incorporated: Managed Democracy and the Specter of Inverted Totalitarianism*. Princeton, NJ: Princeton University Press.

Žižek, Slavoj, ed. 1994. *Mapping Ideology*. London: Verso.

Žižek, Slavoj. 2001. *Did Somebody Say Totalitarianism?: Five Interventions in the Misuses of a Notion*. London: Verso.

———. 2002. *Welcome to the Desert of the Real! Five Essays on September 11 and Related Dates*. London: Verso.

———. 2008. *Violence: Six Sideways Reflections*. New York: Picador.

Index

www.ingramcontent.com/pod-product-compliance
Lightning Source LLC
Chambersburg PA
CBHW030408270326
41926CB00009B/1320